Beyond Privatization

Advances in Political Science: An International Series

As an expression of its commitment to global political science, the International Political Science Association initiated this series to promote the publication of rigorous scholarly research by its members and affiliated groups. Conceptual and theoretical developments in the discipline, and their explication in various settings, represent the special focus of the series.

Titles include:

Christa Altenstetter and James Warner Björkman (*editors*)
HEALTH POLICY REFORM, NATIONAL VARIATIONS AND GLOBALIZATION

Dirk Berg-Schlosser and Jeremy Mitchell (*editors*)
CONDITIONS OF DEMOCRACY IN EUROPE, 1919–39
Systematic Case-Studies

Klaus von Beyme
PARLIAMENTARY DEMOCRACY
TRANSITION TO DEMOCRACY IN EASTERN EUROPE

Ofer Feldman
THE JAPANESE POLITICAL PERSONALITY

Justin Greenwood and Henry Jacek (*editors*)
ORGANIZED BUSINESS AND THE NEW GLOBAL ORDER

Asha Gupta
BEYOND PRIVATIZATION

Mino Vianello and Gwen Moore (*editors*)
GENDERING ELITES
Economic and Political Leadership in 27 Industrialized Societies

Advances in Political Science
Series Standing Order ISBN 0–333–71458–X
(*outside North America only*)

You can receive future titles in this series as they are published by placing a standing order. Please contact your bookseller or, in case of difficulty, write to us at the address below with your name and address, the title of the series and the ISBN quoted above.

Customer Services Department, Macmillan Distribution Ltd, Houndmills, Basingstoke, Hampshire RG21 6XS, England

Beyond Privatization

Asha Gupta
Department of Political Science
Bharati College
University of Delhi
India

Foreword by

Klaus-Dieter Schmidt
Kiel Institute of World Economics
Kiel, Germany

First published in Great Britain 2000 by
MACMILLAN PRESS LTD
Houndmills, Basingstoke, Hampshire RG21 6XS and London
Companies and representatives throughout the world

A catalogue record for this book is available from the British Library.

ISBN 0–333–79165–7

First published in the United States of America 2000 by
ST. MARTIN'S PRESS, LLC,
Scholarly and Reference Division,
175 Fifth Avenue, New York, N.Y. 10010

ISBN 0–312–23259–4

Library of Congress Cataloging-in-Publication Data
Gupta, Asha, 1952–
Beyond privatization / Asha Gupta.
p. cm.
Includes bibliographical references and index.
ISBN 0–312–23259–4 (cloth)
1. Privatization. I. Title.

HD3850 .G678 2000
338.9'25—dc21

99–087196

This book is printed on paper suitable for recycling and made from fully managed and sustained forest sources.

10 9 8 7 6 5 4 3 2 1
09 08 07 06 05 04 03 02 01 00

Printed and bound in Great Britain by
Antony Rowe Ltd, Chippenham, Wiltshire

To the most cherished memory of
Devi Puraskar Pandey
a global citizen and a true Gandhian in thought and deed

Contents

List of Tables and Figures

Tables

Figures

Foreword

For half a century, the state has played a dominant role in most economies. It has run factories, banks, railway and telephone services, it has manipulated or regulated commodity, capital and labour markets and it has generously distributed – at the expense of taxpayers – various public goods. But, over time, the fascination of the state as a 'Jack of all trades' has diminished. In fact, stagnant growth, rising unemployment and inflation and bursting budget deficits in most countries of the developed and less-developed world are a hallmark for success. Now, the pendulum is swinging back. Market-based reforms such as privatizing state-owned enterprises, liberalizing markets and balancing governments' budgets are moving to the top of the agenda all over the world.

The counter-trend from state to private has become the stuff of many books and articles – most of them enthusiastically praising the benefits of privatization. However, we should not fool ourselves. Privatization is far from being popular. Democratic governments do not win elections because of privatization, but in spite of it. The reason for this is simple: while academics tend to debate on privatization in an abstract way, politicians and ordinary people face an existential problem: politicians are afraid to lose voters, ordinary people may lose their jobs.

We are indebted to Dr (Mrs) Asha Gupta for her book which does a brilliant job in surveying the state of the art in debating privatization – with respect to both pros and cons of privatization. The book reflects the author's wide depth and grasp of knowledge in this field. Clearly organized and written in lively prose, it is an educational as well as an enjoyable read. It should become a standard reference work for all who wish to get a clear and thorough overview of the issues covered. The objective of the book is to make the reader familiar with privatization trends in developed as well as in developing countries. It looks, in particular, at the United Kingdom, East Germany and India. This set covers the wide range of differences among countries with respect to their history, level of development, political and economic system and, last but not least, cultural environment.

Accordingly, the book stresses the importance of national, regional and cultural differences – what David Stark has called the 'path-dependency' of privatization. The message is that the move towards privatization should be different around the world, with respect to both its forms and its settings, because the economic, social and political circumstances are unlikely to be the same everywhere. In the words of the author, the 'road to privatization' should have many lanes – allowing for diverging speed and sweep.

The book does not take an uncritical view on privatization. It argues 'in favour of a healthy balance between state and market, economic growth and human development, public and private sector, autonomy and accountability, national and international interests, economic growth and social justice, economic development and environmental conservation, sovereignty and governability, privatization and democracy, etc.'. It warns of 'indiscriminate privatization', which might fuel 'reactionary backfire', paving the road to re-nationalization and re-regulation. In the author's understanding, privatization can be the cure as well as the cause of economic ills.

In fact, the book is rich of controversial issues. Although – or despite – it carefully balances out the arguments in favour and against privatization, it might meet not only applause. Some readers might argue that government should invest much more energy into privatization than the author suggests. A gradualistic approach might have only little success – or might make matters even worse. However, as the author states, the debate on privatization is just at its beginning, not at its end. Looking ahead, we should be open for all kinds of serious arguments.

Every book has its omissions. This book has flown from the pen of a political scientist. Somebody might find that it underexposes the contributions of economists to the debate who have prepared the ground for it. Neither Ronald Reagan nor Margaret Thatcher would have arrived in the political world without economists' new understanding of the marketplace. The cross disciplinary, multivariate approach adopted by the author unavoidably imposes some constraints. Rather than to blame the book for its omissions it should be considered as a necessary and valuable complement to what economists have to say in favour of privatization – as well as against it.

Klaus-Dieter Schmidt
Senior Research Fellow
Kiel Institute of World Economics
Kiel, Germany

Preface

The debate initiated around the neoliberal themes of privatization, deregulation, denationalization and destatization is based on the new political economy – economic politics applied to political markets. It signifies political action in economic markets with the definite aim to maximize profit and utility – the underlying themes of neoclassical economics. In the era of globalization and interdependence, we find a close relationship between political philosophy and attitudes towards economic relations. Whether it is described as Thatcherism, Reaganomics or the contributions of Milton Friedman, the fact remains that in contrast to the ever-expanding role of the state since the Second World War, it is now being held that 'it is none of the business of government to remain in business'.

Although the interaction between the political and economic aspects of the changing role of the state is often assumed, it is rarely studied. The waves of privatization in the so-called first world, second world and third world cannot be explained straightforwardly in terms of either economics or politics. It is difficult to say whether privatization is good economics or good politics. Privatization may be viewed as good politics in terms of reducing the tax burden on the individual, while still maintaining and expanding the quality and quantity of services and products. It may also be viewed as good economics in terms of opening new opportunities for entrepreneurial innovations. In fact, two political legacies of the 1980s have influenced the economic policies of the 1990s: (1) the renewed enthusiasm for private enterprise and market economy, and (2) rolling back the frontiers of the state. The confluence of these two trends has propelled the privatization drive across the world.

The spread of privatization to the liberal democracies, post-communist societies and developing countries – comprising military or authoritarian regimes alike – is really remarkable, and more surprising is the rapidity with which this phenomenon has unfolded across the world. It is rare in history for any economic and monetary policy to catch up so quickly in the developed and the developing world simultaneously, as has privatization. It can be seen to be a part of the general rehabilitation of market forces as an intellectual disillusionment with the Keynesian approach to economic management, and a failure of socialism as a serious intellectual force. The ethics of privatization is based on the validity of private as opposed to state property rights.

Privatization refers to the transfer of various activities from the public to the private sector. It can mean the sale of state-owned enterprises either fully or in part. It can also mean a partnership between government and business through the transfer of responsibilities from the public to the private areas. In fact, privatization can signify something as broad as the shrinking of the welfare state, or it may imply simple association of the private sector with areas hitherto reserved for the public sector. It covers a wide range of ideas and policies both in economic theory and political practice.

As such, it can mean different things to different people. While in the case of the United Kingdom it may imply shifting the balance from public to private, for the United States it may only imply the blurring of boundaries between the public and the private. In a country like the United States with a very small public sector, privatization virtually amounts to the involvement of the private sector in carrying out public responsibilities. Therefore, the dynamics of privatization have to be explained both in a domestic and international context.

In fact, the move towards privatization in the developed and developing world has been so diverse in forms and varied in settings that the causes and consequences are unlikely to be the same everywhere. If political ownership had diverse origins and designs, privatization is bound to have diverse origins and designs too. While faster growth, higher efficiency and wider competition have been cited as the prime objectives of privatization in the developed world, external pressures and budgetary constraints have been the prime factors responsible for privatization in the developing world. In post-communist societies, privatization aims at quick mobilization of private investments from abroad and legitimization of the informal sector and parallel economy at the national level.

Surprisingly, in the wake of 'deideological recasting' of the concept, a variety of measures have sailed under the flag of privatization. The techniques of privatization have varied from case to case and country to country; they may take the form of divestiture involving the sale of a particular unit, the sale of a state-owned enterprise or the sale of a limited percentage of shares. Other arrangements could be contract management, franchising or leasing.

Usually, discussions on privatization have been restricted to the transfer of ownership of the public sector to the private sector. But this amounts to mere 'explicit' privatization. In the case of developing countries, privatization can also be implicit or concealed. For instance, a government may scrap cash subsidies and introduce freely tradeable exim scrips for export–import purposes. Besides providing incentives to exporters, this helps in keeping imports tied to the growth in exports. Some governments may also resort to mere marginalization which may prove to be politically less volatile than divestiture or liquidation.

While fiscal objectives dominated the privatization debate in advanced and developing countries, ideology played a major role in the shift from nationalization to privatization in post-communist societies. Ideologies do change, not always due to their being corrupted, or the end of their role or through political opportunism, but mainly due to changes in circumstances. New situations warrant new explanations and shifts in paradigm. The puzzle and intrigues of massive privatization in the former USSR and Eastern Europe can be better explained in terms of politics than economics. Since the transformation of post-communist societies was generally seen as a once-and-for-all shift from one coherent order to another, rapid privatization became the hallmark of economic reforms and transformation.

However, it would be futile to locate the causes of privatization within the state itself. Nor should it be seen as a simple matter of transferring public assets and services to the private sector. We should not forget the hard fact that politicians can never afford to be market-dependent. In the process of the privatization debate, only governments decide who will enter or exit the marketplace and under what conditions. Prior to privatization, the role of the state was to protect the economy from disruptive external forces, but it is now required to adjust the domestic economy to external exigencies. This has led to a 'domestication of international politics' and 'internationalization of domestic economies'. It has not only freed domestic economies from state regulation, but has also exposed them to greater vulnerabilities both at the domestic and international level.

Each country occupies a distinctive position in the international arena, and since its patterns of behaviour and outcome are affected by domestic politics and economics, the dynamics of privatization can be better understood in the international context. Although it is difficult to say whether privatization constitutes the cause or the consequence of globalization, one thing is certain – it is the process of globalization which has made privatization imperative and desirable in more than a hundred countries in less than a decade. The penetrability of national economic borders, pressures on public resources in the wake of a welfare state crisis, disenchantment of the public with the quality of public services, and the rise of neoliberalism raised the problems of competitiveness and sternness of the public sector in general and the efficacy of economic agents in particular.

The OECD, the IMF, the World Bank and various international lending agencies and think-tanks played a very important role in propagating the ideology and rhetoric of privatization. Multinational and transnational corporations also encouraged this type of thought and practice to harness differential endowments in a 'borderless world'. These corporations hoped to reap quick economic benefits out of privatization in the form of joint ventures.

But the international phenomenon of privatization cannot be explained in terms of a unidimensional model, it has to be explained in terms of a multidimensional model. Different countries may react to different problems in different ways and the policy outcomes may have a common appearance only by chance. Or there may be certain common factors responsible for certain economic and political changes but various countries may not interact with, learn from or induce change in other countries. Or different countries may or may not face similar problems yet they may try to emulate certain policies through interactions with one another.

Primarily because of the media focus and high attention being paid to privatization as an instrument of economic and political management in advanced economies, emerging economies tried to emulate privatization despite having an altogether different sociocultural and economic milieu. Technological advances and fast means of communication helped in electrifying the speed of emulation. External inducements and social learning also helped in diffusing the very idea of privatization across the world.

Undoubtedly, the hope of privatization in a given society is set by socioeconomic conditions, and the political culture and management expertise available therein. It may be easier for those countries to reduce the role of the state in the public sector if they have accorded considerable legitimacy to the private sector, but it may not be easy to reduce state intervention in those countries which have been emphasizing the redistributive role of the state in the name of social justice. Like all economic reforms, privatization, too, has distributional consequences. It may favour certain groups at the cost of others and, as such, it may end up shifting the 'concentration of economic power' rather than 'diffusing economic power' *per se*.

If privatization is seen merely in terms of achieving economic growth, productivity, efficiency, competition, wider choice, reduction in PSBR, bridging fiscal deficits, generation of additional resources and foreign exchange out of economic and political compulsions, to the neglect of the sociocultural context, it may very well fail. However articulate a privatization policy may be, it cannot be implemented successfully if the other factors are against it. In all societies we find a nexus among power, wealth and politics. It constitutes the political culture of a given society and the prospects of privatization depend substantially upon this nexus. The prevailing political culture, the level of economic development, geographical size, bureaucratic capabilities, entrepreneurial skills, managerial strategies and political sagacity can also affect the future prospects of privatization. An incompetent government can never lead to successful privatization.

As such, privatization has no intrinsic value of its own; it is neither good nor bad in itself. It is neither a quick fix nor a panacea. Nor can it lead to economic growth and economic development *ipso facto*. On the contrary, its success or failure depends on many other factors. At the most it can be seen as an important economic device, a political strategy or an administrative tool, but certainly not an end in itself.

The present study promises to take the reader for a drive on the Road to Privatization, mapping the developed and the developing world, covering the political, economic and sociocultural dimensions, pointing out the impediments and hazards on the way and providing a preview of the path that lies ahead. This long tour of a vast analytical territory in the shortest possible time allows only brief stopovers at the United Kingdom, East Germany and India. These stopovers in the itinerary have been selected after a careful scrutiny. The

UK experiences in privatization still remain the most widely noted and widely imitated, while the *Treuhandanstalt* provides a unique and unsurpassed example of a trustee playing a key role in privatizing and transforming the entire economy of the former GDR into a market economy in just four years.

A late arrival on the privatization horizon, India provides a typical example of a developing country where privatization implies a break with the past rather than a continuum of the past. Even if, the 'national mind' agrees to take a drive on the Road to Privatization, the national heart still remains unreconciled. As such, privatization poses both options and challenges in a big way. It is very difficult to arrive at a concensus in a country like India where apparently contradictory characteristics and structures exist simultaneously.

We may find development and underdevelopment, very rich and very poor, feudal and capitalist structures coexisting in an uneasy harmony. Even the political culture is quite mixed. No wonder, despite fulfilling all the prerequisites of privatization in terms of parliamentary democracy, deep rooted cultural and social traditions, a mixed economy, free and fair judiciary, strong media and appropriate legal structure, India suffers from a bad image at the international forum for being ambivalent, unpredictable or unreliable as far as privatization efforts are concerned. Its policy has been 'one step forward and two steps backwards' and its approach too cautious.

The objective of the present study is to make the reader familiar with the theoretical and practical aspects of privatization. It discusses the emerging trends in privatization in the so-called first world, second world and third world alike. It makes an attempt to analyse the various factors responsible for the shift in paradigm from nationalization to privatization in the context of globalization. An attempt has also been made to unravel the intrigues of privatization in an objective manner.

The study is equally concerned with the causes and consequences, pros and cons, retrospects and prospects, theoretical and practical, implicit and explicit aspects of privatization. It does not look at the privatization debate in terms of state versus market; rather it highlights the need towards establishing a healthy balance between the state and market, economic growth and human development, the public and private sector, autonomy and accountability, national and international interests, economic growth and social justice, economic development and environmental conservation, sovereignty and governability, privatization and democracy, and so on.

An endeavour has also been made to look beyond privatization by focusing on its non-economic dimensions. Privatization cannot and should not be seen in ahistorical, apolitical, acultural and non-institutional terms. It may yield different results in different contexts; it may be a total success or a total failure in two different contexts or two different periods of time. As such, there can be no perfect or foolproof model of privatization. To make an enterprise more market-responsive and open to technological changes, privatization is not always warranted.

Privatization can provide only partial solutions to resolve our fiscal problems either by 'recapitalization of capitalism' or 're-mixing the mixed economy'. It cannot provide a lasting solution to our economic ills, nor can we separate the economic problems from the sociocultural and political context. We can either begin or end our explanations with economic factors but cannot do both. As such, we will have to look beyond privatization if we wish to highlight the very presence of human beings on this earth, not as predators, polluters and consumers, but as caretakers, protectors and producers. This is certainly not the end of the debate but only a humble beginning.

ASHA GUPTA

Acknowledgements

I shall be failing in my duty if I do not acknowledge with deep gratitude all those who have been gracious and helpful in the preparation of this study. First of all I would like to thank the University Grants Commission of India for providing me with an excellent opportunity to pursue this study under its Career Award Scheme in Humanities. I am equally obliged to the Department of Political Science, University of Delhi, for providing me with the necessary affiliation, cooperation and administrative support.

Besides collecting data at the Delhi School of Economics, the Centre for Contemporary Studies, the British Council Library, the American Centre at New Delhi, the Indian Council for World Affairs, the India International Centre and the Indian Institute of Public Administration, I also benefitted from various other research fellowships awarded to me for the collection of data abroad. I express my sincere thanks to the Indian Council for Social Science Research, the Shastri Indo-Canadian Institute and Friedrich Ebert Stiftung at New Delhi for providing me with an opportunity of collecting relevant data on the United Kingdom, Canada and East Germany respectively.

I simply feel beholden to Professor V.V. Ramanadham, Professor Nick Woodward, Professor John Hill, Professor Stephen Ingle, Professor Bhiku Parekh, Dr Subroto Mitra, Professor Stein Kunhle, Dr Veena Gill, Professor Tatu Vanhenen, Professor Dirk Berg Scholasser, Dr Dieter Bos, Dr Klaus-Dieter Schmidt, Dr Horst Bucher, Dr Heinz Bongartz, Mr Uwe Siegmund, Dr Maurice Demers, Professor Romesh Mishra, and Professor Richard Ramsay for showing keen interest in my project.

I am particularly grateful to Professor V.R. Mehta, Professor R.B. Jain, Professor M.M. Sankhdher, Professor Subrata Mukherjee, Professor M.P. Singh, Professor Mahendra Kumar and Professor Neera Chandok for their valuable comments and suggestions. I am extremely grateful to Dr T.N. Chaturvedi, Mr Prakash Tandon and Professor Madhu Dandavate for thier constant support and encouragement. My special thanks go to my brother Mr V.S. Jain, Director of Finance, Steel Authority of India for explaining some of the financial intrigues of the privatization debate in India.

I am extremely grateful to my husband, Mr K.K. Gupta, without whose positive cooperation and very active support this work could never have been accomplished. I consider myself very fortunate to have such an understanding husband in an otherwise male-dominated society. My love goes to my teenage children, Anshul and Kakli, who proved to be great assets. Besides keeping me cheerful with their youthful pranks, they provided great help in preparing the bibliography and flow charts with the computation of data. This study is indeed the outcome of great efforts put in by my family members. Owing to the paucity of adequate research facilities at the workplace, a third-world scholar, especially a woman, has to rely a lot on family support.

Last but not least, I am thankful to my friends, relatives and students for their constant encouragement, love and well-wishes. I would certainly like to take this opportunity to thank the Almighty for sparing my life in an accident at Manali. The accident, in fact, provided me the much needed break and an altogether new outlook towards life. It has certainly enriched my research. At this moment, I would also like to express my regards to Shri Jugal Kishore Gupta, who not only proved to be my father *de jure* but my father *de facto*.

The publication of the present study under IPSA – Macmillan collaboration makes my point valid that in the twenty-first century, cooperation should be the guiding principle in economics and politics in lieu of maddening competition. My special thanks to Professor John Coakley, Professor Arian Asher and Mr T.M. Farmiloe for bringing out this book in such an excellent form. This collaboration can provide a model for others.

I acknowledge my debt to the innumerable scholars from various disciplines from whose writings I have benefitted. I will remain thankful to all my readers and critics for thier valuable comments, observations, suggestions and criticism.

ASHA GUPTA

1
Emerging Trends in Privatization

Moments come rarely in history when one age draws to a close and another dawns, when we stand poised between a collapsing past and uncertain future, when established landmarks disappear and the new ones are yet to arrive. Poised at the turn of the century, the world today is facing both quantitative and qualitative changes – quantitative in terms of economic growth and technological changes, and qualitative in terms of a new paradigm of a new society governed by altogether different values and ethos.

With the end of the cold war and the fall of communism, we are left with a world that is more fluid, fragmented and multipolar than ever before. The process of trade liberalization and privatization has led to a trend towards economic integration of markets at the global level. Technological innovations in transport and communications have also helped in compressing the 'economic space' dramatically. Although the world is divided into 187 sovereign states, we find only the four Ts sweeping across the world – telecommunications, television, travel and trade.

In an era of breathtaking speed and sweep, the concept of the nation-state defined as 'the power whose acts are not subject to control by another' is already under attack. In today's world, it has almost become impossible even for the most dominant states in international affairs to set their own agendas and manage their own affairs unaffected by the external affairs and exogenous ambiguities. The globalization of the economy is one of the most important factors causing the erosion of the public policy autonomy of the states. In the wake of economic and fiscal integration at the global level, states are caught in a spiral of competitive deregulation on the one hand, and domestic regulatory limitations in terms of capacity on the other (Gupta, 1996: 38–51). It has widened the gap between the rising expectations and potential output of the state institutions.

A vital debate has begun, or perhaps an old debate become renewed, about the proper role of government. In the wake of the globalization of the economy during the late 1970s and early 1980s, the political legacies for the 1990s have been: (1) renewed enthusiasm for the market economy, and

(2) rolling back the frontiers of the state. The confluence of these two trends led to great hopes for privatization, cutting the ideological barriers for the first time in recent history.

The globalization of the economy propelled governments all over the world to resort to structural adjustments at the political level. Various measures towards liberalization, deregulation and privatization aim at facilitating the shrinkage of the state on the one hand, and the empowering of citizens on the other. The purpose of these reforms is to shift the focus from a bureaucratic model of public management to a market model.

Neoliberalism, under the populist forms of Reaganomics and Thatcherism, is based on the four principles that:

1. the market mechanism should be used wherever feasible;
2. competition should be encouraged wherever possible because it leads to efficiency and customer-orientation;
3. individualism and individual choice should take precedence over collective choices and planned provision; and
4. state provision should be kept to the minimum. (Flynu, 1989: 97–109)

The 'new right' preference is for a situation in which the supply-side structure is competitive and privately-owned, and where the demand-side consists of individual purchases. When this combination is not possible, alternative arrangements can be made.

The normative theories justifying privatization as a shift in public policy draw their inspirations from *laissez faire* individualism and free market economics. To them, these promise greater efficiency, smaller government and wider choice. Privatization signifies withdrawal from the 'whole' to the 'part' – from public action to private concerns. The swing is not from sociability to privacy, but from a civic concern to the pursuit of self-interest. The pursuit of private gains is assumed to serve public interests better. At the heart of the privatization thesis lies the assumption that the public sector is always wasteful, inefficient and unproductive. It is based on the crude division between productive economic relations and unproductive social relations. Under this framework, the profit motive is given the topmost priority.

Four types of government policies can bring about a shift from the public to the private sector:

1. the cessation of public programmes and the disengagement of government from certain responsibilities;
2. a transfer of public ownership and assets to private organizations;
3. the financing of private services through contracts or vouchers; and
4. allowing the private sector to enter into those areas hitherto reserved exclusively for the public sector. (Starr, 1991: 24)

A shift from public to private may result not only on account of government initiatives, but also on account of pressure groups on the one hand, and domestic and foreign institutions on the other.

In fact, privatization can be seen as part of a more general rehabilitation of market forces as an intellectual disillusionment with the Keynesian approach to economic management and the failure of socialism as a serious intellectual force. The rise of Reaganomics and Thatcherism succeeded in advocating the virtues of private enterprise, private initiative and private motive. These advocated rolling back the frontiers of the state in order to promote an efficient and free society. The 'ethics' of privatization is based upon the validity of private as opposed to state property rights. As such, the emphasis on privatization did not occur in an intellectual vacuum.

The genesis

Nationalization, once in fashion, is out. Privatization is very much in vogue, and the followers of this new fashion include people belonging to different political hues. The massive scale on which privatization has taken place during the last decade is amazing. Since 1985, governments worldwide have raised US$328 billion by selling state-owned enterprises (SOEs) (Miller, 1995: 83), and it is expected that this figure will double by the year 2000. Western Europe is expected to raise US$150 billion through privatizations by 1998 (Davidson, 1993: 38–39); France is expected to raise approximately US$36 billion during 1993–8; and privatizations are expected to yield US$27.6 billion in Italy, US$16.7 billion in Spain, US$10 billion in Sweden, US$5 billion in Finland, US$23.3 billion in Germany, and US$26.6 billion in Turkey (Palmer, 1993: 16–17). Sales in UK have raised US$60 billion since 1979, and sales of SOEs in Latin America have amounted to approximately 35 per cent of the total value of privatizations across the world in 1992.

Privatization is essentially a contribution of Thatcherism to the vocabulary of politics. Today's fiscally ambitious and ideologically charged phenomenon began as a British import, and prior to 1979 when Margaret Thatcher became British prime minister, the word privatization hardly appeared in political debate. The word 'privatize' or 'privatise' first appeared in Webster's New Collegiate Dictionary in 1983 and was defined narrowly – to make private, especially to change from public to private control of ownership. However, Peter Drucker, a business writer, used this term as early as 1968, and Anthony H. Pascal, a Rand Corporation analyst in the United States, used the term in 1972 (Donahue, 1989: 4).

Before Margaret Thatcher came to power in 1979, the theme of privatization hardly featured in the election manifesto of the Conservative Party, although the party's desire to 'roll back the frontiers of the state' and promote a 'property-owning democracy' were specifically mentioned. The privatization movement gained momentum only during the 1980s, during which many western and non-western societies tried to follow the privatization lead given by the United Kingdom, though none could reach that far. In most countries, privatization involved not only an economic device but also a political strategy (Gupta, 1996: 38–51).

France, for instance, the most active of the West European countries in implementing the privatization policy, adopted a very cautious approach. In 1981, France had adopted a policy of large-scale nationalization under the leadership of François Mitterrand, but it was only in April 1986 when Jacques Chirac became leader that the French government expressed its desire to sell shares in 65 SOEs, having a total value of FFr250 000–300 000 million with approximately 800 000 employees (Fraser, 1988: 108). In 1988, Francois Mitterrand got reelected and adopted a policy of 'ni–ni' (neither nationalization nor privatization). But it was honoured more in breach than in observance.

Recession, increased expenses on social welfare and a growing budget deficit forced many governments in Western Europe to concede politically what had been long obvious economically – rigid restraints on ownership of the public sector were no longer tenable. Although there were many factors responsible for the economic stagnation in developed economies, the blame was generally put on the poor performance of the public sector. Four factors contributed to the notion of efficiency and the effectiveness of privatization: (1) deindustrialization, (2) public sector productivity, (3) perception of public work and (4) emergence of pro-market ideology. The notion of privatization appealed to the political elites and the masses alike because it was the only notion that promised to maintain services and yet cut taxes (Sclar, 1994: 330).

Just as we notice waves of nationalization not only in Eastern Europe but also in Western Europe in the wake of the Second World War, we find waves of privatization in these very countries during the last two decades. These 'waves' emphasize massive and large-scale ownership changes. While nationalization signifies expansion, privatization signifies contraction (Siegmund, 1996: 5). Nationalization is the process by which the state, in the wake of its sovereignty, takes property away from private individuals or firms either by legal or judicial action. The ethics of nationalization is based on the validity of state as opposed to private property rights, the principles on which the property is to be expropriated, and the compensation due to the previous owners. Privatization, on the other hand, is based on the validity of private as opposed to state property rights, the principles on which property is to be distributed, and the compensation due to the state (Calvert, 1991: 3).

At one time, the public sector was regarded as a major instrument of economic growth. The International Monetary Fund and the World Bank refused to provide loans to developing countries during the 1960s unless and until they resorted to nationalization of the key industries. The same very instructions are now keeping pressure on developing countries to privatize their public sector enterprises before applying for loans. During the 1960s, industrialized countries opted for the public sector to achieve social and political stability, while developing countries opted for the same for attaining self-confidence, developing heavy industries, creating employment opportunities and reducing the scope of exploitation by the private sector (Anand, 1994: 55).

The pendulum has now shifted in favour of privatization, and the shift should be seen as a historical phenomenon. There are many factors responsible for this: the public sector, for example, received a major setback in the middle of the 1970s due to the sharp rise in oil prices, making it difficult for many economies to adjust to the situation quickly. This inability to adjust quickly was attributed to the inefficiency of the public sector in general. The proliferation of transnational and multinational corporations pushed the logic of nationalization to the background. Having sufficient resources for new industrial projects, they found the prevailing government policies inconsistent with the globalization of their national economics. It was felt that the crisis in the form of economic decline and recession in advanced economies could only be solved by market-oriented policies and economic liberalization (Hawarth, 1992: 16–35).

With the increased flow of international capital, the demand for economic liberalization became more widespread in the advanced economies during the 1980s and for developing countries during the 1990s. The conditions of competition and organization of interfirm economic relations changed with the centralization of private capital during and post-Second World War period. The circumstances which warranted nationalization in industrialized countries were no longer valid. Nationalization was resorted to in these countries primarily to curb the financial powers of private capital and TNCs. The second important reason was to 'cartelize' the markets through administrative measures. Thirdly, it was argued that the large corporations, engaged in monopolistic practices in sales and raw-material markets, blocked scientific-technical progress and ignored the interests of the labour force (Kuznetsov, 1993: 9).

This trend towards nationalization and statization of economic life was ideologically sustained by the Marxists, institutionalists and the followers of Keynes alike. During the 1970s, the crisis in the welfare state was castigated in terms of conflict between the public sector and private enterprise. Against the background of recurring fiscal crises, it was no longer possible to support welfare state as an appendage of economic growth. As such, the ideas of self-reliance, user charges and means-testing began to dominate the economic and political discourse in advanced welfare states. Systematic attempts were made in these countries during the 1980s and 1990s to shift responsibilities towards human welfare from the state to society through privatization (Gupta, 1994: 94–122).

From nationalization to privatization

The need for the state as an entrepreneur, which was felt strongly during the 1940s and 1950s, disappeared during the 1980s and 1990s. Economic liberalization, deregulation and privatization became the topics of national and international discourse on political economy. However, these policies did not become popular immediately after the oil crisis during the mid-1970s. For the first few years, the SOEs (state-owned enterprises) were used as an instrument for supporting global demands.

Although governments all over the world generally imposed more restrictions and obligations on SOEs than on private and commercial enterprises, the SOEs were made the scapegoats for the huge financial losses incurred due to the adverse public policies. While the SOEs were under obligation to maintain jobs and fulfil social obligations, they were not allowed to raise the prices of their products and services or raise capital from the open market to meet the rising costs and inflation. They had to depend willy nilly on budgetary support and state subsidies. This resulted in huge fiscal losses and dismal economic performance. For instance, during 1989–91 the losses of SOEs as a percentage of GDP reached 9 per cent in Argentina, 8 per cent in Yugoslavia and 5 per cent on average in sub-Saharan Africa. In 1991, approximately 30 per cent of the SOEs in the People's Republic of China were found to be loss-making (Kikeri, Nellis and Shirley, 1992).

The globalization and internationalization of domestic economies and transformations in the wake of oil-shocks, the penetrability of national economic borders, pressures on public resources in the wake of crises in the welfare state, public disenchantment with the quality of public services, the rise of the new-right and end onto neoconservatism in favour of market economies raised the problem of the competitiveness of economic agents and the efficacy of administration and management of the public sector (Mascarenhas, 1993: 319–28). The OECD, the IMF, the World Bank and a chain of international rating agencies and think-tanks played a very important role in propagating the ideology and rhetoric of privatization across the world. Adopting methodological individualism as their base, the neoconservatives and the new right groups advocated economic liberalization, deregulation of the economy and privatization of the public sector enterprises and services.

In the late 1970s and early 1980s, privatization gained political acceptance in advanced capitalist countries. While declining growth rates, rising unemployment, a decline in investments and rises in inflation led to the privatization drive in most of the industrialized countries, an acute debt crisis propelled the privatization debate in most of the developing countries and put it on the national agenda. With the fall of the communal economy in the former USSR, Eastern Europe and People's Republic of China, the post-communist societies became the testing ground for privatization on the massive scale.

However, the problem of post-communist economic transformation proved to be predominantly political. Prior to the fall of the Berlin wall, the problem of transformation in Eastern Europe was seen overwhelmingly as a political problem – the problem of liberalizing and democratizing the authoritarian regimes as early and as fast as possible. With the sudden collapse of the communist regime, the focus shifted from political to economic transformation. Western economists and international financial institutions also encouraged mass privatization and 'shock-therapy' in Eastern Europe and post-communist societies. Some of the scholars on post-communist societies even went to the extent of visualizing economic transformation as a precondition for democratic transition and not vice versa. To them, the ascendancy of neoliberal views in Central and Eastern Europe should be seen as an ideology of transformation rather than a transformation of a theory (Feigenbaum and Henig, 1992).

Privatization, like nationalization, aims at establishing a new pattern of ownership. It is not only the outcome of the groups in power but it also helps in forming and shaping these groups. For instance, an analysis of privatization programmes and policies in ASEAN (Thailand, Philippines, Indonesia, Malaysia and Singapore) reveals the role played by the government in changing the pattern of ownership in these societies. In these countries more and more politicians got into the business of privatization, and business terminology began to permeate the political horizon. Privatization became a means towards personal enrichment. For instance, we find an alliance between the political leaders and conglomerates in Indonesia – the former supplying licences, import monopolies and contracts to the latter. In Singapore, too, privatization policies and programmes have been used in the past to confirm and legitimize rule by the political elite.

Privatization not only alters the ownership patterns but it also alters the agent–principal relationships, having considerable impact on the performance of a firm. Under the public sector, the public acts as the principal while the politicians and top civil servants act as agents. The boards of SOEs and various departments comprise the second tier of agents. These agents are supposed to work in the public interest, although Hayek and others have questioned that, arguing that the ballot-box cannot provide a sufficient mechanism to ensure the public interest, especially when the public generally lacks the necessary information to be able to check on bureaucrats, public sector managers and politicians. After privatization, the very principal–agent relationship is changed: now the shareholders of a firm become the principals and the managers become the agents. Managers are now required to manage firms in the interests of shareholders, although there is no dearth of evidence of managers cheating their shareholders.

In fact, privatization alters the very internal and external business environment (Parker, 1993). Increasing pressures to internationalize the domestic economy cannot be compatible with the principles of public accountability and national interests inherent in public sector and state ownership. Destatization became necessary in the beginning of the 1970s just as nationalization had become necessary during the 1930s, 1940s and 1950s in industrialized countries, and in the 1960s and 1970s in developing countries. If the legal norms regulating the activities of private enterprises are extended to state enterprises working on commercial lines, we may call it 'destatization', but not privatization. Strictly speaking, privatization connotes changes to the entire social relationship network, not only in economic terms but also in terms of political, moral and informal social relations. While privatization alters the very environment of business by creating new opportunities for production, investment and trade, it also leads to uncertainties and vulnerabilities in the wake of swift changes in economic and political policies at the local, national or global level.

Types of privatization

The conventional approaches to macroeconomics are found inadequate to understand the worldwide phenomenon of privatization. Nor can the approaches based on pure economics or public administration help us in understanding the political underplannings, the timing and various forms and techniques of privatization. These may present privatization as an administrative tool to set the political and economic apparatus to order, or a necessary exercise in terms of structural adjustment. These are unable to explain the politics behind privatization programmes and policies in a given society and its effects and consequences on political ideas, institutions and behaviours.

In fact, privatization has been adopted in different countries in different contexts, and each country may have its own rationale behind adopting the privatization policy. The objectives may vary from country to country depending on their socioeconomic conditions and prevailing political culture. The administrative objectives may aim at making the government function better by reducing the burden on public bureaucracy on the one hand, and raising additional resources through user's charges, vouchers, asset sales and contracting out on the other.

The economic objectives behind the privatization drive could be: achieving economic efficiency, more competition, wider choice and people's capitalism on the one hand, and reducing the government's operating deficit, public sector borrowing requirement and external debt through debt swaps on the other. The political objectives could aim at reducing the role of the state, the elimination of government interference in economic management, the diffusion of economic and political power among the supporters of the ruling elite, the appeasement of Bretton Woods institutions and curtailment of trade union powers (Suleiman and Waterbury, 1990: 2).

On the basis of administrative, economic and political objectives, privatization efforts can be classified into three categories: (1) pragmatic,

(2) tactical and (3) systematic (Feigenbaum and Henig, 1994). *Pragmatic privatizations* are usually carried out by the bureaucratic units. Top bureaucrats like to resort to privatization when they find it cost-saving to purchase a service from outside or when new technologies render older forms of organization obsolete. Privatization occurs when top bureaucrats and politicians involved move beyond traditional 'make–buy' decisions and allow private organizations to take over the provision of goods and services hitherto reserved exclusively for the public sector.

Tactical privatization aims at pursuing short-term political goals – to attract voters, reward supporters or achieve product-differentiation. For instance, the privatization programme of asset sales during 1986–8 by the Chirac government in France primarily aimed at attracting voters. It was a deviation from the economic policies of the French socialists. From the very beginning, the Chirac government had made it very clear that it believed in widening the shareholder base and expressed its desire to dispose of the state's interests in 65 banks and other companies by the end of March 1991, many of which had been brought into public ownership by the socialists themselves in 1982. These included nine industrial companies, thirteen insurance companies, four finance companies, thirty eight banking companies and one communication agency (*The Economist*, 13 April 1991: 52). It can be termed a tactical form of political product differentiation. As long as the electorate believes their elected officials and political representatives, it does not matter whether it is true privatization or not.

All attempts towards *systematic privatizations* aim at shifting the very balance of power by lowering expectations of the government, reducing government capacity and transforming political stakes. A deeper analysis of privatization programmes, policies, techniques and priorities reveals the articulations behind the privatization ideology (Samson, 1994: 79). Sometimes, socio-economic problems are invented by the elite to justify particular solutions. The 'big government' existed even prior to the Reagan administration in the United States, but it was not treated as a burden on the exchequer or a threat to the moral fibre. Similarly, the problems of overload, fiscal crisis or welfare state crisis were not at all new, but these were flagged by the 'ascendent right' in politics only in the 1980s in the form of Thatcherism and Reaganomics in UK and the USA respectively.

As such, privatization cannot be seen merely as an outcome of the actions of the groups in power, it also helps as an agent in forming and shaping these groups. But the different techniques and modalities of privatization have different influences on the producers and consumers. Like all economic reforms, privatization, too, has distributional consequences. It can favour certain groups at the cost of others. As such, some governments may be found reluctant to sell assets to 'undesirable' domestic and foreign investors. While the lure of certain benefits may bring forward certain domestic or foreign investors, these may create new sources of economic and regional disparities leading to political instability or social problems. For instance, in Malaysia the privatization policies aimed at strengthening the role of the *Bhumiputras* in business at the cost of others.

Similarly, the modalities of privatization in post-communist societies were conditioned by domestic politics. For instance, the choice of direct sale or free vouchers to all adults in Russia could not be justified on economic grounds, but it certainly helped in legitimization of the new leadership. In the wake of the hegemonic nature of neoliberal ideology, its anti-communist and western stance and widespread hopelessness and resulting decline on reaching any consensus on economic reform, privatization appeared to be the only hope and no alternative could be found. However, the neoliberal view in post-communist societies should only be seen as an 'official ideology' – distinct from the 'operating one'. Many significant social groups in these societies still remain unrepresented.

In fact, the very privatization process has led to a number of political controversies in post-communist societies. While during the command economies the planners reigned supreme, in the nascent market economies the lawyers and the economists have an upper hand. On the one hand, these lawyers and economists assist their governments in framing rules and regulations, on the other hand they advise foreign investors, SOEs and prospective clients on how to work within their new and fragile systems. As such, they have been acting both as the rule-makers and rule-interpreters simultaneously, creating a lot of scope for manipulation and quick gains in the process. For instance, spontaneous privatizations in the form of illegal appropriation of public assets in Poland, Hungary and Russia allowed the *nomenklatura* (the former elite under the communist system) to retain and even enhance their wealth and power.

It is now becoming visible and obvious that those in power can use the state machinery to propagate the ideology of privatization in their own self-interest. However, privatization is likely to cover a more lasting source of benefit if the government assets are divested once and for all. The decisions about the beneficiaries may be influenced by the government depending upon the degree of control it exercises. It may favour those who are politically committed to it. Privatization by contracting out or leasing may be given or taken away according to fluctuations in the degree of government favour enjoyed or according to the fluctuations in the government's powers (Milne, 1992: 23).

While some countries may adopt privatization for its long-term implications, others may resort to it for short-term political gains. The immediate need for the generation of cash resources led to privatizations in the early 1980s in many western societies, although pragmatic privatization can be traced back to 1932 when many municipal services were privatized in the United States through user fees. But such efforts were usually treated as the expansion of the public sector rather than the shrinkage of government (Henig, 1990: 657).

Under tactical privatization, public assets may be sold at a discount as a form of patronage; contracts may be awarded to campaign managers, supporters and contributors; regulations may be reduced to serve the interests of political supporters or unpopular taxes may be avoided to please friends in business. Under systematic privatization, ownership patterns may be changed, new interest groups may be formed, governmental intervention may be delegitimized or the powers of the trade unions may be curbed (Wolfe, 1989: 20).

Systematic privatization may also take three forms: (1) a change in the capacity of already mobilized interests, (2) a change in the rules, culture and expectations of the public and (3) a change in the legal, political and economic institutions of the society. When there is a substantial decrease in the power of one group or groups of people at the cost of others, the first type of systematic privatization occurs. For instance, privatization may lead to a curb on the powers and influence of trade unions. This was certainly one of the chief motives of privatization in the United Kingdom.

The second form of systematic privatization aims at delegitimizing the public sector. The Thatcher government succeeded in making the privatization programme popular by making an unapologetic case for the virtues of capitalism, individualism and the profit motive (Brittan, 1986). On the other hand, privatization in developing countries has occurred in an entirely different socioeconomic and cultural milieu than the one prevailing in advanced economies (Woodward, 1990: 266–83). It is easier for those countries to reduce the role of the state which have accorded considerable legitimacy to the private sector than those emphasizing the redistributive role of the state in pursuit of social justice. Privatization leads to cultural hegemony of the privileged elites and delegitimization of the state itself (Carnoy, 1984: 75–6).

Frankly speaking, managing change through privatization requires a great deal of political sagacity and administrative expertise. No government can implement privatization programmes and policies without active cooperation from top bureaucrats, legal experts and financial analysts. All privatization efforts require a lot of restructuring prior to privatization – selecting the enterprises or parts to be privatized, obtaining loans, establishing long-term guarantees, floating shares, creating debt–equity swaps, and so on. Very few advocates of privatization know that instead of raising additional revenues and resources, privatization may actually cost money.

Similarly, instead of reducing the role of the government and public bureaucracy, the privatization process may actually enhance it (Jain and Bongartz, 1994). In the privatization process, the conceiving, planning, goal-setting, standard-setting, performance-monitoring and evaluating parts still remain with the government. If these are done badly, public interests still suffer. An incompetent government cannot lead to economic efficiency, even if it decides to privatize. Some governments have made deliberate attempts to internalize a particular world-view using the state machinery to propagate the ideology of privatization in their self-interest. Some governments are forced to resort to the rhetoric of privatization owing to domestic compulsions and international pressures.

Privatization and globalization

It is difficult to say whether privatization constitutes the cause or consequence of globalization. It was the globalization of the economy which made privatization imperative and desirable in more than 100 countries the world over. The globalization process has to be understood in terms of the internationalization of production to harness differential endowments for the domestic benefit of the country or region concerned. Information and rapid means of communication also play an important role in this process. Multinational and transnational corporations have encouraged this type of thought and practice, requiring an environment in which capital, technology and inputs (raw materials or component parts) and outputs (finished goods) can have a free flow across borders. Privatization can prove to be a boon in terms of joint ventures between multinational corporations (MNCs) and SOEs across the world. MNCs can now take advantage of cheap labour where it is to be found and 'robotization' where it cannot be found.

Prior to privatization, the role of the state was to protect the economy from disruptive external forces, but now it is required to adjust the domestic economy to external pressures. In the era of economic interdependence, while certain countries have been able to reap the benefits of prevailing modes of global production, marketing and distribution, only a few countries are in a position to play the strategic role in policy-making. Most often, the leaders are now found to be acting as conduits between global trends and domestic requirements. Many ministries (Finance; Industries; Labour) at the state level are no longer tied to domestic constituencies but to the apron strings of international bodies. They are required to carry out the global policies reached at various international economic summits, even if they had no decisive role in deciding them. Privatization and destatization seem to be the logical and natural outcome of this trend.

The economic expansion stimulated by Keynesian demand management and Fordist industrialism also led to a new economic conjuncture. Even the advanced economies found it difficult to sustain the social policies committed during the decades of economic growth and development in the era of economic recession and decline. They had to borrow heavily from avid lenders. Even the United States became one of the largest debtor nations. This led to the growing ownership of US industries and real estate by foreigners. As the debt problem became more acute, the governments' accountability to foreign creditors became more overwhelming than to their own citizens. Investment banks do play an instrumental role in identifying and setting the priorities for privatization in a given country; they also motivate the potential investors (Gallo, 1993: 197–205).

Privatization got political acceptability at the global level primarily because of the rise and efforts of the 'new right'. The globalization of the economy, in the wake of new innovations in science and technology and rapid means of transport and communication, provided the perfect setting to the privatization drama. Privatization and globalization helped in changing the old definition of core and periphery (Cox, 1991: 340). In the late twentieth century, enterprise corporatism shifted from the economics of scale of Fordist mass production to the economics of flexibility and quality-production of post-Fordism. In fact, the post-Fordist practices in key sectors helped in the resurgence of Asia-Pacific in the late twentieth century.

In the Asia-Pacific region, the states have played an important role in shaping the development of their economies. The patterns of production and distribution in this region are built upon long-term supply and subcontracting networks in contrast with vertically integrated American corporations; small and medium-sized manufacturing firms in contrast with costly and highly specialized production machinery; and innovations in the process of production in contrast with the creation of new products (Bernard, 1994: 219). The proponents of A-CASH (Alternative Capitalist System Hypothesis) have also argued that there are significant differences between the capitalist mode of development and these differences are evident in organizational arrangements, institutionalized roles and the sociocultural environment.

In the present scenario, where governments can create sound policies and institutions, they cannot create ground rules and regulations to be followed by the private sector, multinational and transnational corporations. As such, firms and managers cannot be seen only as the agent of the market, rather they have to be seen as the players of the game, setting their own rules and regulations in the process (Teece, 1993: 199–225). The hyper-liberal tendencies in the form of deregulation, privatization and destatization facilitate the restructuring of the labour force and social relations of production to serve the vested economic interests of the elite.

During the 1980s, in advanced countries, the stress used to be on the separation of the state and the market, while in the post-cold-war 1990s, the stress is on cooperation between the state and the market. In the context of globalization of the economy, the whole debate on privatization needs to be seen in a new perspective. So far, cooperation among the economic actors in advanced economies, particularly in the United States, was seen as anti-competitive, collusive and undesirable. Of late, business schools in the west have started advocating the litany of cooperative in lieu of competitive strategies (Nielsen, 1988: 475–92). We find widespread examples of complementary cooperation in East Asia where interfirm networks are common, and the number of firms cooperating in this way can be very large. For instance, approximately 30 000 business units serve as networks supplying autoparts and services to the Toyota Motor Company itself (Fruin and Nishiguchi, 1993: 225–46).

It is no longer impossible for different systems to interact with one another in mutual and global interests. We find tremendous flows of capital, goods, technology and human resources between Canada, China and Japan – three different systems altogether. What is important is that the individual actors should be like-minded. As such, business firms can be more successful than their political counterparts in finding out ways of accommodating various differences within a state or within a region by employing various management strategies. As such, the very future of globalization and privatization depends on the prospects of economic cooperation and systematic tolerance of the vast differences prevalent across the world. We cannot resort to 'systematic compatibility'. Governments and corporations are also required to evolve their own rules and regulations to cope up with the vast complexities and uncertainties prevalent in today's world.

Privatization and democracy

A serious threat to privatization can come from organized democracy. The other part of the risk involves political mobilization of those who become marginalized in the process of structural adjustments. These dangers have already been predicted by the neoliberal ideologues researching on the problem of ungovernability of modern democracies (Crozier, Huntington and Watanuki, 1975). The mutually supportive relationship of a 'mass-democracy' and 'welfare state' is no longer valid. On the contrary, the present symptoms indicate that the democratic mass politics may not work in the direction of expansion or maintenance of the welfare state. The same logic can apply to privatization efforts across the world. It may lose political support when its true social costs are revealed to the masses. Therefore, in view of regular swings of nationalization, privatization and re-nationalization in the form of re-regulation is not ruled out. Nor can we rule out a threat to political repression or central planning. There is only a remote possibility of the participatory type of economic management and public policies inspired by the motto of economic growth with social justice (Stackhouse, 1994: 100–18).

Although it is possible to develop a market economy without a democratic political system or run a democracy without a market economy, both are complementary. Chile, Korea, Mexico and Taiwan provide examples of the successful development of a market economy under semi-authoritarian political systems. India provides an example of successful democracy in terms of the political process even before the economic reforms were launched in 1991. The fall of communism in Central and Eastern Europe in 1989 ushered in a new era of the consolidation of economic and political forces towards a market economy and political democracy simultaneously. These post-communist societies are facing a cruel dilemma: transforming their economies is necessary for the survival of political democracy even if it proves fatal in terms of the political careers of the leaders involved in this process.

Most post-communist societies badly need foreign investments and transfers of technology to modernize the old firms and create new industries in the wake of competition for markets at the global level. Privatization seems to provide the only practical solution. It has also become crucial for the successful transition to democracy. In these societies, it is difficult to mask the underlying tensions between indigenous firms and foreign investors, between free markets and economic nationalism or between economic efficiency and social justice. As such, local leaders have to function under many domestic constraints. Privatization implies a break with the past, rather than the continuance or expansion of the past political and economic policies. They have to row against the wind. Indiscriminate privatization can fuel the reactionary trends in fragile democracies.

The structural adjustment programmes and policies in these societies aim at restructuring the economy by reducing the role of the state and subjecting economic activities to market forces. Liberalization, privatization and adjustment programmes are designed to overcome the fiscal crisis on the one hand, and achieve higher indexes of economic growth on the other. These have become the constituent element of the democratization process the world over. While Latin American countries are trying to transform the free market capitalism already prevailing therein, the post-communist societies have just introduced it. But in all cases, these complex changes are bound to affect the state, civil society, the political regime and socioeconomic relations in the process. Venezuela, for instance, is facing the deep crisis of governability in the wake of structural adjustment programmes and policies on the one hand, and consolidation of democracy on the other.

The Venezuelan political system used to be cited as an apt example of an institutionalized and committed democratic stability situation (Azhar, 1990). Here the democratization process began as early as 1958. But, in 1989, disturbances were made by marginal sectors from urban areas to thwart the structural adjustment programme. It was also affected adversely by military interventions, military coup d'etats in 1992, and institutional conflicts between the President and the Congress. It raised the crucial question: whether the Venezuelan political system has the capacity to sustain the structural adjustment programme and the democratic political order or not?

Other such examples have put a questionmark to the issue of compatibility of privatization with democracy. Some scholars have even raised doubts about the validity and desirability of democracy in the twenty-first century. Ample studies have been made in the past to trace the growth from feudalism to democracy, and many scholars have opined that capitalist development is associated with democracy. To them, the growth of democracy helped in weakening the landed upper class and strengthening the working and middle class (Moore, 1966) – the prerequisites for democracy. In fact, the theory of democratic capitalism is based on the commitment on the part of 'non-proprietors' to accept capital's private property, and commitment on the part of the 'proprietors' to accept the existence of some political institutions through which the non-proprietors can try to influence the political process on the way in which resources are invested and production distributed (Przeworski and Wallerstein, 1982: 52–68).

Many contemporary scholars, on the other hand, have argued that neither capitalists nor the capital market, but the 'contradictions' of capitalism advanced the cause of democracy (Rueschmeyer, Stephens and Stephens, 1992: 7). They have argued that the 'new rights' basically aim at achieving economic autonomy from political control by delinking the market from the state. They have also argued that it is not the business of government to remain in business and this is not possible without disarticulating all forms of politics and undermining democratic institutions. They aim at giving birth to new actors and new macropolitical systems by propagating the theory of the invisible hand and market economy, with a definite aim to curb the process of the state, reduce the public sphere and dimension of public policies.

Paradoxically, all the policies and programmes of structural adjustment (deregulation, liberalization and privatization) are launched by democratically elected governments, even if they appear to be against the interests of the state on the one hand, and 'non-proprietors' on the other. While the better-off sections of society gain through structural adjustments and privatization programmes, the lower strata have to foot the bill in terms of economic and regional disparities, retrenchment, and cutbacks in welfare and social benefits. In post-communist societies, the communist *nomenklatura* and in other countries the 'business–politician–bureaucrat' nexus have been able to reap economic gains in the game of privatization politics.

To some, privatization has proved to be a hurdle to the growth and development of institutionalized democracy in post-communist societies, and the sustenance of democracy in other countries. In a democracy, state action is identified with the public interest, while privatization tends to nourish the private interest. While 'public' is supposed to contain the whole, 'private' denotes only a part. Moreover, 'public' signifies common interests, while 'private' signifies personal interests. By shifting responsibilities from the government to the market, privatization alters the very institutional framework through which citizens in a democracy promote their interests. Moreover, privatization is bound to divide society into losers and gainers. For instance, the substitution of market-determined price for subsidized price is bound to affect many people adversely. In a democracy, the losers are unlikely to accept their lot; they can resort to politics, litigation and other means of confrontation which is bound to create feud and disharmony in the society.

Neoliberalism and neoconservatism in the form of structural adjustments and privatization can cause strain, stress and contradictions in a political democracy, and we may not find harmony, compatibility and mutual reinforcement between privatization and democracy in the next century.

The present symptoms indicate that democratic mass politics may not support structural adjustment and privatization programmes and policies. Loud resentment by feminists, environmentalists and social workers can already be heard.

Another crucial question that arises in this context is that of autonomy versus accountability. While entrepreneurship requires autonomy, a personal vision of the future, secrecy and risk-taking behaviour on the part of top managers, the 'democratic administration' calls for accountability, citizen participation, openness and transparency in policy-making and stewardship. In coming decades, a conflict may ensue between entrepreneurial autonomy and democratic accountability. While privatization may enhance the autonomy and discretion of managers and entrepreneurs of privatized agencies, it may make them less accountable to the public. Only effective citizen participation can provide the necessary check. For this, we again need a democratic structure. As such, the relationship between privatization and democracy remains tenacious.

2
The Concept, Objectives and Techniques of Privatization

Privatization as a 'fuzzy concept' and as 'an art', has been growing in terms of importance ever since the 1980s. In less than one decade, the privatization movement has become a worldwide phenomenon. The emerging trends in privatization all the world over clearly demonstrate the desire to strengthen and expand the market at the cost of government. Generally speaking, privatization refers to the transfer of activities from the public to the private sector. It can mean the sale of state-owned enterprises either fully or in part. It can also mean a partnership between government and business through the transfer of responsibilities from the public sector to the private sector. It may also be described as an attempt to recapitalize capitalism both by reducing the size of the public sector and by providing ready-made markets to the private sector.

Privatization should be seen as an approach towards economic policy in a given political system, rather than a policy in itself. It is based on the assumption that market provision is always more efficient than public provision. At the heart of the privatization thesis lies the belief that the private sector is more efficient, competitive and cost-effective than the public sector. Its support is rooted in the ideological desire to shrink government under the banner of pragmatism (Sclar, 1994: 329–36). Some look at it as a political strategy for diverting demands away from the state, reducing the load off government thereby (Gupta, 1996: 38–51).

What is privatization?

Privatization is, in fact, a very vague concept (Starr, 1988: 1101), and difficult to define. Etymologically, the term privatization implies 'withdrawal of the state from the production of goods and services or transfer of ownership from the public sector to the private sector' (Webster's New Collegiate Dictionary, 1983). In the narrow sense, it refers to the sale or leasing of assets in which the state has a majority interest, contracting out publicly provided services, substitution of user charges for tax finance, and liberalization measures aimed at providing competition and efficiency in enterprises hitherto reserved for the public sector (Heald, 1983).

Strictly speaking, attempts at liquidation of publicly owned assets, the sale of minority shares while retaining governmental control, deregulation of economic activities and efforts to make public sector enterprises behave like private ones, cannot be cited as instances of privatization (Walle, 1989: 611). Nor can all attempts at liberalization and deregulation be termed privatization. Nor can revitalization of public sector enterprises be called privatization as such, although such attempts may lead to privatization in due course.

In the broad sense, the concept of privatization can be used to describe any activity implying the rolling back of the state or government. It can take various forms: it can be both explicit or implicit; it can come from above or below. A distinction can be made among mega, micro and macro-privatizations. Mega-privatization refers to the general roll back of the state, macro-privatization refers to market orientation and micro-privatization to the strengthening of the enterprise culture without changing the ownership *per se*. While mega-privatization is concerned with the values of freedom and choice, macro-privatization is concerned with the value of the efficient allocation of resources, and micro-privatization with efficiency at the operational level (Sankar and Reddy, 1989).

Different countries at different stages of economic development may adopt different policies in the name of privatization. Surprisingly, privatization came into practice first and the theoretical framework was provided much later. Its genesis can be traced back to the ideological swing to the right in the United States and United Kingdom with a mild shift in economic policies taking place in the former USSR and China. As the term privatization gained currency, the economic reforms in Eastern Europe, the redefining of relations between government and public enterprises in Western Europe, liberalization measures in India and Pakistan, the liquidation of public enterprises on a very small scale in Africa, and debt–equity swaps in Latin America were all described as privatization, particularly by the western media. Implicitly, privatization was seen as a process and not as a cherished goal.

In the United Kingdom, the process of privatization began under the leadership of Margaret Thatcher in the late 1970s and early 1980s, largely out of frustration with the deficits and perceived ineffectiveness of state enterprises or parastatals. Although efficient operation of these enterprises was a legitimate concern, often the more pressing motive for privatization was the fiscal drain on the government exchequer (Christiansen, 1989: 597).

Initially, attempts were made to look at the possible savings in government and the availability of additional resources by selling some of the public enterprises without indulging in any serious political debate. Gradually, privatization became an end in itself. The government purposefully emphasized the ownership as the key variable in economic performance. In the context of the United Kingdom, privatization symbolized denationalization and divestiture implying change in ownership from the public to the private sector. It also signified withdrawal of government from business in favour of the private sector.

In the United States, the role of the public sector has been both qualitatively and quantitatively different from that of the United Kingdom. According to a study, the total public sector in the United States accounts for only 35 per cent of the national economy. About one-third of it is spent on social security, another one-third goes to compensate government employees, ranging from the President of the USA to the rugby coach at a university. The final one-third goes to purchase goods and services form non-governmental entities (Savas, 1987: 255).

Private organizations have been involved with the public sector throughout American history. As such, there is very little scope for privatization in the United States in the sense of denationalization or divestiture. American-style privatization implies private delivery of goods and services that are still paid for collectively. The general assumption is that contracting results in better and economical public services. For instance, the government may turn to the private sector for collecting waste, the disposal of waste, extracting energy from the coasts and treating hazardous waste.

By privatizing, the public sector retains its responsibility but exercises it in a 'superior manner' by relying on the skilled expertise of the private sector. In this way, a service can continue to be produced privately while still being financed by public authorities. In reality, it is very difficult to draw the line where public ends and private begins. For instance, a publicly-owned bank with a minority equity holding in a private company may control that company quite effectively, or a private company in the defence industry have the government as their sole customer (Bienen and Waterbury, 1989: 617). Privatization may be said to have taken place only when the responsibility for a service or a particular aspect of service passes wholly or in part from the public sector to the private sector, and when market criteria such as profit or ability to pay are used to provide or distribute certain benefits and services to the general public (Walker, 1984: 25). For instance, a commuter may be required to pay a nominal toll tax for using a road maintained by the private sector.

Privatization needs to be discussed in an altogether different context in developing countries and underdeveloped economies. A crucial debate is going on in most of these countries about the proper role of the public sector in the economic development and the pros and cons of privatization. While some believe in getting rid of loss-making public enterprises, others believe in revamping them. In some countries, the sole purpose behind privatization seems to be to woo international aid donors without any regard to the fundamental political and economic issues involved (Heald, 1990: 15). In such countries, there is more rhetoric than actual implementation of privatization.

In most developing countries the term privatization has been used as an umbrella term covering various economic activities such as deregulation, liberalization, liquidity, withdrawal, disinvestment of a limited percentage of shares, and so forth. The sole purpose behind financial reforms seems to be the generation of additional resources to solve the fiscal crisis, rather than any ideological commitments towards reduction of a government's role in the economy. Politicians in these countries are motivated by short-term gains, rather than long-term improvements in the economic structure *per se* (Bishop and Kay, 1989: 643).

In the 'deideologized' recasting of the concept, a variety of measures have sailed under the flag of privatization (Glade, 1989: 674). Where capital markets are nascent, financial resources scarce, the local private sector weak and not fully developed, foreign investors are not acceptable, and where adequate institutional arrangements are lacking and public enterprises cannot be sold *en bloc* (Nellis and Kikeri, 1989: 668), privatization can be conceived only as a part of structural adjustments either at the behest of international aid donors or owing to the economic and political compulsions at the domestic level. Privatization may help in combating the problems of fiscal deficit, a balance of payment crisis, mounting debts and lack of foreign exchange by grabbing an 'extra-loan' from the World Bank and the IMF, deferring the real problems to be solved at a later date, if at all.

In fact, very little privatization has taken place in the developing countries in the form of divestiture. By the end of 1987, only 30 examples of divestiture were found in Africa, 165 in Latin America and 250 in Asia (Berg, 1987: 481). Owing to various constraints – political, legal, social, economic and cultural – the domestic constituency for divestiture is very small in developing countries. Franchising or contracting-out, too, has limited scope. In the absence of a welfare net, liquidation involving massive retrenchment cannot be recommended either.

In fact, we find less-formal privatization taking place in these countries. It can be classified into 'internal divestiture', 'creeping divestiture' and 'backdoor privatization' (Berg, 1987: 484). By internal divestiture we mean shedding activities of the state-owned enterprises which are least profitable or which are loss-making. For instance, in Panama some of the unviable sugar mills were simply closed down or leased to the private sector. In the same way, national aircraft can be leased to international carriers in order to reduce costs without holding any public debate on the matter.

In some developing countries governments have curtailed budgetary support, access to credit at commercial banks or slimmed down staff before finally closing an enterprise. It can be termed creeping divestiture. It too involves secrecy and no public announcement may be made by the government to avoid stiff resistance.

In some other countries we may find cases of backdoor privatization. For instance, a government may decide to contract out a service or part of it to an individual or group of individuals without making it public. Or it may decide to sell a poorly-managed government hotel to some private concern without inviting competitive bids. Such small activities are less likely to meet public hostilities.

In some cases, privatization may imply throwing open areas reserved for the public sector earlier to the private sector without involving any change in the ownership or management of a public enterprise. We may call it incremental privatization. For instance, private companies may be associated for exporting arms or the private sector may be involved at the initial stages only. It can finance a project, operate it for sometime and transfer it back to the government after recovering the minimum return.

Therefore, the connotation of privatization is much wider than the mere transfer of ownership or management from the public to the private sector (UNDV Report on Privatization, 1988: 13). Broadly speaking, privatization implies involvement of market forces to ensure greater competition and economic efficiency on the one hand, and reduction in the role of the state as a regulator, facilitator, provider and producer of goods and services on the other. It also refers to attempts at deregulation and liberalization, unleashing the forces of competition and introducing market forces into an economy (Dhameja, 1991: 121).

In a narrow sense, it refers to divestiture, implying transfer of ownership from the state to private hands on the one hand, and non-ownership options such as load-shedding, franchising, leasing or contracting out public services on the other. To some, abandoning or postponing proposals for starting new enterprises under the public sector or expanding and diversifying activities of existing public enterprises also amounts to privatization.

Why privatization?

Privatization can be seen as part of a more general rehabilitation of market forces following an intellectual disillusionment with the Keynesian approach to economic management, and the failure of socialism as a serious intellectual force. The rise of Thatcherism and Reaganomics succeeded in advocating the virtues of private enterprise, private initiative and private motive. It emphasized rolling back the frontiers of the state in order to promote an efficient and free society. The ethics of privatization is based on the validity of private as opposed to state property rights; as such, the emphasis on privatization did not occur in an intellectual vacuum.

All the world over, governments are resorting to privatization for multiple reasons: improving efficiency and competition, reducing public deficits, generating additional cash, eliminating political interference in the management of various enterprises, and widening the ownership of economic assets through disinvestment of equity in select public enterprises (Gupta, 1990: 9). It is generally assumed that the private sector is more efficient than the public sector. The myth prevails that what the public sector can do, the private sector can do better. Also, the non-productive public sector is considered to be a burden on the productive private sector and a drain on the national exchequer.

At the heart of the privatization movement is the assumption that the public sector is always wasteful, inefficient and unproductive. It is based on the crude division between productive economic relations and unproductive social relations. Under this scheme, the economic motive is given more weight than social motives. This, in fact, is a diluted version of *laissez faire*. Honestly speaking, there can be no productive gains from social services, and therefore the convention prevails that the more a society spends on public services, the lower is the rate of economic growth. It provides legitimacy to the privatization movement the world over.

Privatization is mainly concerned with the narrow form of economic efficiency rather than social equity. It is generally believed that privatization leads to economic efficiency, but technically speaking, economic efficiency implies the least-cost notion of efficiency. It is achieved when the value of what is produced exceeds as much as possible the value of resources used. By introducing the element of competition and market forces in the working of various enterprises, one can hope to improve their operational performance.

Some of the advocates of privatization see it as an end in itself. They operate from the ideological premise that as many functions and activities as possible should be in private rather than government control. The government has no business to govern business, and business activities suffer if subjected to unnecessary political control. Others see privatization simply as a means for correcting the deficiencies of public sector enterprises. They find in privatization a pragmatic rather than an ideological solution (Wortzel and Wortzel, 1989: 23).

Usually, the privatization policy in any country is adopted with three goals in mind:

1. to manage public enterprises more efficiently;
2. to make markets more competitive; and
3. to offer new opportunities to citizens to invest in shares and thereby provide help in the growth of these enterprises.

In this way, privatization is supposed to be beneficial to employees, customers, clients and taxpayers alike (Gupta, 1989: 76).

The most important reason for privatization lies in the grossly unsatisfactory performance of public enterprises in general. The questions arise: (1) can the huge investments in public enterprises be made more productive or profitable, (2) how long can the loss-making public enterprises be subsidized in a financially precarious situation, and (3) is there any alternative available? Privatization seems to provide the desired remedial measures on pragmatic grounds.

It is argued that public enterprises have contributed to budget deficits in a big way. Governments in many developing countries have over-taxed themselves, especially when they get involved in the direct management of industry. Furthermore, government procedures which inevitably find their way into management of public enterprises are often very cumbersome. Also, we find these enterprises over-administered and less-managed. Bureaucrats, who happen to be at the helm of the affairs, are only trained to run government; they lack the proper expertise to manage an enterprise efficiently on commercial lines. As such, the privatization policy is adopted in some countries just to provide the necessary work culture and impetus to public enterprises (Chidambram, 1989: 14).

Moreover, privatization allows government to concentrate on governing. It releases the government's administrative and policy-making talents for the jobs they are fit for. It reduces government's time and resources by replacing some of the governmental activities with private ones. These include introduction of public insurance, running the public transport system, funding the health services, contracting out hospital cleaning, and so on. Privatization is worth trying in those areas which need not have been in the public sector in the first place. It can take the unnecessary or extra load off government, thereby improving further the performance of the erstwhile public enterprises.

Privatization can also reduce the burden on the government exchequer by passing loss-making public enterprises to the private sector or by eliminating or reducing subsidies offered to them. It also helps in distinguishing the true government fiscal deficit and in reducing the public sector's net worth. If privatization leads to greater efficiency or lower financial losses, there will be a reduced call for budgetary support. The government can also hope to earn extra revenues from the enterprises turned into profit-making units following privatization. As such, privatization can promote competition and efficiency on the one hand, and save the limited resources of the government on the other.

In fact, in some countries the policy of privatization was adopted to generate extra resources by selling off the assets and equities of select public enterprises. The efforts on the part of the British government to sell shares to employers, employees and the general public have gained worldwide attention. Because of the long-running share markets and deliberate underpricing, individuals were encouraged to buy shares on the implicit assumption that prices always go up and never go down. The transfer of public assets to private hands is highlighted as the victory of economic democracy and people's capitalism (Heald, 1990: 11).

In Britain, in the first phase of privatization the sale of publicly-owned property was more significant than the sale of shares. Since 1979, over one million publicly-owned houses were sold under the right-to-buy scheme. It fetched the government about £15 billion. In December 1986, the shares of

British Gas were sold for £5434 million. British Airways was sold for £9000 million, Rolls Royce for £1363 million and British Airports Authority for £1225 million. By the end of 1988, the disposal of public assets had yielded a handsome £1250 million (Bishop and Kay, 1989: 647).

The government's objective behind the privatization programme in the United Kingdom was not merely to relinquish control over state-owned enterprises, but also to dispose of its equity stakes in them. Financial arguments were central in the privatization debate in the UK. Besides financial benefits, the government also looked forward to diminishing the strength of the trade unions in the public sector. The government also hoped to reap political benefits by propogating the theory of 'wider share ownership'. The number of shareholders in the UK indeed rose from 3 million in 1979 to 8.5 million in 1985, due largely to the privatization programme launched on a massive scale (Lawson, 1987). The government did not mind sacrificing the loss of revenue to secure people's capitalism. Ideology apart, the immediate financial gains seemed to provide the necessary motivation.

The British experiment on privatization, highlighted as a great success story by the western media, was bound to have its impact on other developing economies. While in the United Kingdom once the political decision was taken to divest, the key question revolved around financial matters. In developing countries, on the other hand, the crucial question was who the potential buyers would be. In deciding who should be allowed to buy the assets and equities divested, various political, economic and sociocultural factors had to be kept in mind.

In fact, each country has its own rationale behind adopting the policy of privatization ranging from immediate financial gains, increase in revenues, economic efficiency, enhanced competition, wider share-ownership and political popularity. Undoubtedly, the scope of privatization in a given society is set by the socioeconomic conditions and the political culture prevailing therein. In a society infested with ethnic, religious or regional tensions, with the dominance of particular groups, privatization is likely to pose serious problems.

As such, each government has to work under various economic, political and sociocultural constraints. Most of the time the governments have been opportunistic in selecting public enterprises to be deregulated, liberalized or privatized. Nor can there be any uniform policy or consistent philosophy behind privatization. It may vary from enterprise to enterprise, from time to time, and from country to country. Some countries may be forced to adopt the privatization policy at the dictates of international aid donors, while others may give it mere lip service to accrue immediate political or economic gains.

Therefore, the motivation for privatization may vary from country to country. According to an interregional workshop on privatization (UNDV, 1988: 15–16), the chief objectives could be:

- to relieve a situation of financial losses and burdens on the government budget;
- to relieve budgetary strains, implying inadequate funds for public investment purposes or for release of other purposes of government;
- to meet a situation of inefficiency and non-viability of public enterprise performance by creating market disciplines and promoting competition;
- to minimize governmental interventions;
- to improve the national savings rate and growth, and to improve allocational efficiency of investments;
- to develop capital markets;
- to eliminate unfair competition with private enterprises;
- to withdraw from activities more suited to private enterprise especially when the original objectives are fulfilled or are no longer valid;
- to improve income distribution and eliminate inequitable subsidizations;
- to relieve the administrative burdens of the government;
- to encourage a share-ownership democracy;
- to increase indigenous ownership;
- to raise productivity of employees through stock-ownership incentives.

To sum up, privatization, by pushing back the frontiers of the state, can lead to innovative management and promote economic efficiency. It can help raise revenues for the treasuries; it can increase savings, investment and growth; and, finally, it can lead to further economic democratization through increasing participation in the ownership of national assets. In short, the motives for privatization can be classified into two basic categories: (1) privatization for immediate gains, and (2) privatization for ideological purposes. The distinction is useful because privatization involves tremendous costs – social, economic and political.

How to privatize?

Depending upon the motivation, privatization may take different forms in different countries. In advanced economies it involves an attempt to reinvigorate a badly run state enterprise through divestiture or spreading ownership more widely by selling shares to the general public. In developing economies it may involve liquidation or economic policy reforms such as deregulation and liberalization. The economic environment in the two sets of countries is altogether different, and as such the modalities of privatization may also vary. Various measures may be adopted for privatization such as:

A. *Ownership measures*
- divestiture or denationalization,
- joint ventures,
- liquidation.

B. *Organizational measures*

- leasing and management contracts,
- restructuring of public enterprises,
- economic policy reforms such as deregulation and liberalization.

C. *Operational measures*

- contracting out or franchizing,
- user charges,
- incentive rewards,
- fixing targets,
- resort to capital markets,
- rationalization of governmental control,
- abandoning or postponing proposals to start new public enterprises or to expand or diversify activities of any of the existing public enterprises.

The divestiture of public enterprises or denationalization constitutes privatization in the strictest sense. The government's desire to privatize a public enterprise can be fulfilled either by selling it or by deregulating entry and allowing the private sector to expand and displace it gradually. This would eventually lead to withering away of a public enterprise and *de facto* load-shedding. The British brand of privatization has been mostly used as a divestiture of public assets and transfer of ownership by the sale of state-owned enterprises directly or indirectly.

The Thatcher government (1979–90) sold off all or part of its holdings in automobiles, aerospace, ports, telecommunications, postal services, chemicals, oil, gas, steel, coal, electricity supply and waterways. The proportion of GDP attributable to state-owned enterprises dropped from 9 per cent to 5 per cent, and about one million jobs were transferred from public to private sector (Dhameja, 1991: 119). For instance, employment fell from 232 410 to 104 400 in British coal, from 244 084 to 15 748 in British Rail, from 186 000 to 53 720 in British Steel, and from 159 825 to 131 398 in Electricity Supply from 1979 to 1988 (Bishop and Kay, 1989: 684).

Divestiture has been adopted by many developed economies quite successfully. It has also been adopted by some developing countries such as Argentina, Bangladesh, Brazil, Mexico, Nigeria, Philippines, Thailand and Turkey. Instead of formal divestitures, we also find examples of less-formal divestiture in some developing countries where capital markets are thin, potential buyers are few and political constraints are too many.

In those cases, where it is not feasible to sell off a public enterprise in its entirety it may be better to convert it into a joint venture. In a joint venture, government may dilute its equity holdings either by public issue or by offering them to private entrepreneurs or foreign business houses. Management is left in the hands of private entrepreneurs subject to the condition that they will produce a minimum rate of profit, failing which they may be removed from management. In a joint venture, ownership remains both with the government and the private entrepreneurs; the joint venture is considered a useful modality in the privatization process. In some cases, potential buyers may ask for hundred per cent ownership transfer to avoid undue government interference. In other cases, private capital may look forward to governmental partnership as a guarantee of better chances of successful operation.

For instance, in Qatar, the Qatar Fertilizer Company was partially privatized in 1984 with a European company becoming a minority partner with an exclusive management and marketing contract (Heller and Schiller, 1989: 764–5). In every case of foreign capital involvement, joint venture or partial divestiture modality, a country is at some disadvantage, but it becomes unavoidable for the future growth and development. However, it would be wise on the part of the government to adopt a cautious approach in such matters.

It may not be possible to sell off the loss-making public enterprises at all. In such cases, attempts must be made to sell off the profitable segments or subsidiaries to private concerns. Alternatively, they can be given away to the employees or to the public. If all such attempts fail, they can be liquidated. Liquidation can be considered a form of privatization in as much as it restores assets to a more productive use in the marketplace, and ends the need for subsidies (Savas, 1987: 243).

In fact, some developing countries have preferred liquidation to privatization. They contemplate slow death for these enterprises because it is less likely to attract public attention and therefore creates less nuisance for the government (Berg, 1987: 484). For instance, in Côte d'Ivoire some sugar-processing complexes and rice-mills were closed (Heller and Schiller, 1989: 764), and in Somalia the government was committed to closing financially unviable public enterprises, particularly those whose services were deemed unessential, and in 1981 three such enterprises were phased out of operation (Nellis and Kikeri, 1989: 670). In Mexico, 500 public enterprises were eliminated during 1982–8 through liquidation and mergers. In fact, liquidation outnumbered sales by three to one.

There are many factors which influence the selection of public enterprises for divestiture such as: obtaining immediate income or foreign exchange, reducing expenditures, improving efficiency, encouraging industrial development, encouraging foreign investment or loans, encouraging private entrepreneurs or pursuing a free market economy. Privatization of a public enterprise is fundamentally a political act, requiring political commitment from the very top of the government for its success.

However, divestment is not a simple and straightforward process of identifying the parasatals and announcing their sale. It involves a tedious process and has to cross many hurdles on the way. As such, the first public enterprise to be divested should be an attractive one. The ideal strategy for denationalizing the profitable enterprise is to deregulate the industry, allow competition and ultimately sell off the assets to the newly-formed private enterprises. Another strategy could be to auction them at a price equal to the appreciated value of their assets plus the highest bid for the percentage of annual profits to be paid to the government. This strategy was applied in the case of the US Postal Service at the national level, and public buses at the local level (Savas, 1987: 244).

Divestiture of equities can be partial too. However, anything less than 50 per cent may bring in cash but no other benefit expected of privatization, the control still being with the government (Gupta, 1991: 6). Yet partial divestiture can be profitable both for the government and investors. For instance, the British government sold just over half of Cable & Wireless for £182 million initially, but within two years it sold another quarter for £263 million (Young, 1986: 1–23), reaping the benefits of an improved public image.

Once a political decision has been made to divest, the key questions revolve around financial matters such as: finding the investors, getting the correct valuation of the assets, underwriting the price of the shares to be floated, and so forth. In some cases, the existing management may buyout with the hope of increasing efficiency and profits once freed of government controls and regulations (Berg, 1987: 482).

Divestiture may be a very difficult, time-consuming and tedious process in developing countries owing to political, social, economic and cultural constraints. Multinational corporations, foreign business-houses and local entrepreneurs belonging to particular minority groups may not be allowed to invest. Furthermore, the government may face opposition from trade unions, managers and bureaucrats alike. For instance, Ghana, Senegal and Turkey are facing difficulties in implementing their policies of divestiture.

The government itself may not like to divest. Divestment leads to decentralization and very few governments in developing countries would like to lose their grip. Whether a country is developed or developing, any strategy for divestment must take into account the interests of all those who are likely to be losers on account of denationalization or divestiture, as a technique of privatization. Privatization is a zero-sum game in which one can win only at the cost of others, although some economists may very well refute this. When divestiture involving transfer of ownership of public assets to the private sector is not feasible, 'marketization' involving greater use of market forces may be encouraged with a definite aim of promoting competition and efficiency. This implies a reduction in the role of the state as a regulator, facilitator, welfare-provider and producer (Sankar and Reddy, 1989: 23).

As a special case, economic reforms in a socialist society may be carried out with a view to enhancing competition and marginal ownership among the economic agents. Privatization may be said to have taken place with the transfer of management, without any significant change in the ownership pattern *per se*; leases and management contracts fall into this category. Governments may lease the public enterprises to private entrepreneurs with an understanding that the latter will pay royalties for using the facilities provided by the public sector enterprises. This scheme has an edge over others in not asking for huge investments form private entrepreneurs on the one hand, and guaranteeing a regular source of income for the government on the other.

This is only a mild form of privatization because ownership and control still remain with the government. Another device could be to lease a company to private concerns with certain lucrative incentives for the managers to make the management more efficient. And nobody can deny that efficient management is crucial for the success of any enterprise, public or private. Privatization liberates managers and employees by allowing them to reach their full potentials. It helps in reducing the economic inefficiencies associated with public ownership. An increase in efficiency implies lower costs and higher value attached by customers to the quality of the goods and services produced.

Leases and management contracts have recently been tried in many countries. In Philippines and Chile, they have been utilized in hotels and other service activities where partial privatization of management is considered sufficient (Yotopoulos, 1989: 684). In some other countries, management and employee buyouts have taken place, and in such cases foreign participation is allowed to only a limited extent. In China, state-owned enterprises have been leased out to individuals, and families. In fact, privately-owned shops and restaurants are mushrooming in the former communist regimes since the fall of the Berlin Wall.

Privatization requires financial restructuring of loss-making enterprises. It may be done before transferring units to the private sector by writing off their accumulated losses. Alternatively, the privatization agreement may provide for the accumulated losses by suitably adjusting the terms of payment. For instance, a proposal for privatization of waterways in the United Kingdom incorporated a provision to write off debt of US$4.9 billion before the sale and to inject US$1.2 billion cash to cover US$300 million of external third-party debt, and to help pay for environment improvement (Accountancy, 1989: 32).

The government can also fragment public monopolies into regional operating companies to make room for more competition. Restructuring on these lines yields three advantages:

1. it promotes competition among the various units making them more efficient;
2. it reduces the size of the enterprise making it more operative; and
3. it provides an opportunity to compare the performance of various units.

Restructuring has been successfully resorted to in road-haulage and ferry businesses in the United Kingdom and telecommunications in the USA. In Japan, too, the government decided to restructure the Japan National Railways (JNR) by splitting it into several regional companies. In fact, seven private railway companies sprang up from the divestiture of deficit-ridden JNR in 1986, and got on the 'right business track'.

As such, privatization should be seen as one of the components of the restructuring programme in a given country and not an end in itself. For instance, in Mexico privatization is taking place along with credit contradiction, fiscal austerity and trade liberalization. The effects of fiscal austerity and credit contradiction may be greater than those attained from divestiture of liquidation of public enterprises (Bienen and Waterbury, 1989: 622). If competition, rather than ownership, is the key to efficiency, then it is better to reform public enterprises by opening them to competition and allowing new entrants to areas hitherto reserved for public enterprises. Deregulation of express services in the United Kingdom provides an apt example of incumbent-advantage. The National Express was able to exploit the market advantage of a preexisting national network, and exclusive or dominant access to city-centre terminals, to reinforce its position (Bishop and Kay, 1989: 644).

In many cases, inefficiencies may be the result of overregulation and overinterference. Privatization, in itself, cannot overcome the economic and political forces that undermine public production, unless and until it is accompanied by liberalization measures. Privatization cannot be a prelude to deregulation. All attempts at deregulation may be thwarted by vested interests. For instance, in some cases, in the name of social justice, the government may itself oppose the economic reforms leading to privatization.

In the absence of liberalization and deregulation, the effects of privatization can only be modest. In some cases liberalization and deregulation can bring more gains than half-hearted attempts at privatization, but in other cases such reforms can be meaningful only if accompanied by privatization. There can be no general presumption that privatization is a *sine quo non* for a successful liberalization campaign, or vice versa (Walle, 1989: 611). In some cases, privatization may turn out to be a prerequisite for other liberalization reforms, in other cases liberalization may make subsequent privatization redundant. However, restructuring may also prove to be too costly and beyond the reach of most developing countries.

Within the two extremes of divestment and deregulation, various other techniques can be adopted. These include contracting out services, user-charges, resort to capital markets for raising additional resources, fixing targets and judging performance accordingly. In the United States, major privatization has taken place in the form of contracting out certain services such as garbage collection, sewage disposal, public transportation, fire protection and so on. In India, the private sector is now allowed to supplement government efforts in constructing roads, building bridges, generating electricity and so forth. Certain services can be contracted out to the private sector on the basis of open bidding, in which case adequate provisions should be made for monitoring complaints, citizens' surveys, field observations and checking records from time to time. Contracting should not be seen as an alternative to regulation, but as a form of privatization that seeks to use some of the desirable incentive properties of competition.

Franchising is another privatization device for providing various services. While government pays the producer in the case of contract services, consumers pay the producer in the case of franchise services. Franchise is an award of monopoly privileges to a private concern to supply a particular service, usually with price regulation by a government agency. It is suitable for providing toll goods; electric power, gas, water distribution, telephone services, bus transportation, cable television, and so on. In the United States, concessions on limited-access highways, parks, stadiums, airports and other public properties have already been franchised.

Another privatization strategy could be to impose user-charges, wherever practical, to cover the full cost of services provided. The objective behind such charges is not to raise funds but to reveal the true cost of the service provided to curb wastage, overuse or misuse of the same. Citizens can opt for an alternative if they feel that the service provided is not worth the price. User-charges can be seen as a privatization device because by revealing the true cost of the service provided, it prevents squandering of resources and helps to end the subsidy. And ending the subsidy can be regarded as a first step towards successful privatization. It means satisfying people's demands in a cost-effective manner, but it may prove to be quite expensive in terms of votes. Most leaders in developing countries may not be in a position to afford it.

The most popular form of privatization is to enter into markets by floating shares, debentures and bonds. Government may prune budgetary support to public enterprises in difficult financial situations, and it may allow some of the select public enterprises to float non-convertible, taxable or tax-free bonds to raise additional resources. Public offerings of shares, debentures and bonds may result in widespread ownership in developed economies, but may prove to be a very difficult exercise in developing countries owing to undeveloped or underdeveloped capital markets. Where successful floatation is not feasible, sale of assets through private or quasi-private placements is advisable. For instance, in Jamaica nearly Jm$500 million of assets were privatized through public share offerings, the sale of assets, leasing and management contracts during the 1980s. In Guinea, partial privatization of 15 public enterprises was conducted with Guinean shareholding remaining at 50 per cent (Nellis and Kikeri, 1989: 668).

'Ancillarization' could be another technique of privatization. Government can encourage small-scale ancillary units to undertake production, providing the necessary raw materials and technical know-how. The products manufactured by these units can be utilized by public sector enterprises. For instance, Bharat Heavy Electricals Ltd in India has been encouraging large numbers of entrepreneurs belonging to private sector units through ancillarization. This is similar to contracting out public services.

Yet another form of privatization could be the dilution of the social and welfare goals of public undertakings. At present, public sector enterprises are expected to be model employers, which puts an extra burden on accommodation, medical-aid, bonuses, leave and travel concessions and some other perks. Therefore, they are often not able to generate sufficient surplus for their own expansion and growth. In most of countries, public enterprises have to meet multiple objectives such as the redistribution of income, regional development, filling in for a deficient private sector, strengthening economic sovereignty *vis-à-vis* multinationals, and building national strength through the defence sector. It would be better to divest public enterprises of this dual role. They can be economically viable only if they are allowed to work on commercial lines.

Either a separate fund should be created to fulfil social obligations or, if the social obligations are to be provided by public-sector enterprises, the costs of such obligations should be measured appropriately and the relief provided through the budget. Public sector enterprises should not be criticized unduly for being a drain on the exchequer for no fault of theirs. Nor should they be allowed to conceal their inefficiencies in the name of social obligations. Government may also be advised to use stringent measures to avoid inegalitarian and wasteful misuse of government funds by the better-off sections of society. Savings from reducing subsidies can be used in a more effective way for improving the status of those who are in need of government support.

In view of serious resource limitations, governments may very well defer launching new schemes and projects or diversifying the activities of existing public-sector enterprises. It is better to have fewer projects in hand which can be completed successfully in time, rather than have a large number of ambitious plans which are bound to face rough weather in the absence of adequate resources. Abandoning the launch of avoidable enterprises can also help in reaping some of the benefits of privatization, though indirectly.

In fact, there cannot be any blueprint for privatization; nor does it call for dogmatic or doctrinaire treatment. Each case must be examined on its own merits. Government can use various techniques to increase efficiency and competition, as well as to raise additional financial resources. While divestiture calls for a one-time decision on the part of government, leasing, contracting, franchising and hiving off certain responsibilities call for continuous commitment towards the market economy. While divestiture involves a difficult political decision and is a 'hard' economic option, marketization involves a 'continued determination' (UNDV Report, 1988: 26).

Colin Samson, a sociologist, has presented 'three faces' of privatization (Samson, 1994: 79–94). According to the first face, privatization is seen as the result of power exercised by the agents involved in the process – politicians, voters and consumers. They act within the parameters of politics – lobbying, elections and legislation.

The second face concentrates on those elements which are hidden by the first face or are obscured deliberately. For instance, while advocating the benefits of privatization, the social costs might be deliberately obscured.

According to Samson, the two-dimensional power is exerted through the ability of particular actors to steer certain issues off the political agenda. This dimension allows for concealment of the ways in which decisions are prevented from being taken on potential issues over which there is an observed conflict of interests.

The third face of privatization is seen as something more than a technical political solution. It serves to promote a distinct cultural agenda – we must privatize because everybody else is doing so. It may entail the use of manipulation, authority, influence, media and cultural signifiers, which advertently or inadvertently contribute towards the internationalization of a particular world view. It conceptualizes privatization as a form of hegemony.

Privatization has become a part of a cultural mission. The privatization device, as a panacea to socioeconomic problems, has been over-sold, which is why Henig and a number of other scholars have been arguing that privatization should be seen as a political strategy rather than an economic or fiscal device. There are close links between political-setting and macro-economic stabilization. A strong government is required to carry out the economic and fiscal reforms to their logical conclusions, and the inability of a government to manage the process can result in a slow-down of the implementation of privatization programmes and policies, causing severe economic, social and political costs. Privatization cannot succeed without an effective mandate from the public, especially in a democratic framework.

3
Impediments to Privatization

Privatization has become one of the most controversial themes in the current political and economic discourse all over the world. The very word privatization causes a lot of misunderstanding, premature polarization and arguments that are beside the point. Some believe it to be an attempt at restoring the market economy, while others interpret it as an attack on the ideals they cherish the most – the ideals of brotherhood, sharing and community life (Savas, 1987: 277).

In fact, two strings of thought share the same concept of privatization. The first involves the transfer of certain responsibilities, activities and assets from the collective realm to the private. The second implies the retaining of collective financing while delegating the delivery of certain services to the private sector. The term privatization, in fact, can signify something as broad as the shrinking of the welfare state, on the one hand, and the simple association of the private sector with areas hitherto reserved exclusively for the public sector, on the other. Contentious in nature and scope, privatization may mean different things to different people. It is a term invented by journalists to explain economic policies. It is not only an inelegant term but also lamentably imprecise. It is perhaps designed not to clarify an issue but to dramatize a conflict, and, as such, its meaning remains uncertain and often tendentious (Donnison, 1984: 45). That is why the privatization process has been so slow, uneven and plagued with unforeseen obstacles (Walle, 1989: 608).

Some of the problems have arisen due to not understanding the concept of privatization in its true spirit. In most cases it has proved to be a political strategy rather than an economic device (Gupta, 1996: 38–51), whilst in others, economic constraints have superseded the political objectives behind the privatization drive. In some cases, privatization is seen merely as an administrative tool to galvanize the ailing economy and state machinery.

The approach to privatization has been either too ideological or too pragmatic. Privatization cannot be seen as a panacea, nor can there be any standard formula or blueprint for privatization. At the most, privatization can be seen as a constituent of economic reforms and not an end in itself. Admittedly, privatization involves a complicated process and is usually fraught with nagging uncertainties (Humphrey, 1991: 9). Some problems have also arisen due to the lack of preparatory work, and, moreover, we often find a positive attitude towards privatization missing.

Privatization is usually resorted to because the preceeding system seems to have failed. The stress is on getting rid of something rather than constructing something new, with very little thought given to the systematic planning of long and short-term objectives or implementational modalities. The general perception is: 'let's privatize because everybody else is doing so'.

While some want to try it just for the sake of a change, others view it as the lesser evil. While some economists view it as a more efficient and profitable way of managing an economy, politicians may view it as a golden opportunity to reap political dividends. In some cases, the latter may have to resort to it under mounting domestic or international pressures, but, deep down in their hearts, they may still feel comfortable with the economy largely run and controlled by the government. They may only resort to the rhetoric of privatization.

This explains why very little privatization has actually taken place in most countries, despite the widespread claims made. In fact, profound economic changes cannot take place without *pari passu* or prior transformation of the ideological climate. In this set of affairs a package of economic reforms is of little relevance if the political will is lacking to implement them, or the socioeconomic and cultural conditions prevailing in a given society do not warrant them. For instance, a military coup was attempted in Venezuela on 4 February 1992 to cap the mounting discontent prevailing in the country undergoing economic reforms prescribed by the IMF (*The Times of India*, 5 February 1992: 18). While these reforms are expected to correct the economy in the long run, there is much hardship involved in the short run, not only for the working class but also for the middle class.

Political constraints

Undoubtedly, the scope for privatization in a given society is set by political, economic, social, geographical, environmental and cultural factors. The issue of privatization calls for a trade-off between the multiple interests of the poor and rich, consumers and producers, workers and managers, bureaucrats and politicians, and so forth. As such, substantial barriers may occur both at the policy-making and the implementational stages. Moreover, governments may have on their agenda other items which may interfere with the privatization policy itself (Austin and Coburn, 1986: 57–67).

The politics of privatization consists of holding out future gains to the general public as well as specific beneficiaries. The gains have to be weighed against immediate costs to those who lose their jobs or influence. It involves great political risks because the beneficiaries of the status quo may be able to jeopardize the privatization move before the future beneficiaries are able to organize themselves. Once a public enterprise has been in public hands for a significant period of time, there develops a strong inertia willing to keep it in the public sector regardless of ideology or pragmatism (Haggard and Kaufman, 1988: 25–6).

Ideology does play an important role in assigning the role to the public enterprise. It may be comparatively easier for those countries to reduce the role for the state who have accorded considerable legitimacy to the private sector, than for those emphasizing the redistributive role of the state in pursuit of social justice. The latter may find it difficult to reduce state intervention and privatize without calling into question the legitimacy of the regime (Bienen and Waterbury, 1989: 624).

Like all economic reforms, privatization too has distributional consequences. It may favour certain groups within a polity at the cost of others, in which case the losers are likely to organize against privatization, particularly if it covers only a small group (Lal, 1987: 273). The termination of certain consumer subsidies or import tariffs can also mobilize the concerned groups against the reform. In most countries, unorganized and organized labour as well as lower and middle-income groups have been party to social pacts by which these groups gain political support for protection of their standards of living through continued state commitment to redistribution. Advanced industrial nations have dealt with this problem through the pacts known as Keynesian ententes. When this pact is broken by de-indexing or linking wages to productivity, it is likely to be resisted by all concerned (Bienen and Waterbury, 1989: 625).

The lower and middle stratas just cannot afford to forego benefits such as free medical and educational services, high levels of consumer subsidies and implicitly indexed wages. Privatization may bring about a reduction in income and a more uneven distribution of economic power, and it may undermine the balance of economic power between the public and the private sector by changing the very rules of the game (Raza, *The Times of India*, 10 May 1989: 3).

It is generally assumed that the widening of public ownership would help diffuse economic power, particularly in developing economies. A more even distribution of economic power cannot be achieved without the intervention of the state. Privatization may result in a mere shift in the seat of concentrated economic power and not in a diffusion of political power or democratization *per se*.

Privatization can be distinguished from other economic reforms in the sense that its costs are likely to be borne by a large number of people, while its benefits are likely to accrue intensively to a very small number of people. The 'public choice' theory suggests that in such a situation collective action is likely to be against the reform, which is equally relevant for developed as well as developing economies. The more a country advances, the less tolerant people become of free-riders. The number of job-seekers may surpass that of job-providers, so that privatization is unlikely to enjoy the requisite popular support.

Moreover, privatization can achieve economic efficiency only by cutting costs on personnel: there is indeed a human dimension to retrenchment. Managers and workers may resist it, but except in the case of liquidation, privatization may not always lead to labour compression. In most cases, the new owners are expected to keep a large proportion of the workforce, and the government may also be called upon to compensate the proportion of the labour force which is curtailed or to extract an agreement concerning layoffs from the new owners. For instance, the Treuhandanstalt, the fudiciary agency responsible for privatization in East Germany was able to effectively negotiate job contracts in many cases.

Yet the rehabilitation prior to actual privatization may include reductions in personnel to make an enterprise appear profitable. It is difficult to find a parallel example to that of the massive restructuring of mining concerns in Western Europe which laid off tens of thousands of employees, depressing the economy of an entire province in the process (Walle, 1989: 609). In Latin America, privatization was more successful because it did not involve retrenchment on a massive scale. For instance, in Brazil, only one out of 17 public enterprises had more than 1000 employees by 1985. Similarly, in Costa Rica, the 18 firms to be privatized constituted less than 1 per cent of the entire labour force (Berg, 1987: 4–5).

Nevertheless, job-creation still remains a crucial responsibility of government in most developing countries. The general pressures on government to ensure a high level of employment are very high, so that the reform process and privatization are usually well-apprehended by organized labour. Few workers can be persuaded to accept the future prospects of employment in the private sector at the cost of prevailing public employment, and, besides, there are limits to which labour can be pushed. Labour, organized or unorganized, cannot be easily persuaded to give up secure jobs in the public sector for insecure jobs in the private sector.

Trade unions may succeed in blocking the attempts at privatization in some countries depending on their bargaining strength. For instance, in Senegal privatization proved to be a contentious and difficult proposition owing to a parliamentary system coupled with strong trade unions. In Niger, on the other hand, the privatization programme faced fewer obstacles due to absence of well-organized labour groups. Similarly, trade unions have been relatively weak in South Korea but quite strong in Argentina (*The Economist*, 6 August 1988: 57). Where labour is united it can make deals, where it is fragmented it may find it difficult to strike bargains. But in all cases there are tremendous risks involved in alienating the labour force.

Privatization is also likely to undermine the powers of the trade unions because they are typically concentrated in the public sector. Unions may react strongly against privatization, not only because of its direct impact on employment, but also because of the apprehension that their political powers and influence might be jeopardized after privatization and the *modus vivendi* with the government upset.

In fact, one of the primary motives for adopting a privatization policy in advanced capitalist economies has been to curb the powers and influence of the trade unions (Calder, 1988). In Turkey and Chile, even the military authoritarians had to strip the trade unions of some of their legal rights before resorting to privatization. On the other hand, the top brass in the military regimes of Asia, Africa and Latin America succeeded in either managing their economies directly or becoming crucial partners with dominant coalitions. And they tried to create their own industrial or commercial enterprises to provide jobs to ex-soldiers (Bienen and Moore, 1987: 489–516). However, their attempts to have full control over trading companies, transport companies, farms or pension funds were widely resisted in Argentina, Chile, Venezuela and Egypt.

In many other developing economies where political instability abounds or the polity is infested with ethnic, religious or regional tensions with the dominance of certain groups, privatization is likely to pose serious problems. It may not be politically acceptable to allow certain groups to gain economic and political ascendency at the cost of other groups. For instance, in Kenya the prospects of privatization are quite limited, and Kikuyu or Asian business groups are not likely to be allowed to buy public assets. Similarly, in Cameroon, there is a general apprehension of Bamilekee dominance (Yotopoulos, 1988). In many other countries, foreign investment is resented by the general public and by opposition parties.

In some cases, the private sector may also resist privatization moves. Already provided with shelter from foreign competition, it is actually the biggest beneficiary of public sector enterprises. It receives inputs produced by them – chemicals, steels, fertilizers, electricity and fuel – at subsidized or nominal prices. In addition it may not like to forego the benefits offered by the public banking system absorbing financial risks, rolling over credits, deferring payments, refinancing sick units and occasionally covering private debts to public equity.

Moreover, if closely held private conglomerates were to bid on public assets, if divested, they would also have to open up their books and operations to public scrutiny, which very few of them can afford in reality. Government can also ask private enterprises to share not only the benefits of state patronage, but also the social costs of development. If the government is either unable or unwilling to provide a safety net to retrenched workers, privatization may prove to be a highly risk affair.

Sometimes, the managers of public enterprises have also opposed privatization, but the evidence of managerial opposition is meagre (Waterbury, 1988). Here one must distinguish between political appointees and professional managers, and it is the former who are more likely to resist the privatization drive than the latter. Professional managers can easily move into the private sector, and in fact, they may be welcomed because of their knowledge of bureaucratic procedures and links established with policy-makers. In Kenya, Nigeria, Ivory Coast, Senegal, Mexico and India, the governments themselves are encouraging public sector managers to shift to private enterprises or to start their own business.

However, the privatization move is more likely to be thwarted by middle-level bureaucrats whose primary function is to control and monitor public enterprises. Privatization is likely to cut their functional *raison d'être* directly (Bienen and Waterbury, 1989: 626). Top-level civil servants may not have the same options to exit as enjoyed by top managers, and as such much of the political opposition is likely to revolve around the prerogatives of the bureaucracy. In some cases they are found exerting influence on the regulatory bodies to make sure of their continued role over the privatized enterprises (Kay and Thompson, 1986: 18–32).

Government may also continue to influence enterprises even after privatization. Since many enterprises in the pre-privatized environment were used, at least partially, to achieve public policy objectives, the government may wish to continue this situation even after privatization, and this can be done formally or informally. Formally, the government may require continued control over the Board of Directors or in the appointment of managers. They may demand prohibition on the elimination of certain production facilities, products and services or reduction of employment opportunities. Informally, the government may make an appeal to influence employee-leaders, they might threaten to renationalize or to invoke new legislation.

If a privatization programme enjoys a high level of acceptance from the major political parties and the general public, the threat of renationalization is of little concern. But if the privatization programme is seen as a 'favoured programme' of the ruling party with little political or popular support, it is more likely to be resisted by the opposition parties and the affected sections of society. If an enterprise is handed over to a multinational corporation, resistance may be still stronger. Many developing countries bear the scars of colonialism and neoimperialism, and opposition parties may seize upon the privatization opportunity to gain political ascendency by appealing to public anxiety over foreign ownership and foreign control (Cowan, 1988).

In some cases, the government itself may use a multinational corporation as a foil to dispose of a 'sacred cow'. It may find it difficult to close down an inefficient and loss-making enterprise, to reduce employment or suspend services due to political pressures, and privatization may enable the government to make these changes comfortably. Sometimes government may privately support economic liberalization, deregulation or privatization, while continuing to criticize them publicly to retain political support. A government's ambivalent stand on privatization programmes and policies adds to the prevailing confusion among the masses (Molz, 1990: 22).

There may be significant resistance from various interest and pressure groups to privatization efforts by the government. In many developing economies there are certain groups who enjoy tremendous economic power despite remaining outside the government. They are quite influential and have close links with top government leaders, and they may adversely affect the movement of public sector enterprises towards the market economy. For instance, in 1988 the sale of Aerolineas Argentinas to Scandinavian Airlines had to be withdrawn owing to mounting pressures from opposition parties, trade unions and disaffected potential buyers: interest groups exerted a lot of influence in this particular case (Molz, 1990: 22).

As such, privatization may result in bitter conflicts with the state's elites. In a number of cases, opposition to privatization may come from the management of the concerned public enterprise, and sometimes it has extended to the concerned ministry as well. In other cases, particular elements of the bureaucracy have opposed it, not wanting to lose the special benefits and privileges enjoyed by them, but envied by the other sections of public bureaucracy. For instance, public sector employees in India enjoy certain perks which are denied to other government employees at the same level. In the Philippines, the Aquino government's privatization efforts were approved by the technocrats, while bureaucrats linked to the Marcos regime resisted them. In fact, we can notice an interplay among individual interests, ideological conflicts and bureaucratic politics in the Philippines (Haggard, 1988: 91–122).

The most unlikely opponent to privatization is likely to be found in the state apparatus itself; it is likely to be wary of losing valued rents and prerogatives. Large-scale privatization can disturb the very balance of power between the public and the private sector, thereby arousing much more popular opposition than would have followed the distributional consequences. The state is likely to maximize its own utility in terms of income-perquisites and power, instead of seeking the welfare and well-being of its citizens.

Even those leaders who emphasize the need to reduce the role of the state in the economy and to support divestiture, may not like to lose control of crucial political resources. For instance, Turgut Ozal, the Turkish Prime Minister, had to face the dilemma of reducing the role of the Turkish state in the economy and utilizing available resources to maintain his political support. In most developing countries the public sector expanded owing to greater authority of political leadership over these societies than the faith in any particular ideology. The public enterprises provided the political leadership with patronage power, allowing them to distribute jobs, funds and status to their political supporters. In such regimes, even if a few public enterprises have to be privatized, the benefits are likely to be accrued to political allies only. For instance, in Zaire and Ivory Cost the respective presidents intervened personally to make sure that the public enterprises were sold at advantageous terms to their supporters (Ernest, 1987).

The leadership has opposed privatization in all those countries where their political support is based on the labour force itself. Tanzania and Turkey come into this category (Lees, 1988: 149–78). In these countries, the leadership can contemplate reforms only when the economy becomes unsustainable and their political survival becomes dependent upon economic reforms (*ibid.*: 741). The conflicting objectives behind economic liberalization may also add to the confusion. Privatization efforts in most cases combine partly inconsistent motives of restoring fiscal balance and increasing economic efficiency with those of wresting control over political resources away from hostile groups. As a result, implementation may slow down and the original momentum for reforms may abate. The leadership may find it difficult to shoulder the gigantic challenge of freeing the economy from the clutches of the state and cater to the needs of the needy, poor and deprived sections of society simultaneously.

In the wake of globalization, the powers of national governments to act independently and vigorously have declined. One of the consequences of globalization of the economy at the political level has been the growth of fragmentation and the rise of interest groups. Governments have to play a very difficult role of balancing national interest with international ones, and they may have to depend on external advisors for privatization. Privatization involves complicated transactions in cross-border acquisitions, foreign investment regulations and multiple business cultures. The 'sellers' (government, a public sector enterprise or a privatization agency) and 'buyers' (a multinational or dominant local economic groups) may have altogether different perceptions. There may be strategic, cultural or professional differences between the two, and differences in language may also make effective communication difficult. Government officials might be more concerned with the press rather than the outcome of privatization, causing undue delay in the implementation of privatization programmes and policies (Gallo, 1993: 196–205).

Implementational constraints

Besides barriers at the policy-making level, there can also be formidable obstacles to privatization at the administrative level. Privatization programmes require considerable administrative time, effort and resources. It involves a tedious exercise of finding willing buyers, developing mechanisms for valuation and transfer of public assets and public equities, and training efficient entrepreneural managers. Even the administration of the privatized enterprises demands specialized skills on the part of the regulatory authorities who are required to be well-informed about the privatized enterprises and yet to remain at arm's length. They are also required to control certain activities of a privatized firm without being harsh to its employees.

Where financial resources are scarce, capital markets thin, the private sector weak and over-protected, adequate institutional arrangements are lacking and foreign investors and experts not tolerated, extensive privatization programmes simply cannot be implemented. Political uncertainties can also spell doom for privatization policies in a large number of countries. Despite good intentions, political weakness can result in poor or no implementation at all. Furthermore, there may be technical constraints related to both managerial deficiencies and economic weaknesses within a polity. The privatization programme may also face difficulties inherent in implementation, such as a shortfall of skilled government personnel, legal obstacles, protracted negotiations with employees, and differences with regard to the terms and conditions of the sale (Nellis and Kikeri, 1989: 668).

The very selection of candidates for sale and divestiture may also pose tremendous difficulties. A prime issue is the specification of criteria for sale. Often governments provide strategic importance to certain public enterprises in categorizing them to be divested, liquidated or retained, rather than financial viability. On this basis, those public enterprises may be selected for sale which are unattractive to buyers; usually, governments like to dispose of those enterprises first which are loss-making, but such enterprises can prove too difficult to privatize because of the risks involved.

Moreover, private investors may look upon privatization programmes and policies with suspicion, given unfulfilled government promises of reform in the past. Or they may decide to wait for policy changes in the regulatory environment, without which investment in the public enterprises may not appear very lucrative.

Governments, too, would like to set up appropriate regulatory structures to monitor newly-privatized enterprises, especially if they happen to retain monopoly power or carry out certain social obligations. Further, it may be difficult to find buyers for national monopolies, since these monopolies were set up in the public sector exactly because the private sector was either unwilling or unable to make huge investments. The private sector may not respond positively unless perception of non-reversibility is guaranteed, which very few governments can afford. It may be easier to find buyers for modest businesses than those requiring huge investments. Yet the dilemma remains unresolved; no government would like to sell a profitable enterprise, and getting rid of a particular loss-making enterprise may prove to be inversely correlated with its sale ability (Killick and Commander, 1988: 1477).

Moreover, agreements on which public enterprises are to be sold may involve a protracted process resulting in long delays. For instance, it took more than a year to agree upon the broad classification of public enterprises to be privatized in Niger. In Senegal, two public enterprises were abruptly removed from the list of the ten public enterprises to be sold as the implementation deadline neared. In 1988, the Senegalese government rejected all the five bids received for a food distributing public enterprise; all the bids were found unsuitable because they had demanded special privileges and concessions. If a government is under pressure to provide certain tax concessions, incentives or monopoly powers to potential buyers, it may not be able to derive microeconomic gains from privatization at all.

A serious and important impediment to privatization has been the lack of budgetary resources to finance the contingency liabilities of the privatized enterprises. This has come as a rude shock to many governments; instead of generating resources, privatization may actually cost money. For instance, privatization programme came to a halt in Ghana where the government could neither meet its contingent liabilities nor could pay generous severance allowances.

Existing legal provisions such as giving protection to workers may also pose a serious challenge to the privatization movement. In fact, a successful privatization programme may require certain changes at the institutional level such as competition policy, corporate disclosure and corporate ownership provisions. Procedures to ensure transparency when public assets are transferred to the private sector are easier to recommend than enforce. On the other hand, the lack of transparency in making specific deals could pose a serious problem. Competitive bidding procedures might be ignored in some cases, and prices set without getting them adequately valued in others (Heald, 1990: 10).

Problems have also arisen in some cases due to the lack of well-established and competent consulting groups, accounting firms and commercial banks providing technical advice. Problems may also arise if there is a lack of an arbitration authority to intervene between competitive claims regarding the valuation of the public enterprise to be privatized. The valuation, in itself, may also take considerable time, exacerbated by the poor records kept by public enterprises. Even governments may be sensitive about the valuation exercise because it may raise questions about the public management and investment decisions made in the past (Berg and Shirley, 1987).

Therefore, the privatization process may lead to a number of political controversies causing long delays in the process. Once a public enterprise's assets are evaluated, a certain level of administrative capacity is required to assess the bids made by potential buyers, arrange finance and insurance cover, and deal with the complex legal issues. Very few countries actually possess the desired administrative and planning capacity. In some cases, the government may be reluctant to take the risk of transferring strategic activities to private hands, and privatization may be resisted on ideological grounds in others. Planners committed to centralized planning may refuse to cooperate, and the judiciary, too, may not be prepared to cope with the additional load of work in the wake of the legal and constitutional disputes following privatization (*The Times of India*, 5 February 1992: 15).

Privatization can also affect the centre–state relations under a federal democracy. The changes in legal and institutional arrangements promoting parallel systems in the cooperative sector and decentralization can affect the federal systems to a great extent. Contracting out and franchising arrangements may also demand a review of the existing arrangement (Vuylsteice, 1988: 97–101). For instance, in Czechoslovakia politicians in Slovakia demanded shares in Slovak businesses to be sold only to the inhabitants of Slovakia. This could have crippled Czechoslovakia's infant free market even before it learnt to walk (*The Economist*, 2 February 1991: 79). Differences also arose between the Federal Finance Minister and the Czech Ministry on Privatization over the question of the supervision of the sales and sale-proceeds.

It is also feared that privatization can lead to the concentration of wealth in the hands of undesirable domestic or foreign groups. As such, governments may be unwilling to sell assets to potential foreign investors, while the private sector or local banks may not be in a position to finance the purchases. Capital markets may be weak, poorly regulated or simply non-existent, or not able to absorb the sale of the equities on a large scale. The shareholders, on the other hand, may be willing to bear the risks involved in buying select equities and paying interests on the loans undertaken. The internal tax system, too, may not encourage investments in privatized enterprises (Reddy, 1988: 97–101).

Sale of public assets may be easier than public flotations in developing economies. But asset sales can also involve significant transactions costs and uncompensated wealth transfer especially when the public assets are sold at a discount to the market value. A government cannot expect to be paid the true market value for its assets, and must either lower the actual prices to attract buyers, or provide them with certain concessions or protection from foreign competitors. Large discounts may reinforce the position of privileged political and business elites, thereby routing the notion that privatization promotes competition or people's democracy. While the lure of certain benefits may bring in dynamic investors and entrepreneurs, the distortionary concessions may create the new sources of economic disparity and inefficiency and set a dangerous precedent for future privatizations (Nellis and Kikeri, 1989: 669).

Changes in institutional arrangements, promoting parallel systems in the corporate sector and decentralization may meet with stiff resistance from financial sectors. Privatization may be helpful as an innovative source of finance, but its efficacy is limited and application capricious. No country can bank upon the privatization itself. For instance, former Yugoslavia, at one stage presented a dilemma – whereas an 'alternative of loan' could bring its disintegration, 'to opt out of loan' could perhaps save it (Panda, 1990: 136).

Privatization in the form of divestiture runs the risk of replacing a public enterprise with a private one, and possibly a foreign one, which helps nobody except the purchaser. A quick glance at the implementation record of the conditions attached by the World Bank and other international donors suggests that delays and outright failure of implementation are more common where privatization has been attempted than in the cases of modest public enterprise reforms (Mosley, 1987).

The legal structure, too, may require drastic changes before a privatization programme can actually be implemented. Law and politics affect the financial structure of the public corporation in the same way as does economics (Roe, 1990: 7); a simple sale of nationalized industries or its assets is simply not possible. Creating specific assets that could be sold to the private sector has been a varied task and to a large extent dependent upon the legal framework in most cases, especially in Eastern Europe and Russia after the collapse of communism.

For instance, the auction of 16 shops in Czechoslovakia was marred by last-minute claims under Czechoslovakia's new law allowing restitution to former owners whose property had been confiscated by the communists long ago. Consequently, *The Moskva* restaurant had to be removed from the auction list owing to the claim made by a businessman that the restaurant belonged to his father during the Second World War. Such disputes cannot be solved for years to come.

In most cases, plans to privatize large numbers of public enterprises are even more confusing. The necessary legislation may not be passed by the concerned body in the absence of adequate public support, and in some countries the legal entity responsible for the transfer of public ownership into private ownership is found missing. The first formal step towards privatization requires the creation of such an entity (Prosser, 1986: ch. V), followed by detailed legislation. In the absence of appropriate legal bodies, rules and regulations, charges of corruption and nepotism cannot be ruled out. Furthermore, all efforts towards privatization involve the removal of a 'cash packet' from the ambit of the public sector enterprises.

In fact, with privatization the very legal nature of an enterprise alters. In the eyes of the law, a registered company or corporation is a 'person' quite distinct from the shareholders who own it; these companies have limited liability. The executive, comprising of the Board of Directors, is controlled by the Articles of Association and Memorandum of Understanding between government and the company. It may have certain general obligations also imposed by company law. Privatization alters the very legal relations between an enterprise and its consumers.

In a public enterprise, the customers cannot sue it for breach of contract or negligence. A nationalized industry is supposed to provide a service under a statutory scheme and not under a contract, and is therefore presumably immune from legal action from its customers or third party litigation barring public interest litigation in some cases. A privatized firm's first objective is to protect the interests of the company and its shareholders, with less and less emphasis on social obligations. As such, an entirely different system of accountability prevails. Privatization does not imply mere change in ownership but it also implies change in the property rights of the company as a whole (Veljanovski, 1987: 121).

In any event, the transition from the public to the private sector is not likely to be smooth sailing. The most important obstacles to privatization have been related to implementation rather than reform proposals, and in most cases very little thought has been given to the design and process of reform implementation. This neglect on the part of policy framers can prove to be extremely costly since reforms usually arouse the greatest opposition once the implementation programme is launched (Bery, 1990: 1129).

The dramatic and publicly visible reforms also reflect the failure of conventional economic management, posing a threat to the decision-making system. The real issue seems to be the overall capacity of the administrative and decision-making system to plan ahead and execute the plans willingly. Too often a lack of political will is held responsible for unsuccessful attempts at reforms, and the average person is not able to differentiate between the lack of a sound policy and action plan and lack of political will.

Usually, planners are not able to assess the political opposition likely to be encountered and the political resources needed to counter that opposition. There may also be cases where, despite adequate resources, the conditions for implementation may be highly unfavourable. In those cases, policy-makers may shy away from initiating drastic changes, thereby jeopardizing future prospects for reform. The reform packages which collapse during the course of execution can prove very costly both in terms of politics and economics (Bery, 1990: 1130).

In fact, there is a close association between power, wealth and politics in all societies, and these factors constitute the political culture of a given society. It may be more obvious in certain developed countries and conspicuous in developing countries. It is not because the underlying processes in developed countries are different in nature from those prevailing in developing ones, but only because they are less studied and less understood. As such, each country must design its own policies to suit its requirements or capabilities. A policy, successful elsewhere, may not work in another society owing to the lack of adequate human or financial resources, administrative skills or political expertise, an appropriate environment or cultural traits. A policy may be given up or reversed owing to inadequate preparation or implementational constraints. However articulate a policy may in design, it cannot be implemented successfully if the prevailing circumstances are against it.

Furthermore, implementation of complex socioeconomic reforms requires a great deal of political expertise and administrative skills. It also requires a well-chalked-out action plan, besides a well-thought-out policy design. This explains why the pace of privatization has been so slow in most countries worldwide. The pace may vary from country to country depending upon their political cultures, levels of economic development, geographical size, bureaucratic capabilities, entrepreneural skills and cultural traits.

We should not forget that privatization has many non economic dimensions – political, normative, cultural or social. It cannot and should not be seen in ahistorical, apolitical, acultural and non-institutional terms. As such, we should study privatization experiences and efforts in various countries in their proper contexts, and be aware that privatization may yield different results in different contexts. Although no privatization model can be duplicated or adopted elsewhere in the same vein, we can learn and unlearn a great deal from privatization experiences across the world.

4
The UK Experience

The UK experiences in privatization have been the source of more articles, debates, seminars and workshops than any other policy matter during the 1980s and 1990s. The privatization movement in the UK has now come of age, and this new status is evident from the seriousness assigned to it even by its critics. The Tories were elected consecutively for the fourth time despite the decline in popularity of Margaret Thatcher in 1992. The Thatcherites still bloom in 'Labour colours' (Ahmed, 1996: 12). Despite criticizing privatization as the hallmark of Thatcherism, the opposition parties in the UK have not been able to provide an alternative till today.

Relative to other countries, privatization experiences in the UK have been the most widely noted and widely imitated. These have been notable both in scale and high profile, and they have already set the world record by pushing faster into more controversial areas than anywhere else. This has stimulated the privatization drive in advanced economies, former command economies and developing economies alike. If a political idea could be copyrighted, perhaps former British Prime Minister Margaret Thatcher would be well on the way to achieving a runaway international best-seller (Jonquicres, 1986). Indeed, the UK has been a pioneer in the theory and practice of privatization.

The UK privatization programme was launched in October 1979 with the offer of 5 per cent of the government's shares in British Petroleum. During 1979–83, 12 SOEs were completely or partially privatized, raising net proceeds of £1625 million. During 1983–87, the Conservative government was able to raise the net proceeds to £10 983 million through the upswings in privatization of 24 companies, and during 1987–91 was able to yield net proceeds of £22 514 million through the privatization of British Steel, Water Supply and Sewage, Regional Electricity Companies, and so on. During the fourth term, the Major government was involved in the sale of Trust Ports' Properties (Medway, Clyde and Tilbury Ports), Northern Ireland Electricity and the government's remaining shares amounting to 21.8 per cent in British Telecom.

In 1991, the net proceeds from privatization totalled £21 551 million. By the end of October 1993, approximately two-thirds of the UK's nationalized industries and 940 000 jobs had been transferred to the private sector (Table 4.1), and by 1994 the privatized companies amounted to approximately 20 per cent of the UK's overall stockmarket value. The government also tried to investigate the possibilities of privatizing the Atomic Energy Authority, British Coal, British Rail, Crown Agents, Forest Enterprise, Northern Ireland Airport Authority, Nuclear Electric, Parcel Force, Red Star (a package delivery service), the Patent Office, Royal Post and three horse-racing courses near London (Bowden, 1994: 81–2).

Table 4.1 Net proceeds of major privatizations in the UK including privatization by share offer, 1988–93

Company	*Sale date(s)*	*Net proceeds (£ millions)*
British Steel	1988–90	2425
National Bus Company subsidiaries	1988–91	149
Professional and Executive Recruitment	1988–89	5
British Gas (debt)	1988–91	1400
	1922–93	350
Giroleasing	1989–90	339
Harland and Wolff	1989–90	8
Motorway Service Area leases	1989–93	16
Rover Group	1989–90	150
Scottish Transport Group subsidiaries	1989–93	49
Short Brothers	1989–90	30
Water Holding (debt)	1989–90	73
Water Holding (shares)	1989–92	3395
British Gas Onshore Oil assets	1990–91	130
Electricity Industries (debt)	1991–93	1870
Electricity Industries (shares)		
England & Wales	1990–93	6930
Scotland	1991–93	2718
Girobank	1990–91	112
British Technology Group	1991–92	25
British Telecom (shares)	1991–93	8844
Insurance Service Group	1991–92	13
National Telecommunications	1991–92	70
Northern Ireland Electricity		
(debt)	1993	70
(shares)	1992–93	497
Scottish Transport Group subsidiaries	1989–93	49

Source: A.N. Miller (1995) *Columbia Journal of World Business*, vol. xxx, no. 4: 88–9, Winter.

According to Stephen Dorrell, the financial secretary to the treasury under the Major government, the UK's central and local governments still had holdings of over £300 billion that could be privatized as of 1990. These included British Shipbuilders, British Waterways, the Civil Aviation Authority, London Authority, Scottish Nuclear Ltd., Bank of England, Docklands Light Railway, Her Majesty's Stationery Office and the Royal Mint. The question before the British government was not what to sell but what to keep. The Major government continued with the 'privatization programme' in 'public interest'. It tried to free the British Gas and electricity completely. By the end of 1998, British Coal and British Rail were already under the process of privatization.

The context

We cannot fail to notice the context of privatization in the UK. It is very surprising that within a short span the UK has moved from private enterprise to nationalization, and again from nationalization to privatization. A deeper analysis of the functioning of public enterprises over the years explains how these have been used as policy instruments both in the case of nationalization and privatization. Not long ago, the UK excelled in an ambitious programme of nationalization (Buckhaus, 1990: 161): during the postwar era the dominant assumption was that the market could no longer be left free to play its own tune. The state was required to intervene to improve industrial and economic management on the one hand, and to curb the harmful effects of capitalism in terms of inequities of income and opportunity on the other.

The individualistic nature of management and innovation, in consonance with the economic liberation of the first industrial revolution, was found to be no longer relevant at the time of the second industrial revolution. Britain was found ill-equipped for the requirements of institutionalized, systematic and science-based activities. After the Second World War, large-scale production and nationalization were seen as the most appropriate and effective ways of achieving economic growth and efficiency. Britain's weakness in terms of its international position was noticed only during the 1950s and 1960s, politically through its inability to hold the Empire together and economically through its failure to match the growth rates of other OECD countries.

It was argued that the plight of many industries was bad due to their small number, inefficiency and outdated technology. Nationalization was considered the best way to plan the economy and promote social welfare. In those days, social development was treated as an end in itself by the industrialized countries, with the state as an agent of social responsibility. The focus used to be an resource-inputs as symbols of progress and commitment to the neglect of outputs (Gupta, 1994: x). Gradually it became the duty of government to provide the basic facilities, services and a decent standard of living to all of its citizens on egalitarian and citizenship grounds.

The goal of social welfare somehow became linked with most of the nationalized industries, resulting in cross-subsidization of services on the one hand, and prevention of competition from the private sector on the other. The idea of nationalization gained political acceptability. New technologies in the wake of industrial development also gave credence to the notion that the state could play an important role in industrial planning, research and development. Moreover, continuing military demands on industry during the post-cold war era also affected industrial sectors under state control. The UK had been only second to the United States in terms of per capita commitment to defence R&D, and its development of nuclear weapons meant a substantial commitment of public resources to aerospace, shipbuilding and electronics (Walker and Sharp, 1991: 269).

During 1964–70, when the Labour Party was in power, the state in the UK assumed the role of prime mover. The salient features of public policy during this period were (1) rationalist optimism reflected in the form of Keynesian macroeconomic management, (2) partnership between government and industrial management, (3) expansion of education as a prerequisite for economic and technical advance, (4) an emphasis on manufacturing in order to promote exports and substitute imports, (5) an emphasis on scientific discovery and innovation and (6) enlargement of enterprises in order to reap the benefits of economies of scale. For instance, the government supported the mergers of engineering industries such as GEC in electrical and electronics engineering, British Leyland in automobiles, ICL in computers and Alfred Herbert in machine tools (Sharp and Shepherd, 1987).

In the 1970s, the oil crisis and stagflation led to disillusionment with the Keynesian policies of macroeconomic management in general, and the performance of the nationalization industries in particular. The UK had the lowest economic growth in Europe. In 1979, the rate of return net of subsidies and depreciation was 0.86 per cent. The National Enterprise Board, which was set up in 1975 to catalyze new developments in industry, turned into a rest house for lame ducks. Similarly, the nuclear power stations based on advanced technology of AGR became a drain on the national exchequer (Henderson, 1977: 159–205).

Despite many efforts towards revival, the domestic economy did not prosper and international trade shares continued to decline. Under these circumstances, interventionist policies became easy scapegoats. In 1976, the British government had to seek the help of the IMF to keep the economy running: it faced severe problems in terms of its public sector deficit and balance of payments. In 1978, the UK faced a rough winter in terms of public sector strikes and a succession of inflationary wage claims. Privatization, as a hallmark of Thatcherism, was a natural response to the perceived failure of nationalization in terms of the public sector performance. Fast changes in the underlying economic situation and technological innovations also required a shift in public policy – the economy became less controllable, for example,

Table 4.2 Structural change in the British economy, 1979–89

	1979		*1983*		*1989*		*GDP (US$) per employee 1979–89 (constant prices)*
	GDP (%)	*Employment (%)*	*GDP (%)*	*Employment (%)*	*GDP (%)*	*Employment (%)*	
Agriculture	2.1	1.6	2.0	1.7	1.5	1.3	172
Energy, Water	8.0	3.1	11.5	3.1	5.2	2.1	230
Manufacturing	28.2	31.3	23.5	26.2	22.2	23.0	245
Construction	6.1	5.3	6.0	5.0	6.9	4.7	251
Distribution, Hotels	13.2	18.4	12.7	19.5	14.2	20.3	190
Transport. Communications	7.6	6.4	7.0	6.4	6.9	6.0	180
Banking, Finance, Insurance[1]	11.5	7.1	13.6	8.9	19.7	11.8	131
Other services	23.3	26.7	23.7	29.2	23.4	30.9	165
Total	100	100	100	100	100	100	206

Note: [1] excludes leasing.
Sources: Sharp and Walker (1991) *Political Quarterly*, 62(3) July–Sept, : 319.

because of advances made in information and telecommunications technology. This led to the weakening of government authority (Table 4.2). Earlier, telecommunications was considered to be best served by the public sector, but later it was found that such services could be provided more efficiently by the competitive private sector. As such, modern technology became an ally of market forces (Howell, 1986: 167).

Moreover, there has also been a theoretical reassessment of the ability of the market to adjust to the changing demand and supply conditions. In micro-economics, the contestability theory has shown that a monopolistic market, due to economy of scale, may not necessarily require government regulations on entry and exit or the pricing policy of an enterprise, if potential competitors could make a hit and run entry to the market. In fact, the market approach to macro-economics has been used successfully to explain the phenomenon of cyclical fluctuations, unemployment and inflation in an equilibrium framework (Taniuchi and Taguchi, 1990).

Such attempts at theorizing the economy also proved useful in supporting and enlarging the role of market forces in the last two decades. In fact, normative arguments about the appropriate size and range of government activities paved the way for privatization. As such, a unified theory of public enterprise can accommodate both nationalization and privatization and explain the cycles where nationalization is followed by privatization and privatization is followed by reregulation. Although it is difficult to foresee the length of such waves, the existence of them cannot be denied.

Objectives of privatization

Like nationalization, the objectives of privatization in the United Kingdom have been vague and sometimes conflicting too, and so far the government has not produced a comprehensive document about the objectives and techniques of privatization. In fact, the objectives have varied from time to time depending upon the economic conditions, political circumstances and changing public attitudes. Initially the momentum of privatization was influenced by dissatisfaction with the size and performance of the SOEs, later by short-term budgetary constraints and finally by share ownership and distributional concerns.

The origin, content, process and forms of privatization were affected by the context in which privatization took place in the UK. During 1980–81 and 1991–92, the share of GDP for the nationalized industries declined from 9 per cent to just 3 per cent. The process of privatization began in the form of political realignment in the 1970s, which saw the Conservative Party adopt policies support of a market economy. The proponents of privatization saw a zero-sum relationship between government and the economy (Starr, 1987), and to them the bigger the public sector the smaller was the private economy;

the greater public spending, the less private savings and investments. This oversimplistic view provided a boost to the privatization drive. Explaining the objectives of privatization, John Moore, the then financial Secretary to the Treasury stated:

> Our policies have been specifically designed to further a number of objectives. They are designed to lead to greater efficiency ... They reduce the role of public sector and provide substantial sale receipts. They allow employees to take a direct stake in the companies in which they work and this leads to major changes in the attitudes. And, importantly, they provide a major stimulus to wider share ownership. (1986, London: H.M. Treasury)

The reality behind the apparent multiplicity of objectives shows the lack of a coherent policy towards privatization. In the initial years, the Thatcher government made no substantial changes to the structure of the nationalized industries, despite their poor performance in terms of profitability. Gradually, it tightened the financial constraints imposed upon them and sought to introduce more market-oriented management. In the case of British Steel it experimented with the introduction of performance-related incentive contracts for the top managers, which resulted in a considerable improvement in productivity performance. For example, British Coal's output per man per year increased by 22.6 per cent in 1986–87. But no similar tendency was found in other major public utilities.

In the early 1980s, the government resorted to a medium-term financial strategy for steady reductions in the rate of growth of the money supply and the public sector borrowing requirement (PSBR). Pursuit of the PSBR objective was, in fact, the key factor that resulted in shifting the government's attention from the sale of more marginal state enterprises to the privatization of the larger public corporations. In fact, privatization of state-owned enterprises had a direct and immediate effect on the PSBR. When an enterprise was transferred from the public to the private sector, its borrowings no longer contributed to the PSBR. The proceeds from asset sales were no longer classified as borrowings in the government accounts. As such, the sale proceeds in a given year reduced the PSBR in that particular year. According to the prevailing accounting convention in the UK, asset disposals were treated as negative government spending, so that for all practical purposes sale proceeds were actually treated as a reduction in governmental expenditure (Vickers and Yarrow, 1989: 218).

In this way, privatization allowed the government to meet its fiscal targets without actually reducing government expenditure or enhancing taxation as would otherwise have been imperative. The importance of fiscal objectives was clear from the early privatizations during 1979–83. Moreover, privatization also helped in increasing short-term government revenues. For instance, revenues from the sale of nationalized industries grew from £377 million in 1979–80 to approximately £5000 million in 1986–87. The government was expected to receive around £26 billion by the end of 1987 from the sale of public assets (Veljanovski, 1987: 5).

In fact, when the government sells fixed assets held by it previously for its own use, the sale proceeds are treated as capital revenue. When the government sells part or all of its interests in a public enterprise, the transaction is treated as a sale of equity and the sale proceeds are recorded as a loan repayment. As such, asset sales tend to be a once-and-for-all reduction in the overall deficit unless the market price is less than the income that would have accrued to the government (Mansoor, 1988: 181).

The pace of privatization in the UK seems to be more influenced by macroeconomic goals than microeconomic goals of promoting competition and increasing efficiency. With the sale of British Telecom, attempts were made to rationalize and legitimize privatization. Regulated private monopoly was seen as a more effective and efficient form of production than nationalized public monopolies, and it was argued that the private monopoly produced goods and services more efficiently than the public monopolies, and that the abuse of monopoly could only be controlled by a new regulated agency set for this very purpose. That is why the Office of Telecommunications (Oftel), the Office of Gas Supply (Ofgas) and the Office of Electricity Regulation (Ofer) were set up in the UK.

However, it was the floatation of shares in the UK with the definite purpose of widening share-ownership that gained maximum attention worldwide. During 1979–83, a number of experiments were made with different kinds of floatations. For example, British Aerospace, Amersham and Associated British Ports were offered for sale at a fixed price, while Britoil, British Petroleum Enterprise Oil and Cable & Wireless were offered by inviting tenders. British Sugar was a private placing, while National Freight was an employee buyout. In some cases, preference was given to small shareholders. Loyalty bonuses were also announced for those who held their shares for a longer period than the minimum time prescribed.

This certainly had a dramatic effect of creating windfall gains for successful applicants for shares. It therefore became highly popular with millions of successful applicants, while the losses borne by taxpayers were thinly spread and less visible. The profits were calculated by taking the difference between the value of the shares on the day of issue and their valuation by the market on the first day of trading. The government also reaped political benefits by claiming wealth redistribution via underpricing shares and pushing back the frontiers of the state.

This all led to a massive expansion in the number of shareholders, including the number of employees holding shares in their own companies. During 1979–87, the total number of shareholders in Britain increased threefold. By January 1987, the number of shareholders in British Telecom was 800 000, in British Gas 2 400 000, and in TSB 1 600 000. Approximately 3 800 000 British people held shares in more than one company (Veljanovski, 1987: 104).

During the early 1990s every fifth adult in Britain owned shares in more than one privatized enterprise, utility or service.

The value of these shares increased manifold over the following years. For instance, the value of shares in British Petroleum had increased by 60 per cent by the middle of October 1986; Associated British Ports by 400 per cent, and Jaguar by 219 per cent. The average increase of all issues was approximately 116 per cent (*Investors Chronicle*, 17 October 1985).

In most of the sales of the SOEs there are attempt to encourage workers to buy shares. This helped employees to perceive an identity of interests between themselves and the success of the company for which they worked. Moreover, the policies to promote employee-ownership were found entirely compatible with the objective of promoting wider share-ownership. The proponents of privatization popularized it in the name of creating a property-owning democracy by involving the people directly in the success and failures of the economy. They also hoped for the stage to arrive when the entire public might regard themselves as shareholders, thereby converting the shareholders interests into public interests (Oakeshott, 1988: 177).

In fact, preoccupation with the issue of ownership diverted the attention of the government away from the main objective of privatization – increasing economic efficiency by fostering competition. Greater economic efficiency was not one of the main targets of the privatization programme in the UK; another two important objectives were (1) widening share-ownership, and (2) reducing the public sector borrowing requirement. In the initial stages, the tension between the economic efficiency and other objectives of privatization was not visible because some of the companies, such as Amersham, British Aerospace, British Petroleum, Cable & Wireless and Enterprise Oil, already operated in reasonably good competitive environments. The conflicts between policy objectives became more acute when attention fell on major public utilities such as British Telecommunications and British Gas.

Basically, three factors were responsible for the conflicts in the government's objectives of privatization: (1) the anxiety to make floatations successful, (2) the government's interests in the sale proceeds, and (3) promotion of competition. These three represented the political, fiscal and efficiency objectives (Ramanadham, 1989: 25). Sometimes the government had to achieve success at the sale-counter at the cost of taxpayers; at other times it had to sacrifice gains from economic efficiency in order to promote wider ownership. Sometimes it had to sacrifice competition to attract private investors in the natural monopolies. For instance, in the cases of British Telecom, British Gas and British Airways, privatization left the monolithic size of these sectors undisturbed, while the National Express had to face real barriers of competition.

On the basis of government documents, official sources and the Conservative Party's manifestoes, various objectives of privatization can be identified as follows (Ramanadham, 1989):

1. Reducing the size and scope of government by rolling back the frontiers of the state.
2. Taking the government out of business by promoting the ideology that it is none of the business of the government to remain in business.
3. Reducing political intereference in the management of an enterprise by separating the commercial from the social objectives.
4. Saving scarce public resources for activities other than SOEs.
5. Attracting domestic and foreign investment through divestment.
6. Promoting people's capitalism through wider share-ownership.
7. Reducing the fiscal deficit and public sector borrowing requirement.
8. Generating new sources of tax revenue through higher returns on the capital invested in privatized business.
9. Curbing the powers of public sector trade unions.

Modalities of privatization

The modalities of privatization in the UK varied from time to time and enterprise to enterprise depending upon the objectives involved. Since privatization denotes not only denationalization but all attempts at marketization, it provides scope for a wide range of modalities. There can also be a combination of measures relating to ownership, organizational and operational measures. These include divestment, liquidation, management buy-outs, management buy-ins, joint ventures, leasing, contracting and disinvestment of shares, and so forth. Under ownership measures we can talk about sales of an enterprise in full or partial involvement of the private sector, liquidation in the form of sale of assets and sale of an enterprise to employees through management buy-outs (Ramanadham, 1989: 8–10).

The organizational measures include all attempts towards introducing a market discipline, involving good business and management practices at various levels of the SOEs. For instance, the company may be restructured in such a manner that control is limited to the apex level, while the subsidiaries can enjoy substantial freedom at the market level; or a monolithic organization such as British Steel may be broken into smaller units to promote competition, or a major project line may be converted into an independent company. A public enterprise may lease out large chunks of its assets to the best bidders to achieve economic efficiency, without giving up ownership *per se*. The government can break a big enterprise into smaller units to promote competition from within, or it can deregulate certain activities thereby improving the prospects of entry and exit.

Among the operational measures we can include contracting out, franchising, target-setting, imposing fiscal constraints and reforming the pricing policy, and so on. These are important measures of privatization, though not very spectacular. In the case of the UK, contracting out and franchising have been adopted successfully in a number of areas such as refuse-collection, hospital-cleaning, catering and non-commercial bus services, and so forth. Contracting out involves the decision of an enterprise to acquire an input or service from the market instead of producing or providing it itself. The private sector can also serve as an ancillary unit, and there can be many other options at the intermediate level.

Privatization can also be undertaken in a phased manner. First, lower-level changes may be introduced, and when the results are satisfactory more radical measures may be taken. Government may sell shares in tranches, first selling a few shares to test market conditions. Meanwhile, it can prepare an enterprise by improving its profitability and making it attractive to the market before actually privatizing it. For instance, in the case of British Airways redundancies of labour were systematically dealt with. In the case of the National Freight Consortium, the management buy-out was made easy with the government's offer of £47 million towards the pension fund liability. In the case of British Rail, the government considered hiving off the non-core activities to make it more attractive for privatization purposes.

The government in the UK adopted different techniques in different cases. Many have been public sales, but others have been in the nature of private sales. Public sales were held in the case of British Telecommunications, Cable & Wireless, Associated British Ports, British Gas and British Airports Authority; while private sales were held for National Bus Company, National Freight Company, British Leyland Trucks, Sealink Ltd., British Rail Hotels, British Airways Helicopters and Royal Ordinance (Ramanadham, 1989: 65). The costs of sales and underwriting also varied from case to case ranging from 0.5 per cent of gross proceeds in the case of Rolls-Royce to 13.6 per cent in the case of Associated British Port Holdings in 1983.

The government adopted various techniques of public sales. In the case of British Port Holdings (1983), British Telecommunications (1984) and British Gas (1986), the government offered the shares at a fixed price. In the case of Associated British Port Holdings (1984), British Petroleum (1983) and Enterprise Oil (1984) it preferred to sell by inviting tenders, with the minimum price fixed. In the case of British Airport Authority, the government accepted applications in descending order of the prices tendered.

According to the Conservative Manifesto of 1987, there are several aspects of allocation of shares in the UK which merit special attention:

1. Priority was given to small applicants in order to promote wider share-ownership.
2. Limits were placed on individual shareholdings.
3. Special offers were made to the employees and pensioners of a privatized enterprise.
4. Bonus shares were given to those who held their shares for a longer period of time.

5. Management buy-outs were experimented within labour-incentive corporations.
6. The government retained a special or golden share itself. For instance, in the case of British Airports Authority, those who applied for up to 1000 shares were allotted only 100 shares.

In several cases limits were imposed on individual shareholdings. No person was allowed to hold more than 15 per cent of the voting shares in Amersham International (1982), BAA (1987), British Aerospace (1981, 1985), British Gas (1981), Cable & Wireless (1985) and Rolls-Royce (1987). In the case of British Airways (1987), non-Britons were allowed to own up to 25 per cent and UK nationals up to 15 per cent of the shares offered. In some cases special offers were made to employees at the government's expense. For instance, in Amersham International, 35 shares were allotted free to all employees, and in British Port Holdings the government offered matching shares up to 225 per employee. In British Airport Authority (1987), preferential consideration was made for the allotment of up to 4082 shares per employee or pensioner. In Rolls-Royce, 10 per cent of shares were reserved for employees or pensioners, while 15 per cent of shares were reserved in the case of Jaguar (1984).

The National Freight Corporation provides a special case where a management buy-out was tried successfully. First of all the NFC, the largest road haulage organization, was converted into National Freight Company Ltd. under the Transport Act of 1980, and the management buy-out was carried out in 1982. The new enterprise was named The National Freight Consortium after privatization, and it sought to involve the employees as owners. The shareholders themselves appointed the director, and no single person or family was allowed to hold more than 100 000 shares. Remunerations were profit-oriented (McLachlan, 1989). There are several cases where the British government holds a special share, such as, Amersham International, BAA, British Aerospace, British Gas, British Petroleum, British Telecommunications, Britoil, Cable & Wireless, Jaguar, Rolls-Royce, Enterprise Oil and Sealink Ltd.

The process of privatization

The question arises how could privatization take place in the UK on such a massive scale. It was mainly because deliberate care was taken to design a programme that was not only achievable but also popular. The Thatcher government did not look at privatization only in terms of a financial transaction but also a politically sensitive issue, knowing very well that the cause for privatization had to be argued effectively and enthusiastically. No privatization programme could ever succeed unless it took into account national interests and local sensitivities. Adequate attention had to be given to both the macroeconomic aspects and political strategy (Table 4.3).

Table 4.3 Steps to privatization

	Step one	*Step two*	*Step three*
Stage 1	*Feasibility study* Undertaken by civil servants, merchant banks or management consultants	*Background & opinion* Report to Ministers on the possibility, options and prerequisites of any sale	*Ministerial decision* Decision in principle to proceed, choice of option to be pursued; for example, floatation of shares, etc.
Stage 2	*Select advisers* Usually merchant bank advisers selected for advice leading to sale	*Preparations made* Prepare business by strengthening management team and introducing private sector attitudes and methods. Prepare legislation and pass regulatory measures, if necessary	*See balance sheet* Adjust balance sheet if necessary. Assume the legal power to create and sell a public limited company
Stage 3	*Select PLC* Well-run PLCs with reasonable balance sheets should be selected for sale. Choose merchant banks, brokers and solicitors for sale	*Choose market slots* Decide on the number of shares to be sold, where to sell and how to fit sales with other issues. Decision to be taken whether to under write sale or not	*Build image* Consider pathfinder prospects and build image before actual advertising starts
Stage 4	*Final decisions* Final decision has to be taken to go ahead and price is decided	*Sale takes place* A public corporation may be sold 100%, or a fixed per cent of shares be sold at a time and privatization process completed in tranches	*Process completed* With the sale of a 100% holding the transfer form public to private sector is completed in one go. But it can also be in a phased manner

Sources: J. Moore (1986) *Privatization in the United Kingdom*: 18–21.

It is difficult to say whether privatization is good politics or good economics. It is seen as good politics in terms of reducing the tax burden on the individual while maintaining the quality of services and goods; and it is also viewed as good economics in terms of opening new vistas for entrepreneurs. The politicians, in fact, have been looking for economic devices, such as liberalization, deregulation and privatization, to put their sagging economies back into shape and to reap political benefits thereby.

It is interesting to recall that privatization was not an outcome of a coherent political philosophy even in the UK (Heald, 1982: 333). The privatization drive was set in motion by the Conservative Party's traditional support for private property, and the goals of privatization evolved gradually. In the early days, the objectives appeared to be purely financial and managerial, with the original impetus coming from the desire to discipline the nationalized industries by subjecting them to market forces. The government took care in informing and educating the public why it was considering or resorting to privatization in a particular case, and what were the likely consequences. For instance, in the White Paper *Privatization of the Water Authorities in England and Wales* (Department of Environment, 1986), the government emphasized the benefits of privatization to customers, employees and the nation as a whole, in the following ways:

1. The authorities will free the privatized enterprises from government intervention in day to day management and protect them from fluctuating political pressures.
2. The authorities will be released from the constraints on financing which public ownership imposes.
3. Access to private capital will make it easier for the authorities to pursue effective investment strategies for cutting the costs and improving the quality.
4. The financial markets will be able to compare the performance of individual water authorities against each other and against other sectors of the economy.
5. A system of economic regulation will be designed to ensure that the benefits of greater efficiency are systematically passed on to customers in the form of lower prices and better services than would otherwise have occurred.
6. Measures will be introduced to provide a clearer strategic framework for the protection of the water environment.
7. Private water authorities will have greater incentives to ascertain the needs and preferences of customers and to tailor their services and tariffs accordingly.
8. Private authorities will be able to compete in the provision of various commercial services, notably in consultancy abroad.
9. Private authorities will be able to attract high quality managers from other parts of private sector.
10. There will be the opportunity for wide ownership of shares among employees and local customers.

The question arises: would Mrs Thatcher still have resorted to the privatization strategy had it been economically efficient but politically non-viable? If politics is the art of the possible, the possible is that which the politician is able to get across in terms of what his or her audience is willing to accept, both on rational and political grounds. It is this knack for measuring political circumstances correctly that makes the difference between honest intentions and success.

Margaret Thatcher had this knack in plenty. She was able to convert the privatization policy into political pay-offs; she knew it perfectly well that it was dangerous to assume that the people or institutions would act altruistically or in the public interest. Politically, it was impossible to achieve a policy, however rational or logical it might appear to an economist, unless and until it served the self-interests of individuals. The Thatcher government succeeded in making the privatization programme popular by making an unapologetic case for the virtues of capitalism, individualism and the profit-motive (Brittan, 1986: 33). The Thatcher government was preeminently 'a government of dissenters and outsiders'. Her greatest scorn was reserved not only for the socialists but also for the traditional conservatives since she was opposed to both egalitarian and aristocratic values (Walker and Sharp, 1991: 265).

Privatization became popular in the UK because the Thatcher government was able to highlight its benefits in terms of its ability to increase industrial efficiency, raise money, boost ownership among employees and the general public, and carry domestic and international prestige. The government was also able to refute the charges, such as selling the family silver, taxing the future generation to meet current expenditures, taxing the taxpayers for the benefits of consumers, and so on. It was made possible because of the fact that all of the critical participants in the privatization programme – taxpayers, customers, employees, management, perspective investors, commentators and opponents of privatization – were identified early and dealt with in the most satisfactory manner under the prevailing circumstances (Grimstone, 1989: 116).

Adequate care was taken to involve those who mattered in the process of privatization, due attention being given to the managers and workers involved in order to seek their cooperation: the management buy-out in the case of National Freight Corporation provides an apt example. Care was also taken to involve small applicants through preferential allotment of shares in the case of disinvestment. Different kinds of pricing and selling channels were adopted to attract domestic and foreign investment and expert advice was sought from merchant banks and financial analysts. Media publicity was also well-planned (Ramanadham, 1989: 29–30).

After announcing the objectives and modalities of privatization, the government tried to set priorities and draw a tentative timetable. Privatization in the UK proved to be a highly technical job, and involved three steps: (1) legal and constitutional changes, (2) restructuring of the company to make it more attractive for sale purposes, and (3) the actual sale of the company. All of these steps involved a lot of preparations. Enterprises came under market discipline in the form of performance-monitoring, target-setting and limiting external financing; some enterprises were restructured through capital write-offs or fresh cash injections; while certain *ad hoc* measures were adopted in other cases.

The question arises: should the restructuring have occurred before or after privatization? For instance, the Thatcher government allowed access to the gas and electricity transmission systems as early as the 1980s, several years before the industries were sold, although no entry occurred. While the government rejected the advice of the Monopolies and Mergers Commission to split up the privatized gas industry in 1993, it did split the generation sector before privatizing the electricity industry in 1990–91. However, it maintained the regional distribution sectors intact. In the case of British Coal, the government decided to sell it as five geographical units. The splitting of an industry after privatization was generally perceived as either a failure on the part of the government, or as misleading the shareholders who bought shares in the integrated company according to their expectations of future gains. By splitting the monopoly, the government actually marred the future prospects.

In fact, privatization and restructuring both involve a reallocation of net benefits among three groups – consumers, private producers and government. If a monopoly is privatized intact, the government may get more profits, but it implies loss to the consumers. The costs of restructuring could be less if carried out before privatization, whereas it could be more in terms of high opportunity costs in terms of a legislative programme if done afterwards. Restructuring before privatization could be at the cost of management cooperation, but the government may not be in a position to give direct orders to a firm after privatization. If restructuring occurs before privatization, the uncompensated cost that the producer bears is reflected in the sale price and thereby transferred to the government. After privatization, the government's interests are restricted to the proportion of profits through taxes (Green and Price, 1995: 75–89).

In the UK, privatization has been a governmental commitment and the pace has also been swift and determined. The government did not depend solely on divestiture, it resorted to many techniques of privatization, some of them proving to be novel and somewhat ingenious. But in many cases privatization proved to be a long process and a tedious exercise. For instance, it took the British government almost three years to prepare water and electricity for privatization despite all the expertise available, and the privatization of natural monopolies further required the establishment of regulatory agencies to preserve and protect consumers' interests. As such, licensing systems were developed in order to promote efficiency wherever it was feasible and impose controls on prices wherever necessary in order to enhance productive efficiency.

Privatization and the RPI–*X* formula

In the UK, all the privatized utilities are subject to a regulatory framework. The usual method applied to control them is known as the rate-of-return regulation. It puts a ceiling on prices which the monopoly utility is allowed to charge each year. The ceiling is so computed as to cover the utility's costs and to provide for a fair rate of return on capital. It restricts prices from being raised too high above costs, but it carries the risk of an inefficient cost performance. Under this scheme, management has no incentive to improve performance; the utility's profits are more or less fixed. Since profits are constrained to a specific rate of return on assets, there is no incentive to reduce costs, which may result in poor performance in practice.

To curb the perceived weakness of rate-of-return regulation, a more effective device was proposed by Stephen Littlechild, known as the RPI–*X* formula. This places a ceiling on prices charged by the utility over a period of five years, during which time the prices of the products can be increased by an amount not greater than the increase in the retail price index less *X* per cent. The value of *X* is specified in relation to the anticipated scope for reduction in real costs over the five years. In the case of British Telecom, *X* was set at 3, in the case of British Gas at 2, and in the case of British Airports Authority at 1. The difference in the values of *X* denotes the difference in the impact of technological change on each sector as well as the difference in perception on the scope for productive improvement.

The RPI–*X* formula is an improvement upon the rate-of-return regulation. Under the RPI–*X* formula, any enterprise which is able to achieve more than

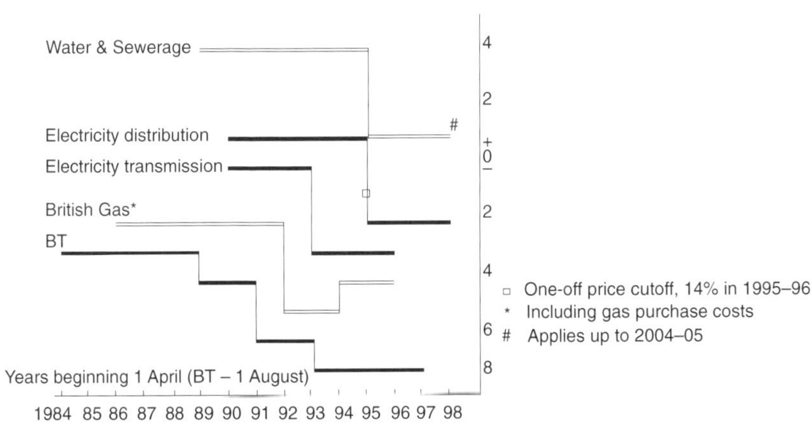

Figure 4.1 The *X* factor: British utilities' maximum annual real price increases (%)
Source: *The Economist*, 28 January 1995, based on Ofwat, Offer, Ofgas and Oftel figures.

the expectations over the five years period can retain the additional margin of profits, while the enterprise which underperforms is deemed to have a poor profit record. In addition to the RPI–*X* formula, there are statutory provisions which prohibit the charging of excessive or predatory prices for individual products within the overall RPI–*X* ceiling. These provisions apply equally to other products also, not governed by the formula.

The success of the RPI–*X* formula depends upon the performance of the newly-privatized enterprises. This approach can be effective if the value of *X* can be set independently of the enterprise's actual performance record and if underperformance results in sanctions in the capital markets. Figure 4.1 shows the maximum annual real price increases of various British utilities in relation to the *X* factor. However, the near-monopoly status and associated financial strength of British Telecom, British Gas and British Airports Authority belie any such hopes. There has been a proposal from Sprint, America's largest international carrier to build a nationwide trunk network in the UK at a cost of £200 million, but it will have to cross many hurdles.

Proliferation of the regulatory watchdogs

The privatization of natural monopolies and public utilities has posed serious technical problems in the UK. It has made it difficult to protect the interests of consumers of these privatized companies without adequate competition and regulation, and has led to the proliferation of regulatory watchdogs modeled on the Office of Fair Trading, such as the National Rivers Authority (NRA), Office of Water Services (Ofwat), Office of Gas Supply (Ofgas); Office of Telecommunications (Oftel), Office of Electricity Regulation (Ofer), and so on.

Regulatory watchdogs have also been established in some other sectors. For instance, in the financial sector the Securities and Investment Board (SIB) and five other Self Regulating Organizations (SROs) have been established under the Financial Services Act. Similarly, the broadcasting sector is now under the regulation of three new watchdogs – the Independent Television Commission (ITC), the Radio Authority (RA) and Broadcasting Standards Council (BSC). These bodies have been established to ensure that the firms' monopoly powers are not misused. Where competition is found lacking or inadequate, regulation has been encouraged to curb the privatized enterprises from unduly fleecing their customers (*The Economist*, 28 January 1995: 76). For instance, Oftel (Office of Telecommunications) was established when British Telecom was privatized in 1984.

Pioneers in privatization, the regulatory watchdogs in the UK do not cap utilities' rate-of-return on capital; rather they try to limit the annual price increase on the basis of the RPI–*X* formula. The regulatory body determines the *X* factor which is reviewed every five years by the Monopolies and Mergers

Commission (MMC). If a utility disagrees with the price cap set by a regulator it can refer the matter to the MMC. In the UK, gas prices have actually fallen by 20 per cent in real terms since privatization, while water charges have risen due to huge investments in environmental projects.

In lieu of the dismantling of the regulatory bodies; their number is likely to increase in the future. For instance, in 1984 the UK government had regarded Oftel as a temporary creation to hold fort till the telecoms market became more competitive. But Oftel believes that it has a big role to play even today; its *quo pro quo* is the fair trading clause inserted in the license of every telecoms firm which allows the regulator to intervene if it finds any firm exploiting its market power in an unfair manner. The fair trading clause is based on articles 85 and 86 of the European Union's Treaty of Rome (*The Economist*, 8 June 1996: 67–8).

Quite surprisingly, the powers of the existing regulatory bodies such as the Office of Fair Trading (OFT), the Monopolies and Mergers Commission (MMC) and the Civil Aviation Authority (CAA) have been extended. For instance, prior to privatization the MMC could only examine the efficiency and cost aspects of the nationalized industries, but now a privatized undertaking can also be referred to the MMC by the Secretary of State. The MMC can also examine the competitive aspects of those utilities which fall under the purview of the private sector. For instance, the MMC has been able to take British Gas to task for overcharging its industrial customers; this would have been inconceivable under nationalization.

These regulatory bodies have vast powers to monitor performance, control prices and quality of service. They provide economic regulation under the RPI–*X* price rule wherever relevant, ensure conformity with terms and conditions, detect anti-competitive practices, provide a forum for consumer complaints, and set licensing terms for the new enterprises. These watchdogs also enjoy considerable discretionary powers, which has led to unaccountable public administration in the UK.

The move from nationalization to regulation has certain advantages too. It has helped in separating management from the task of regulating its own affairs in the public interest, and it has also opened the actions of privatized industries and regulatory bodies to public scrutiny. Regulation is supposed to be more transparent than control through nationalization. It also protects the interests of consumers, and most of the privatized utilities are also subject to investigation by the MMC.

Yet there are defects in the way the new economic regulation has evolved. It has grown in a piecemeal and idiosyncratic fashion, and most cases can be seen as an outcome of the short-term constraints imposed by the need to sell the nationalized industries successfully. Gradually the regulatory framework has become more vague and complex. Instead of promoting competition, it has become a substitute for competition, nor has it been able to lead to genuine cost–benefit appraisals.

The very purpose of the regulatory constraint has been to protect the interests of customers. It is supposed to hold the fort till the competition arrives, and it is inappropriate if competition is unlikely to emerge. It is a temporary safeguard and not a permanent method of control. The one-off nature of restriction is precisely what preserves the enterprise's incentive to be efficient, because the enterprise keeps any gains beyond the specified level. However, repeated pressures for efficiency audit or value-for-money audits may destroy the incentive and encourage nannyish attitudes towards the enterprise (Beesley and Littlechild, 1989: 17).

Much deregulation in the UK has been called reregulation, and we find a shift from structural regulation to rules guiding conduct. Often these rules are more complex than those replaced. For instance, in the financial sector there has been a shift from the structural separation of broking and market-making to the regulation of conduct through detailed new rules for the protection of investors (*The Economist*, 21 January 1989: 73). But the regulators are at a disadvantage. They often have less information about costs than the companies to be regulated, and it is therefore difficult for them to judge whether companies are working efficiently or not. In utilities, regulators can control only those things which are measurable such as prices and profits. But it is not easy to enforce structural regulation. Where it is impossible to tell whether an enterprise faced with potential conflict of interests is acting in the best interests of consumers, it is better to separate markets and prevent the enterprises in one market from entering another.

The biggest challenge has been to bring about a permanent and continuous change in the way companies operate, but turning a state monopoly into a private one is a tedious job. For instance, a battle raged between British Gas and the regulatory authorities including the MMC for two years after it was privatized in 1986. Government cannot leave everything to the market, and privatization has, in fact, increased the need for regulation. When an enterprise imposes costs on others, regulation is needed to restore the balance, but overregulation has to be avoided at all costs (Bishop, Kay and Mayer, 1995).

It is better to encourage competition rather than detailed regulation to reap the benefits of privatization. Economic instruments such as taxes, marketable permits and auctions may prove to be more efficient, economic and effective than legalistic controls. The British experience in privatization leaves much to be desired, and some would suggest that, so far, it has led to sternness without efficiency (Cairncross, 1990: 251). Unless some positive steps are taken, today's regulators will prove no less capricious than yesterday's civil servants. The privatization of organizationally and technically complex enterprises such as public utilities have questioned the very validity of a market solution to public sector inefficiency and monopoly. They have also posed a great challenge to the new regulatory bodies to foster competition.

Organizational effects of privatization

After almost two decades of being central to the Thatcherite prescription, to reinvigorate the British economy, privatization still remains a contentious issue. While some have viewed it as a catalyst, others with firsthand experience shy away from public comment. While government ministers have praised it without reservation, some academics have expressed serious reservations; while some describe it in terms of a strong medicine, just what was needed in the 1980s to save the British economy from decline, others find in it a mere whiff of quackery (*The Economist*, 9 June 1990: 39). The businessmen actually running the affected companies appear to have found privatization more traumatic and more beneficial than what is commonly assumed by academics.

The heads of the recently privatized companies have generally found privatization to be essential to fundamental improvement of their companies' performance. But there has also been an increase in complaints from customers immediately after such privatizations. Both British Telecom and British Gas saw a huge increase in consumers' complaints. Most of the privatized companies also resorted to dramatic cuts in the workforce with 'concomitant gains' in productivity. For instance, British Telecom's productivity increased from 1.9 per cent to 3.2 per cent per year during 1984–89, but it also resulted in massive job cuts. Although productivity increased in most of the companies following privatization, no discernible pattern could be found as a testimony of the improved rate of return on capital employed, return on sales or growth in output.

What has emerged instead is something which cannot be measured easily – the challenge to steer the companies into a fully commercial culture. While many privatized companies indulged in a once-and-for-all shake-up around the time of sale, a sizeable number have subsequently settled down to their old ways. Mere change in ownership cannot change the culture of an organization *ipso facto*; the key to such a change lies in changing the outlook, work culture, work environment, work methods, work values and work norms of organizations. Executives cannot always manage cultural change in their organizations since they are also part of the corporate culture with deeply held views and taken-for-granted assumptions about the proper way of doing things (Woodward, 1990: 366). As such, the process of privatization in itself cannot bring about a permanent and continuous change in the ways in which companies operate.

If privatization is seen merely as a matter of growth, efficiency, earning foreign exchange, neglecting the socioeconomic and cultural dimension altogether, it may fail in the long run. It is generally held by proponents of privatization that it will lead to internal efficiency and better customer service through transferring some of the activities to private ownership to be disciplined automatically by stockmarket processes and enhanced competition or the threat of competition (Woodward, 1991: 65). But how these effects will be achieved is rarely specified.

The underlying model needs some stimulation as well as some form of ecological adaptation. The basic assumption behind the privatization programme in the UK has been the ecological adaptation by organizations in response to external stimuli – greater access to private capital, discipline exercised through the stockmarket and the threat of competition, and so on. These external stimuli are supposed to generate a response in terms of prices, financial viability, operational efficiency and customer sensitivity. On closer inspection of privatization experiences in the UK, one can say that it has certainly resulted in escape from incorporation in government financial constraints and processes on the one hand, and departmental sponsorship and intervention in day-to-day affairs on the other. But there is no hard evidence of any substantial increase in terms of efficiency or competition. Rather, in some cases, customers have complained of reduced service and increased prices.

The biggest drawback of the privatization movement has been the overemphasis on profit-maximization and cost-savings. Nor is it free from complacency, growth of bureaucracy and the destructive pursuit of power and control, to the neglect of a service ethos. This explains the current trend towards management buy-outs, organizational unbundling and cultural change programmes. Frankly speaking, these may only lead to the management of public perception, without attributing anything concrete to efficiency and effectiveness.

It is feared that the dynamics of management careerism may outweigh the dynamics of competitive pressures, if any. As such, the model of ecological adaptation may not fulfil the basic assumptions underlying the privatization programme in the UK. On the contrary, privatization may advocate those values which have proved to be most damaging to an organization; namely, the pursuit of career advancement and personal acquisitiveness in lieu of the desire to work for the common goal, common purpose and common benefits of the organization as a whole, if not society as a whole (Woodward, 1991).

Privatization changes the very business environment both internally as well as externally. It results in a shift in paradigm – a shift from public administration to public management (Gupta, 1996). Once a public enterprise is privatized, the very administrative culture needs to be replaced with an entrepreneurial one. The focus is now on performance-monitoring and public management rather than conformity to rules and regulations. Accountability to the government needs to be replaced with accountability to customers. The government is now seen as a 'steerer' rather than a 'rower', and the managers of the privatized enterprise, too, have to face the challenge of fitting their organizations strategically into the 'chaos border areas between stable and unstable equilibrium' (Stacey, 1993). They have to encourage change, without disintegrating the organization *per se*.

An evaluation

Behind differing perceptions of privatization experiences in the UK lie differences of interest; privatization raises obvious ethical questions. In the privatization process, the formidable problems of ensuring an equitable distribution of assets and obtaining adequate compensation for the state are inherent. In the wake of privatization the sale of national assets deprives the government of resources which could be used for the benefit of its citizens. Lord Stockton, in a pungent speech in the House of Lords, equated it with an historic house owner selling off the Georgian Silver and the Canalettos. Parting with assets could be justified only if the proceeds were to be invested in a more productive field. However, this has not happened in the UK where the proceeds of privatization have been treated as recurrent income or, to be more precise, as negative expenditure to bridge the gap on the current account (Lord Stockton, 1985).

Moreover, it has been one of the dilemmas of the privatization process that under the law of supply and demand, a government keen to privatize national assets can only be expected to receive the lowest possible price for them. The government in the UK obtained much less than their actual price. For instance, the sale of electricity supply companies was estimated to incur a huge loss of £3 billion to the exchequer. Neil Kinnock, the leader of the SDP, called it a great loss to the national exchequer to sell public assets at 40 per cent less than their actual worth.

Besides losing money, the government also lost direct control over the activities concerned. The practical implementation of privatization also affected, in a significant manner, the relationship between the public and specific interests on the one hand, and between specific interests and the government on the other. It made it difficult for the government to act at all times in the public interest. Furthermore, the sale of national assets to special interests could always be opposed on the grounds of public interests.

In view of public criticism, the sale of PowerGen, a power generating company, to a single bidder, the Hanson Trust, for £1500 million had to be cancelled. Objections to the deal were made on two grounds, (1) the sale to a single bidder excluded other possible contenders, and (2) it involved selling at less than the book value of the company. Similar objections were also made in connection with the sale of regional water boards. The public wanted to retain access to large tracts of land belonging to these water boards, which was met on paper by imposing an obligation on the new companies to maintain high environmental standards in these areas (Southern Water Annual Report, 1990: 3–4).

Privatization in the UK has also led to the creation of special interests, and has resulted in inegalitarian use of scarce resources. The philosophy seems to be – it is better to have few families 'thoroughly' than many 'inadequately'. The social costs of privatization have also been high, while the benefits have been uncertain. The British experience has led neither to efficiency nor to less-government, and the original Thatcherite zeal to dismantle quasi-autonomous national organizations has only been replaced with an urge to create new ones.

But the new ones are even more powerful than the old ones. Paradoxically, they have extended their powers to regulate and control private industries to the officials who are appointed by the Secretary of State without being accountable to the state *per se*. Moreover, it is also noticed that these regulatory bodies soon get captured by those very interests whom they are supposed to control. The accountability of regulatory bodies has remained one of the biggest challenges to the very notion of a public interest justification for privatization (Plant, 1989).

The results of privatization in the UK over the past 15–20 years have been mixed. It is equally wrong to say that the private sector is more efficient or that the public sector is more caring. And different groups may look at the results of privatizations in the UK from different angles. For instance, the Conservatives may look at the reduction in jobs in a privatized industry in a positive manner, while the Labour may look at it in a negative manner. The large number of variables involved can also affect the evaluation of privatization experiences in the UK – ranging from the structural framework of ownership to current accounting practices. While the role of government is reduced in terms of GDP and the workforce, its control has increased in terms of regulatory bodies.

The UK government has retained a special share in some privatized enterprises in a bid to prevent unwelcome takeovers, especially by foreign investors. For instance, despite the existence of the European Union, the privatized aerospace industry still receives substantial aid from the government. As such, privatization has only partially succeeded in reducing government control and improving the efficiency and competitiveness of the firms concerned. Despite tall claims of the success of British privatization in terms of reduction in the role of government and political interference, and increases in revenues and efficiency, according to a recent survey it was found that 64 per cent of British voters still oppose privatization, while only 31 per cent favour further privatization (Miller, 1995: 94). Every new privatization is seen with suspicion, if not outright hostility (*The Economist*, 16 January–13 February 1993: 60).

There are obvious reasons for public skepticism about privatization. It is difficult for people to accept the transfer of ownership of public enterprises and assets to the private sector when they consider public assets as their own. Secondly, efficiency in privatized enterprises is generally gained at the cost of jobs. While the elimination of jobs is highly visible, the gains to be accrued from privatization in future remain concealed to the public. The public cannot evaluate gains in terms of reduction in the size and scope of the government or political interference in the management mainly because these cannot be quantified. On the other hand, much resentment may come from the public against the very high salaries and perks paid to the managers and executives of privatized enterprises (*The Economist*, 1 June 1996: 59–61). These can be very much quantified and compared with endowments in other enterprises. This has also led to a low level of public support for privatization in the UK.

As such, the case of privatization in the UK appears to be less strong than what its advocates tend to suggest. It certainly cannot be seen merely as a problem of economic management; has deeper connotations and its consequences can be far and wide. Although the UK model of privatization has limited value for the emerging market economies in Eastern and Central Europe on the one hand, and developing countries in Latin America, Asia and Africa on the other, nevertheless these countries can learn and unlearn a great deal as far as the techniques of privatization are concerned. They can draw some practical lessons from the privatization experiences in the UK since the British privatization programme, to this date, remain the oldest and largest in recent history.

Lessons from the United Kingdom

The UK has benefited in recent years for being more exposed to competitive forces in the wake of privatization and globalization than many other rival economies. For instance, Britain's GDP grew by 2.8 per cent in 1997. Due to the reduction in trade unions' powers in the wake of privatization, employers are now freer to resort to hire and fire. It has also helped in cutting the unemployment rate to approximately 7 per cent of the workforce, and with these cuts inflation is also under control. While the rate of inflation averaged

Table 4.4 Future prospects of the British economy (% change year-on-year unless otherwise indicated)

	1995[a]	*1996*[b]	*1997*[b]	*1998*[b]
Real GDP[c]	2.4	2.2	3.4	2.5
Central government deficit (% of GDP)[d]	5.8	4.7	4.0	3.0
Manufacturing production	2.2	0.7	2.8	2.0
Consumer prices[e]	2.7	2.6	2.4	2.4
Unemployment rate (%)[f]	8.7	8.2	7.6	7.3
Interest rates:				
interbank 3-month offer rate	6.50	5.60	6.20	6.65
20-year gilts	8.26	8.00	8.25	8.13
Current account ($ bn)	–4.6	–3.1	–6.1	–6.0
% of GDP	–0.4	–0.3	–0.5	–0.5
Exchange rates				
DM: pound	2.26	2.31	2.29	2.23
$: pound	1.58	1.54	1.53	1.50

Notes: [a] actual; [b] EIU forecasts; [c] expenditure-based measure at market prices; [d] calender years; [e] all items excluding housing, average for the year; [f] OECD standardized rate.
Source: *EIU Country Report*: 7. fourth quarter, 1996.

13.3 per cent during 1973–79, it stood at 6.2 per cent during 1979–95 (*The Economist*, 8 June 1996: 67). It is difficult to say whether the UK would be able to maintain this growth in the next decade, but one thing that is certain is that the country has definitely benefited from the competitive pressures of Europe's single market, privatization and deregulation (Table 4.4).

Instead of following the Darwinian principle of the survival of the fittest, privatization in the UK has aimed at restoring the health of an enterprise by adhering to the principles of the free market, the enterprise, and value for money. The free market came to be seen as a natural, efficient and dynamic regulator of economic activities. By intervening in the markets, earlier governments disturbed the market mechanisms on the one hand, and encouraged the cosy and corporatist relationship between the industries and the state on the other (Sharp and Walker, 1991: 329).

In fact, under Thatcher, the concept of privatization denoted a broad cultural movement; it encouraged the entrepreneur, for example, to operate a new or expand an old business. The call for value for money also helped in improving the performance of the public sector and reducing public expenditure wherever possible. The public services were contracted out to the private sector on the assumption that the private sector is always more efficient, productive and virtuous than the parasitic and wasteful public sector.

Although the achievements of privatizations are less dramatic than the rhetoric would lead us to believe, we can draw some lessons from the UK experiences as follows:

1. The objectives of privatization should be clearly spelled out, since conflicts between objectives can affect the outcome adversely. Privatization should be seen as a means and not an end in itself.
2. Privatization requires a lot of preparation. Political support has to be sought from the public, trade unions and bureaucrats, and the government must regularly communicate with the public with regard to the aims, priorities and modalities of privatization.
3. The modalities and techniques of privatization may vary from enterprise to enterprise and from time to time.
4. Adequate attention should be given to the allocation of shares in the wake of privatization. Either low-cost shares should be made available to citizens or facilities be provided for cheap credit.
5. The regulatory bodies should keep a check on the profits of the privatized monopolies and public utilities. The government should encourage competition wherever feasible.
6. Priority should be given to long-term objectives, such as efficiency of an enterprise, and also to short-term revenue and fiscal gains.
7. We should never forget that privatization can only bring temporary relief to budgetary deficits. Nor should we expect automatic gains from privatization.

8. The British model can prove more suitable for those countries that have well-developed capital markets and large private sectors than the developing countries with thin capital and undeveloped or under-developed capital markets.
9. There should be transparency in all privatization deals to avoid undue delays and political controversies.
10. The costs of privatization can be heavy. The political and social costs can prove too high for those countries where the resort to privatization programmes and policies implies a break with the past rather than a continuum of past policies.

5
Privatization in East Germany: The Role of Treuhandanstalt

The Treuhandanstalt (THA), popularly known as 'Treuhand', played a key role in transforming the entire economy of the former German Democratic Republic (GDR) into a market economy. The term Treuhand in the German language means a trustee. The Treuhandanstalt was a state trustee agency which was responsible for the privatization of state-owned property of the former GDR. East Germany's experiences in privatization remain unique and unsurpassed both in terms of the massive scale and rapidity of the process. During a short period of four and a half years since German reunification and the culmination of the Treuhandanstalt (1 July 1990 to 31 December 1994), the THA was able to fully or partially privatize all but 192 companies out of a total portfolio of 13 815 holdings. It was able to reprivatize 1588 companies and communalize 265 (Figure 5.1). By communalization, we imply restoration of the state-owned enterprises and public assets to various municipalities at the provincial level.

In the process of privatization of the THA companies and parts of companies, 2983 MBO/MBI (management buy-outs/management buy-ins) agreements were signed, of which 2081 were administered by the THA branch offices and 902 by its headquarters. It was able to secure investment commitments up to DM211.1 bn and job commitments up to 1 508 000, and was able to generate proceeds up to DM66.6 bn. Foreign investors bought 860 THA companies or parts of them for DM6.8 bn and agreed to create or retain jobs up to 155 000. They also promised to invest up to DM25.8 bn (Final Report of the Treuhandanstalt, 1994: 2). In 1994, the growth rate in East Germany was 9 per cent and the GNP had returned to 1990 levels (*The Economist*, 24 December–6 January 1995). The THA was also responsible for the privatization and restitution of 10 000 small shops, restaurants, service firms, 2.3m hectares of arable land, 1.9m hectares of forest and the assets of former GDR political parties, mass organizations, army and security forces (Volkhart, 1994). The THA was, in fact, the world's biggest holding company (*The Economist*, 30 April 1994: 75).

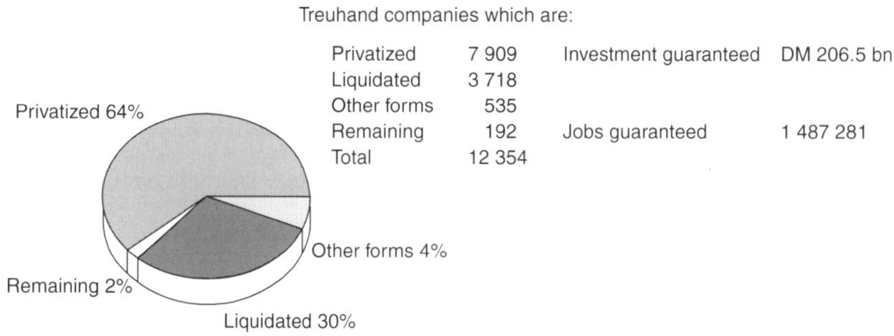

Figure 5.1 Status of privatization in East Germany on 30 December 1994
Source: Treuhandanstalt, 30 December 1994, in Heyden (1995).

The context

It is important to understand the context in which privatization occurred in East Germany in order to understand its unique features: (1) the massive scale, and (2) the short period of time involved. In fact, the privatization of state-owned enterprises in the former GDR was the most crucial and difficult part of the transformation of the planned economy into a market economy. In Germany, the question was not whether to privatize, but how to privatize as fast as possible. The decision for a sweeping privatization on a massive scale was in tune with the spirit of the Federal Republic of Germany (FRG) which had always assigned an important role to private ownership since the Second World War. In contrast to other European countries, there was no wave of nationalization in the post-Second World War FRG.

All transitional economies in Eastern and Central Europe had to face dramatic falls in industrial output in general, but the fall in East Germany was the largest. Output fell not because loss-making enterprises were liquidated, but because the demand for the products of East German companies collapsed. East German producers were unable to compete automatically with West German and world-market goods which were immediately available, and especially when East Germans had a craze for western goods and products. Because of their increased wages through economic unification, they could afford to switch over to western products comparatively more easily than consumers in most post-communist societies (Estrin, 1994: 129).

While demand rose by approximately 10 per cent, production fell in East Germany in the wake of unification. Industrial output fell by approximately 50 per cent during the first half of 1990 to the first half of 1991, and at one stage was just one-third of its original level. The GNP fell in real terms by 28 per cent during this period and the current account deficit was 88 per cent of GNP in 1992 (Estrin, 1994: 130). With the breakdown of COMECON and the collapse of output in Eastern and Central Europe, the prospects for East German firms became bleak. Even before unification, industrial productivity in East Germany was estimated at 30–40 per cent of that of the west. It was essential to privatize to bail the entire East German economy out of the serious crisis. Even the success of the political decision to reunify East Germany with West Germany depended upon the successful transfer of basic institutions to a market economy and liberal democracy (Lehmbruch, 1994: 115). The government's privatization strategy was based on the assumption that, if given an opportunity, West German companies with expertise in management and access to finances would be willing to buy East German firms and turn them into competitive units in the global market. The government expected to achieve economic miracles through huge flows of investment from western enterprises to the eastern firms, thereby raising productivity to high levels.

It was hoped that West German companies would commit themselves to major investments in the new federal states, either in the form of greenfield investments or through the purchase of East German enterprises, in order to avail themselves of the skilled workforce at cheaper rates in East Germany, and the rapid access to Eastern and Central European markets through East German networks (Estrin, 1994: 131–2). East Germany had an almost 50 per cent share in the COMECON trading system prior to unification. However, these hopes could not materialize. With the collapse of COMECON, deep recession in Eastern and Central Europe and the disintegration of the USSR, the value of the East German contacts was lost. This adversely affected western companies' investment in East Germany.

In order to promote investment and privatization in East Germany, the government adopted two policy instruments: (1) investment grants and subsidies were made available to reduce the cost of an investment project by up to 50 per cent, and (2) subsidies could also be provided in conjunction with the privatization of the state-owned enterprises in East Germany by the Treuhandanstalt. The task of privatization of state-owned property was assigned to a fiduciary agency – the Treuhandanstalt. Its job was not only to sell SOEs and property in East Germany, but also to buy investors and secure jobs (Breuel, 1994: 33). It also had many industrial and social objectives to fulfil – almost an impossible challenge (Fischer, Flax and Schneider, 1996: xxiii).

The agency

The THA was founded on 1 March 1990 under the communist government of Hans Modrow. The objective of Modrow's government was to rescue the old economic system rather than to transform it. The initial objective of the Treuhand was to privatize East German enterprises and retain some of the profits and assets for distribution to the workers as a compensation for their hard work, to promote socialism with a human face (Blum, 1992: 6).

The industry in the former GDR was concentrated into 157 *Kombinates* – huge state trusts. The THA was obliged to take over the role of a 'raider' – without an imminent market. It was required to break up the *Kombinate* into pieces that could be sold, but could also recombine the units. It was responsible for evaluating what could be privatized and what needed restructuring and liquidating. When the freely elected GDR government came into power under the presidentship of Lothar de Maiziere, the coalition agreement went into detailed legislation on the tasks and working methods of the THA. Section 1.4 of the Agreement stated that the new THA would continue with the original task of breaking the *Kombinate* and converting them into legal entities. The prime aim was to convert the state property into the property of private persons, and well-justified cases into the property of regional authorities.

The Treaty creating monetary, economic and social union between East and West Germany took privatization for granted (Fischer and Schröter, 1996: 31). On 17 May 1990, the Federal Chancellor's Office and the Federal Ministry for Economic Affairs presented the 'Bonn plan' for the Treuhand Act. They envisaged three different organizations to deal with commercial assets, residential property and agriculture. The legal form envisaged was an *Aktiengesellschaft* (AG) – a joint stock company on the pattern of AGs in West Germany. The AGs were found to be more autonomous and flexible for being based on the principles of separation of business and government on the one hand, and codetermination with equal representation from both sides of industry on the other (Fischer, Wolfram and Schroter, 1996: 33). The Treuhand was not designed to become an entrepreneur itself. As such, its managers did not sit on the boards of directors of the companies to be privatized.

A new law defining the tasks and responsibilities of the THA came into force on 17 June 1990, emphasizing privatization in East Germany. After the unification on 1 July 1990, the THA was subordinated to the FRG Ministry of Finance. The agency was set up in Hermann Goering's Luftwaffe building in Berlin. It had to build itself from the scratch, with no blueprint or precedent to follow. The number of employees of the THA increased from a mere 600 in its early days to more than 2500 by the summer of 1991. In August 1990, Detlev Rohwedder became its first president, followed by Birgit Breuel after he was assassinated in April 1991. She provided able leadership to the THA until 31 December 1994.

The structure

Although the THA was a statutory body, it functioned more like an investment bank than a centralized state agency. It was independent of Bonn and had an economic and businesslike orientation. The agency was allowed to run its own debt and its budget was not controlled by the

German House of Commons – *Volkskammer* (Heyden, 1995: 44). Although it enjoyed the status of an institution under public law under the Act of Privatization and Reorganization of State Property, yet it was organizationally a separate part of the federal administration within the meaning of Article 86 and Article 87 of the German constitution – the *Grundgesetz* (The THG, section 2: sentence 1).

The original THA was headed by a directorate, composed of the president and four other members. They were appointed by the administrative board for a period of five years but could be dismissed earlier on serious grounds (The THG, section 3: sentence 2). They were not bound by the instructions given to them. The executive board was required to submit an annual report and accounts to the administrative board, and it exercised supervision over the activities of the THA. The president of the THA was supposed to keep the chairman of the administrative board informed of all important business matters, and decisions of particular significance also required the assent of the administrative board. Its tasks included the preparation of the business plan, drawing of funds from the capital market, establishment of companies, restructuring, privatization and liquidation (Kloepfer, 1996: 44).

The original THA under the Modrow government was to function on the basis of territorial decentralization. It led to the setting up of the headquarters at Berlin and administrative centers in 14 East German cities, each responsible for a separate region. Later on, the external offices were retained by the THA as branches. These were authorized to take decisions on their own with regard to privatization of small and medium-sized companies (Rohwedder, 1990: 1681). The so-called Beirate advisory boards helped the branches in maintaining contacts with the business, political and social forces within the region. The THA established excellent formal and informal networks during the course of its tenure, without which it could not have succeeded in its mission.

The Treuhand had a matrix organization divided into nine executive boards on the basis of functional responsibilities, such as administration, financing and operating responsibilities. The headquarters at Berlin were responsible for enterprises with more than 1500 employees and for firms in the energy, transport, banking and credit sectors. The rest of the companies were dealt with by the regional subsidiaries. In terms of organizational law, the branches were supposed to be subordinate and dependent parts of the institute under public law but, in fact, they proved to be a lower tier of authority. The THA executive board had assigned certain tasks to them to carry out at their own responsibility, and there was no possibility of contesting their decisions at the central office. The THA retained the branches as decentralized business divisions by having recourse to the internal organizational power of the executive board and its authority to issue orders. It recruited staff for itself and other subsidiaries independently.

Functions and responsibilities

The functions and responsibilities of the THA varied from time to time depending upon the prevailing economic and political situation. The original THA was responsible for converting the state-owned *Kombinates* and other organizations into joint-stock companies. Its task was to exercise trusteeship over public property; it was not the owner of state property *de jure*. Yet, it was the holder of people's property for all practical purposes (Kloepfer, 1996: 45), and served the purpose of retaining the people's property as a central agency for the time being. Although it was not directly responsible for privatization, it was authorized to resort to it on a limited scale. Some parties from within East Germany were able to acquire shares, buildings or machinery from state-owned companies through the original THA to establish or enlarge private business, having a *mittelstand* (small to medium-sized) character.

The THG (The Act for Privatization and Reorganization of State Property) of 17 June 1990 dissolved the Resolution of Establishment and Statutes of the Original THA (The THG Act, section 24: 3). It also abolished the existing responsibilities of the THA with effect from 1 July 1990. Instead, the statutes of the THA dated 18 July 1990 formulated new tasks and responsibilities for the THA (The *Gesetzblattder* DDR 1990: 1: 809). *The Rules of Procedure* dated 18 September 1990 further supplemented and expanded these responsibilities (*The Treuhandanstalt Organizationshandbuch*, March 1991).

Privatization became the main responsibility of the THA under the first sub-clause of the Preamble and section I, sentence 1 of the THG. The responsibility of carrying out privatization was laid on the THA by Article I, section B of the THG and Article 25, section I, sentence 1 of the Treaty of Unification. The THA was held responsible for transferring the public assets entrusted to it to private legal entities or natural persons as rapidly as possible and as far as possible (Kloepfer, 1996: 49). However, restitution and communalization were excluded from the definition of privatization (Kloepfer, 1996: 50).

On 1 July 1990, the THA had assumed responsibility for approximately 8500 SOEs with a total strength of four million employees. It required a great deal of political sagacity and economic expertise on the part of the THA to resolve the dilemma – it was required to reshape, reform and restructure the entire economy of the former GDR on the one hand, and preserve the social market economy and jobs on the other (Koch, 1992: 277). Approximately 5 per cent of the entire workforce of the former GDR was employed in social sectors.

Many of these enterprises operated in various branches which had been arbitrarily amalgamated under the centrally planned economy of the former GDR. For instance, in some cases production facilities for tools, kindergartens, lemonade, hospitals, hotels and various other social organizations were grouped together in one single holding company. This had a destructive effect as far as any potential synergy was concerned (Klinz, 1992: 263). These

Kombinates had to be decartelized to enable the new units to survive in the market economy.

It was important to introduce market mechanisms into the state-owned holdings to make them adapt to the structures of the free market economy. The ultimate objective of privatization was to restructure the obsolete centrally controlled economy of the former GDR into a functioning market economy. According to the ex-president of the THA, Dr Rohwedder, its task was to privatize rapidly where that was not possible in the short term, and to restructure with determination and liquidate considerably where neither of these two options was available.

The THA worked on the maxim, 'have as little government as possible and as much government as necessary'. It was also responsible for creating small and medium-sized economic units in order to make them saleable and competitive. As such, it became involved in the process of creative destruction of state-owned holding enterprises into smaller units to make them saleable and economically viable and efficient. The challenge facing the THA was to create units which were small enough to be saleable and large enough to be able to function independently. It had three objectives in mind before dismantling:

1. to make the enterprises competitive;
2. to create transparency in order to enable appropriate reviews and inspections to be carried out; and
3. to change management attitudes of the enterprises.

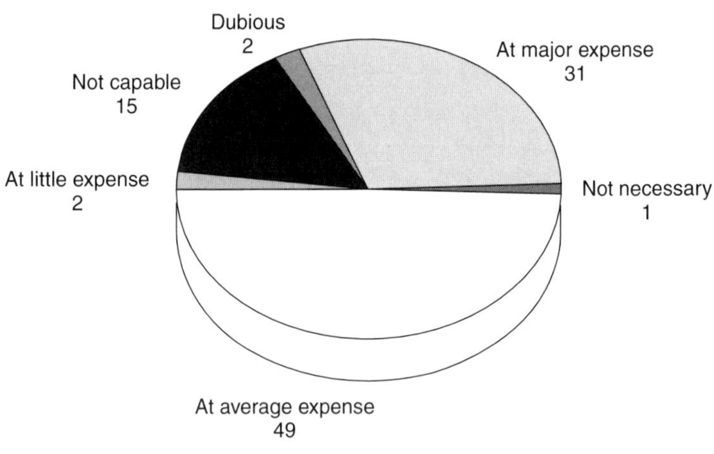

Figure 5.2 Suitability for restructuring in manufacturing companies (rated by THA as of 31 December 1992)
Source: W. Fischer, H. Flax and H.K. Schneider (eds) (1996).

According to the President, Birgit Breuel, the THA's task was not only to sell the state-owned holdings but also to buy investors for them. The key objective in restructuring companies, both during and after decartelization was to find the right buyers to make the companies economically viable and competitive. The job of government through the THA was to create the political, legal and financial framework to support and create viable economic and industrial units. This required a great deal of time, effort and creativity on the part of the THA, whose work was that of crisis management (Koch, 1992: 277). It is still controversial whether the THA should have given priority to restructuring over privatization (Figure 5.2). Many economists have argued that restructuring should have been left to the new investors, but it became quite apparent that most of the enterprises could not be sold without prior restructuring.

Prior to privatization, East German industry was dominated by combines (VEBs), and approximately 15 per cent of employment was in firms having more than 1000 people. The THA had to break them into smaller units to make them saleable, but it also had to recombine wherever necessary. The sole decision on what to privatize and how to privatize rested upon the THA and its supervisory board. It was responsible for evaluating the chances of survival of an enterprise in the competitive market economy, and if it found a company not fit for survival its task was to close it down under silent or formal liquidation or bankruptcy proceedings. It was also responsible for creating and preserving jobs. As such, the THA had conflicting aims and objectives since inception.

Besides these formidable tasks, the THA was required to carry out reprivatization to the extent to which the assets entrusted to it were affected, although formally this task was allotted to the property offices (*Vermogensamter*) under the Property Act of August 1992. It decided by means of an administrative act on the sale, letting, leasing of land, buildings and so on, and was also involved in settling the restitution claims on properties under its possession (Balz, *Rechseinheit – Wirtschaftseinheit*: 46). Under the Treaty of Unification, the assets of political parties and their affiliated organizations, legal entities and mass organizations were to be returned to their previous and rightful ownership. The THA was also responsible for the financing of the Loan Winding-Up Fund and the State Insurance of East Germany. The President of the THA was required to certify that the statutory assignment of basic property to joint stock companies was carried out by means of an administrative act.

Financing

When the original THA was set up, it was presumed that it would generate enough funds for itself through the privatization proceeds and liquidation of companies entrusted to it. Under Article 21, section I, sentence 2 of the Monetary, Economic and Social Treaty, the THA was authorized to enter into debts up to DM17 billion during 1990–91. During the Unification

Treaty, the credit limit was raised to DM25 billion and these debts were supposed to be paid off by 31 December 1995. The Federal Ministry of Finance was authorized to prolong the period of loans and/or extend the credit limits in the event of major changes in the general conditions (*Treaty of Unification*: Article 25: section 4: sentence 3). Gradually, the THA was allowed a credit limit of DM36 billion each financial year, and an additional DM8 billion, with the permission of the Federal Minister of Finance under the THA Credit Act of 3 July 1992.

The THA Credit Act made it easier for the THA to raise credit on the capital market without any prior audit; it was considered a special asset of the federal government in financial terms. But unlike other special assets, the federal government owed the legal liability for the THA obligations. As such, the THA functioned on the basis of a soft budget. It was supposed to raise approximately DM600 billion from the sale of companies (to be used for the upliftment of East Germans), but it left a debt of DM270 billion when it closed its doors on 31 December 1994. The Treuhand's reluctance to liquidate companies, and subsequent subsidies to keep loss-making companies afloat in order to preserve jobs for the time being, proved to be very costly.

For instance, the THA subsidized investments in shipyards at a rate of DM800 000–500 000 more than the cost of sacking a worker. Investment to the Baltic Sea Shipyard totalled more than DM2 billion, and other examples include DM800 million for the EKO Stahl steel plant and approximately DM2 billion for the optical plant in Thuringia, Lothar Spath's Jenoptik (Heyden, 1995: 49). The EKO Stahl GmbH had everything going against it. When the Berlin wall fell, the products were of poor quality, the European markets were saturated with steel producers, it employed 12 000 workers and was losing money heavily. It was a prime candidate for liquidation, but the THA decided that the plant should stay and *Eisenhuttenstadt* should also continue as a steel town. It required DM8300 million to cover the losses and DM8100 million in loan guarantees.

The THA had the tendency to save the biggest and not necessarily the best companies in order to save jobs. It had conflicting goals to fulfil and had to work under sociopolitical constraints. The decision to subsidize jobs in EKO Stahl was designed to preserve the stability of the region concerned. The role of THA is now under question in the case of *Bremer Vulkan* – the largest ship building company in Germany. Its Chairman, Friedrich Hennemann, was charged of divesting public funds to the tune of DM716 billion (meant for an East German shipyard) to the parent company in West Germany. The THA had sold three East German shipyards to Hennemann in 1992 despite misgivings by THA officials and bankers (*Financial Times*, 21 June 1996: 14). It is difficult to justify enormous subsidies to companies like EKO Stahl which had no chance of a turnaround.

Supervision

We should not forget that the THA had to function under the supervision of not only its own administrative board but also under external supervision. It had various internal control mechanisms similar to those within a company in the private sector. The original THA reported to the government, but after the THG came into force its executive board had to report regularly on the progress of privatization to the Council of Ministers. The Minister-President was responsible for supervising the financial behaviour of the THA, and the THA had to seek the approval of the Federal Minister of Finance before finalizing cases for privatization.

As an institute under public law, the THA was subject to control by parliament through the monitoring instruments of formal questions and informal requests for information. The Federal Court of Audit also exercised significant control over the activities of the THA. Parliament set up an independent committee on the THA with 24 members, and the use of a Committee of Enquiry gives enormous powers to parliament to investigate special cases. It is possible for the *Bundestag* and the *Bundesrat* to be informed of any matter of public importance any time.

The East German states also exercised considerable influence through their representatives on the administrative board of the THA and its advisory boards at regional level. The function of the THA economic cabinets was to coordinate the work of the THA and the concerned state government, especially with regard to the labour market. Since the East German states joined the FRG, they became subject to direct control and supervision by the *Bundesrat*. The federal government was under an obligation to report in detail on THA activities every six months to the Commission of the European Community, and the commission could examine individual cases in sensitive areas such as steel, shipbuilding, automobiles, manufacturing, chemicals and so on (The EEC Treaty: Article 293: section 3).

Civil courts are responsible for examining THA decisions with regard to privatization and dealings in companies in which it held equity. The restructuring programmes come under administrative courts. Parties affected by the THA's decisions on investment priority or assignment of property can also make appeals to administrative law. The administrative courts can also be approached in the case of disputes among the THA, political parties or mass organizations with regard to public assets under the control of the THA. It is still a matter of debate whether the civil courts are competent to examine the decisions made by the THA. Since the THA exercised codetermination and supervisory powers over the companies in which it held equity, it was subject to civil law, and as such it was under the control of the civil courts. There are still many cases pending before the civil courts concerning privatization and liquidations carried out by the THA.

The functioning of the THA

The THA resorted to various instruments and methods depending upon the size of the company and the industry in which it operated. In many cases it had to opt for a combination of various methods and instruments; it had no fixed criteria or blueprint. It started the process from scratch and adopted a case-by-case approach. Birgit Breuel supported flexibility on the part of the THA to avoid unnecessary delay and red tape during the privatization process. It aimed at finding commercially active business owners as quickly as possible, and it had to tailor-make different strategies at different times according to the market conditions prevailing at that particular time. As such, it had to rely on formal and informal networks. It had plenty of scope for the manoeuvring needed to carry out its tasks – a complex bundle, ranging from selling SOEs and assets, buying investors, preserving and creating jobs, to realization of proceeds (Schmidt and Siegmund, 1996: 214).

Although there was no hierarchical relationship among the various aims, the THA had set its own guidelines on the basis of experience gained through learning by doing. It gave priority to a privatization that could be carried out quickly. Its endeavour was to sell the company as a whole, if possible, but otherwise it aimed at partial privatization. It pursued a strategy which not only concentrated on the goals but on the means as well. It tried to preserve as many jobs as possible in order to avoid serious unemployment problems at the regional level. It did not follow privatization rules strictly and kept its options open; instead of generating maximum proceeds through privatization, it gave priority to the survival of the company at its location. As such, it gave priority to the investor who was likely to continue the business operation with a reasonable hope of success rather than to the highest bidder (Schmidt and Siegmund, 1996: 216).

Usually, two methods are adopted for selling the companies or part of them: (1) the auction method, and (2) the bargaining method. The auction method can lead to rapid privatization on transparent grounds, but does not guarantee sufficient competition among bidders. The bargaining method, on the other hand, ensures a greater degree of freedom and flexibility for both negotiating parties, but it provides little transparency and is often found to be time-consuming. While the auction method is recommended for mass privatization, the bargaining method can be more useful when there are only a few bidders or suitable buyers. The bargaining method also helps in finding the right buyers and not simply any buyer.

The THA negotiated with interested parties without following any formal procedure. Although this procedure did not guarantee equality of opportunity to all potential investors, the THA found it useful because it could discuss the various stages of privatization – unbundling, initial restructuring, contract-drafting and final sales simultaneously, quickly and efficiently (Schmidt and Siegmund, 1996: 219). The THA resorted to limited tender in the cases of small or medium-sized

Table 5.1 THA companies found suitable for restructuring (as of November 1992)

Classification	*Total*		*of which fully or partially privatized*	
	No.	*%*	*No.*	*%*
1. Company is operating profitably	25	1.7	16	64.0
2. Company expects to enter profitability soon	102	7.1	76	74.5
3. Corporate strategy appears successful	593	41.2	340	57.3
4. Company appears capable of being effectively restructured, but strategy not yet sufficient	347	24.1	163	47.0
5. Restructuring capability appears dubious	70	4.9	34	48.6
6. Company is not capable of being restructured, alternative concept should be drawn up	301	21.0	93	30.9
Total	1438	100.0	722	50.2

Source: W. Fischer (ed.) (1996) *Treuhandanstalt: The Impossible Challenge*: 223.

companies, and public tender for mass privatization. The limited tender was a formal procedure in which the THA laid down a number of conditions subject to further negotiations. The THA used public tender only twice – once for the mass privatization of more than 30 000 retail shops in January 1991, and the second time when larger items came for sale later. It did not resort either to public auction or floating of shares (Schmidt and Siegmund, 1996: 221).

The THA was actively involved in the preparation, execution and monitoring of the privatization process. During the preparatory stage it was concerned with the creation of saleable units by unbundling or merging, the valuation of assets and liabilities, and the assessment of a company's suitability for restructuring (Table 5.1), as well as exploring markets and initiating negotiations with potential buyers. In the second stage, the stress was on the actual sale negotiations. The THA first checked investors' credit ratings and the viability of their corporate strategies. If satisfied, it negotiated in detail on future investments and jobs to be preserved with individual bidders. It also had to take care of the environmental and other liabilities before finalizing the purchase price. Some of the companies had negative value and some were sold just for the token value of DM1. Even after privatization, the THA's job was not over; it had to supervise and monitor contracts and renegotiate whenever necessary.

Privatization through MBO/MBI/management KGs

Since the East Germans lacked access to finance, management expertise and western markets, they could not participate in the privatization process effectively. They applied pressure for privatization from below, and the initiative came from the Eastern managers themselves. Initially, the THA had no scheme for management buy-outs (MBOs) or management buy-ins (MBIs). Only in the autumn of 1992 did the THA establish a fund to provide the MBOs access to consultancy advice, an idea which had emerged at Berlin regional subsidiary level earlier (Carlin, 1994: 146).

In order to give the East German managers a chance to continue managing their companies under the market economy, the THA set up a policy known as *Initiative Mittelstand*. It aimed at providing the managers of small and medium-sized companies an opportunity to carry out management buy-outs. It also developed a programme to help them finance the purchases, knowing full well that the East Germans had no chance of saving money under the communist system (Evans, 1992: 179). Vouchers did not find favour with the THA mainly because they neither brought fresh money nor new technology (Waish, 1995: 1). Moreover, because of the high wage costs, lack of markets and the bad shape of outdated plants, the East German firms could not yield profits. Nobody would have invested in a company with a negative value.

The *Initiative Mittelstand* proved very successful (Figure 5.3). Approximately 18 per cent of the medium-sized enterprises were sold to incumbent or external management, which meant that approximately one-fifth of the THA firms were purchased by East German managers and employees (Treuhandanstalt, 1995a). Nearly 50 per cent of the MBOs were in industry, 25 per cent in services, 13.3 per cent in construction and 11.4 per cent in trade (Treuhandanstalt, 1995b). Approximately 60 per cent of the firms had less

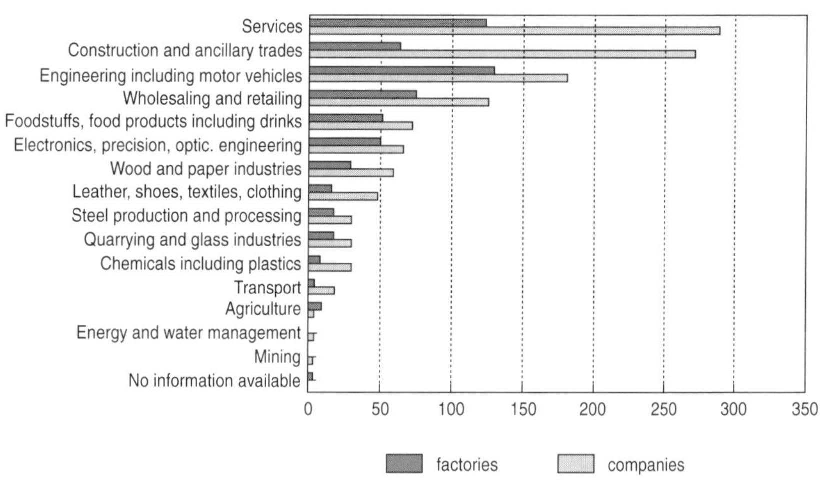

Figure 5.3 Number of MBOs arranged by THA branches (notarized up to 30 June, 1993)
Source: W. Fischer (ed.) (1996) *Treuhandanstalt: The Impossible Challenge*: 393.

than 50 employees, 35 per cent had between 50–250 employees and 5 per cent had more than 250 employees (Treuhandanstalt, 1995c). The average size was approximately 70. Approximately 66 per cent of the firms were purchased by their managers (pure MBOs), 15 per cent by their managers and employees (MEBOs), 15 per cent by East and West German managers jointly (BIMBOs) and 4 per cent by management buy-ins (MBIs) and 'pure' employee buy-outs (EMBOs) (Kokalz and Hufner, 1994).

Through the MBI scheme, the THA tried to attract individual entrepreneurs to establish businesses in East Germany. It launched this scheme in 1992. The advertising campaign elicited 2800 responses, and applicants were shortlisted on the basis of the following criteria (Carlin, 1994: 145):

1. availability of at least two annual salaries as start-up finance;
2. managerial experience;
3. a track record in the industry; and
4. a willingness to resettle in East Germany.

The THA selected 400 candidates after a thorough screening and identified approximately 3000 firms as suitable. The candidates were put in contact with West German and foreign venture capital funds in order to secure participation by the financial institutions. The Deutsche Bank established an industrial holding company in 1991 – the Deutsche Industrial Holding. Its objective was to secure 100 per cent holdings of the THA firms. By July 1993 it purchased 13 of the THA firms guaranteeing 3500 jobs and investment up to DM150 million (*Financial Times*, 2 August 1993: 15). Other private sector investment funds included the *Ermgassen Fund, EGIT* and *Robert Flemings of London*.

In spring 1992, the THA launched a new scheme of Management Companies of the *Kommanditgesellschaft* form (hence: Management-KG's) to introduce market-driven incentives into the restructuring and privatization process while retaining ownership with the THA. This new strategy became necessary when the THA found that even potentially viable enterprises had failed to attract new buyers, and tried to buy time for these enterprises to prove their viability. The advantage of this approach was that the regional and external effects could be taken into account. The biggest disadvantage was that investors had to face market wages and prices *ex post facto*. The THA was required to monitor the employment and investment contracts and had to maintain contacts with the former enterprises for the full duration of the contracts.

An evaluation

An evaluation of the alternative means of privatization in East Germany can be attempted on the basis of following criteria:

1. How successful has been the development of the industrial MBO firms after privatization?
2. What are the decisive factors that caused a positive or negative development of the MBOs, MBIs and Management–KG's?
3. Can these alternative means provide a model to other economies on the verge of privatization?

Although by 31 December 1994, the THA had privatized 2761 firms through MBOs, by Spring 1994 63 firms had already failed, 114 were in the process of liquidation and 213 firms had serious difficulties, 627 firms had satisfactory operations with minor difficulties and only 251 firms were operating successfully. Approximately 31 per cent of the MBOs were in danger of failure or had already failed. Approximately 26 per cent of industrial MBOs were able to realize their strategic objectives (Blum, 1992: 346). Most of the MBOs had difficulties because their new owners did not have adequate knowledge, expertise or experience and their equity resources were too meagre to carry the firms through difficult times at the start-up phase. The managers even had to accept sales concentration because they did not have adequate money for market activities. To Klaus Dieter Schmidt, it would have been better had the THA provided more money to fewer MBOs rather than less money for a large number of MBOs (Schmidt, 22 June 1996).

Despite the failure of the alternative methods of privatization in East Germany in many cases, it cannot be denied that MBOs, MBIs and Management–KG's can provide effective methods of privatization. These methods lead to decentralization and worker-participation in small and medium-sized businesses. This can help in integrating citizens into the country's transformation process, and in stimulating their economic awareness. The MBO, MBI and MKG concept of privatization proved to be promising in East Germany mainly because of the available financial resources, employee integration and terms of privatization. There were some instances of financial irregularities and miscalculations, but they were unavoidable in the situation of rapid privatization undertaken by the THA on a massive scale.

Verkauft and verraten – sold and betrayed – was the basic content of the criticisms of the THA from various quarters within and outside Germany. The Treuhand was commonly criticized for being bureaucratic and secretive; its only concern seemed to be selling the firms off as fast as possible. Buyers and investors had an advantage over the THA since they had better knowledge of the prevailing market conditions than the THA. Buyers extracted as many concessions and favours from the THA as possible, and too much was paid to them in terms of subsidies or fresh capital. The THA was also criticized for showing favouritism towards West German entrepreneurs and companies at the cost of foreigners and East Germans. Some West German entrepreneurs and companies were also reported as having engaged in fraudulent practices.

Many cases are pending before the civil courts and the THA is also under scrutiny by the Federal Audit Commission and the German parliament.

Some critics argued that the THA was in 'super haste' to privatize; it did not invest enough time, money or efforts into restructuring the business enterprises. On the other hand, some other critics argued that it was none of the business of the THA to enter into the business of restructuring; it should have been left to the private investors themselves. Only they could have restructured successfully because their interests and capital were at stake. They argued that the THA was not a competent body to restructure or run 14 000 companies in varying areas (Table 5.2). To them, restructuring was not a viable option in the case of East Germany in the absence of a market economy, managerial expertise and distribution networks. The economic, social and political costs of privatization in East Germany proved to be much more than anticipated.

But any evaluation of the THA can only be made on the basis of a comprehensive analysis covering the basic objectives, process and results of

Table 5.2 Privatization status of East German branches of industry, July 1993

	Total number of companies (gross)		*% of these*[1]		
				Owned by THA	
	No.	*%*	*Fully privatized*	*in liquidation*	*awaiting privatization*
Chemical industry	255	4.3	45.5	25.5	14.1
Plastic, rubber and asbestos processing	179	3.0	38.5	31.3	6.7
Minerals, fine ceramics, glass	462	7.7	56.7	16.0	12.1
Ferrous and non-ferrous metals, foundries, steel products	245	4.1	41.6	24.1	21.6
Steel and light metal structures	203	3.4	39.9	16.3	18.7
Engineering	1102	18.4	46.2	24.0	17.5
Automotive industry	363	6.1	55.4	20.4	11.8
Electrical and electronic industry	491	8.2	38.3	36.7	8.8
Precision and optical engineering	80	1.3	38.8	32.5	10.0
Iron, metal, sheet metal goods, musical instruments, sports equipment, toys and games, jewellery	323	5.4	30.3	35.6	10.5
Wood-working and timber	505	8.4	32.9	31.9	8.5
Paper and printing industries	244	4.1	50.8	27.0	8.2
Leather and shoe-making industries	169	2.8	18.3	54.4	11.8
Textile and clothing industries	519	8.7	19.5	45.3	16.8
Food and allied industries	856	14.3	48.7	28.2	5.8
Total	5996	100	41.6	29.0	12.3

Note: [1] Difference as already liquidated, reprivatized, communalized or partially privatized.
Source: W. Fischer (ed.) (1996) *Treuhandanstalt: The Impossible Challenge*: 229–30.

privatization in East Germany. Despite many criticisms and shortcomings, nobody actually believed that the THA would be able to complete its operative business so successfully during a short span of time. However, the large number of privatizations is no guarantee of the efficiency or success of the THA in its privatization efforts. The results it achieved depend upon the quality of decision-making. For every privatization, the THA had at least one alternative: it could have sold a company to another bidder, could have continued running it for a longer period of time or could have liquidated it straight away (Schmidt and Siegmund, 1996: 211).

Although the THA was designed to be an autonomous body, it had to work under political constraints and had conflicting goals since its inception. It was required not only to transform ownership, but also to secure and create jobs. It was always on a tight-rope between economic and political objectives. The legal provision became an open gateway for political interventions, and although the THA tried its best to resist political pressures, its decision could not be free of ambiguity. The Treuhand was generally misunderstood by the public, and the whole process of privatization was beyond the understanding of the average German. It was difficult for him or her to understand how a company with valuable land but gross losses could be sold for just DM1 (Charbonnier, 1995: 51. The average German was not expected to understand the microeconomics of a company; West Germans were used to seeing their economy always grow without ever knowing why. They could not understand why it now functioned in another way.

Privatization has always been unpopular with politicians and voters. They are more concerned with the distributional aspects than the macroeconomic aspects of privatization. In the case of East Germany, unification raised the publics hopes too high; hopes which could not be fulfilled in the short term through privatization. Privatization cannot transform a command economy into a market economy automatically, and in the case of East Germany many expectations and calculations went wrong. The THA was made the scapegoat for the recklessly optimistic policies of West German politicians. Many West German companies and enterpreneurs hoped to gain rapidly through East Germany's access to East European markets, East German assets and cheap labour. They could not anticipate the sudden collapse of the East German economy. Five factors were responsible for this:

1. monetary union;
2. unrealistic wage rates;
3. the poor quality of goods produced;
4. the collapse of major export markets in Eastern Europe; and
5. economic recession.

Owing to the exchange rates of 1:1 (in lieu of the actual rate of 1:8), East German firms could not afford suppliers from West German or foreign firms, while East German consumers suddenly discarded eastern goods. Also, in the process of revaluation, East Germany's capital stock halved overnight (The Economist, 24 December–6 January 1995: 82). Perhaps the biggest blunder was made when wage contracts were signed to match wage levels in the east with those of the west by 1994 without raising productivity. It was a political and not an economic agreement between the *Gesamtmetall* and *IG Metall* – the West German and East German Association of Managers. Although East German wages were about 70 per cent of West German levels in February 1993, productivity was 7 per cent below that of West German levels, especially in the areas of steel, engineering and electrical sectors (Dempsey, 1993).

The lack of correlation between wages and productivity made investors more apprehensive. For instance, in November 1992, Daimler–Benz cancelled their plan of building a truck factory near Berlin with an investment of DM1 billion. Krupto, the large German steel manufacturer abandoned their plan to take over EKO-stahl, and Audi also cancelled the building of a new engine plant in East Germany. Besides there was less demand for East German products owing to their poor quality. With the fall of COMECON and the monetary union of East and West Germany, trade with Eastern Europe suffered since these countries were not in a position to pay for East German goods in DM. The East German factories could not compete with western markets on technological grounds.

Moreover, Germany was hit by an economic recession – the worst since 1945 – which had significant effects on the privatization efforts of the THA. Many investors backed off and many deals had to be cancelled, delaying the whole process of privatization. The THA had to keep the loss-making and unviable firms under its fold for longer than anticipated, thus raising costs tremendously. West Germans, used to very good economic and living standards, started questioning the very necessity of complete and rapid privatization in the wake of unification. East Germans were also unprepared for price rises, the loss of jobs and other sociocultural problems. All the blame for economic hardships was put on unification in general, and privatization in particular. The false promises by the shrewd politicians left many psychological scars on the public mind.

Although the ex-president, Birgit Breuel, admitted mistakes on the part of the THA, she also made it clear that the THA had no examples to follow. It had to start the process from the very beginning in a very uncertain political and economic environment. While some argued that there was too little support by the THA, others argued that there was too much. While many criticized the THA for its 'Kafka like image' (*Wall Street Journal*, 21 March 1992), some even complained of it being too generous in divulging information. The Achilles heel of the THA was not a conflict between efficiency and equality, but between privatization and restructuring. The THA was always criticized by economists for giving priority to privatization over restructuring. Others criticized it for making tremendous losses by keeping companies afloat till they were privatized. While assets in East Germany were assessed at DM600 billion even by its President, Rohwedder, the privatization process led to a loss of DM270 billion – a difference of DM870 billion (*Der Spiegel*, 1994: 80).

Although privatization was presumed to be the most effective form of restructuring by the THA, it did not guarantee economic efficiency, competition or wider choice. The THA's main target was the continuation of business rather than the purchase price. This is one of the reasons why their privatization strategies caused huge losses. Instead of raising additional funds, the THA had to sell many companies at negative prices. Since the THA was interested in contracting high employment and investment obligations, it had to pay a high price for them; and since the business objective was not the main basis for taking decisions, there was a lot of scope for subjective judgements by the THA. This gave the image of an omniscient agency to the Treuhandanstalt.

Instead of pursuing a privatization policy on economic grounds, the THA had to rely on a political strategy (Gupta, 1996). It became an instrument of industrial and employment policy, and had to pay a heavy price in terms of economic efficiency to make its privatization policy politically feasible. The multiple targets, often contradicting each other, proved to be politically very efficient in terms of optimal obfuscation (Schmidt, 22 June 1996). It was not possible to protect privatization from the political debate, nor was it possible to keep the THA away from political pressures. The blame for the huge costs of privatization cannot be put exclusively on the THA.

The THA sailed in a no-man's-land between policies and economics; legally, it was neither an official authority nor a holding company. It was comparable to the Deutsche Bundesbank in many ways, but in fact it had very limited autonomy and was financed by the Federal Ministry of Finance, co-administered by the management trust (whose members represented various political parties) guided by numerous advisory committees and controlled by parliament (Schmidt, 22 June 1996). Under these situations it could not achieve optimum results. In an endogenous equilibrium, it had to calculate the decisions of other political players and actors, as well as the constraints imposed by various lobbies. It faced a trade off between the high costs of privatization and the high costs of subsidization for a longer period of time. The THA preferred low and negative selling to permanent subsidies (Schmidt, 22 June 1996). In this respect, the THA proved to be a great success.

It is survived by the *Bundesanstalt für Vereinigungsbedingte Sonderaufgaben*, popularly known as the BVS. The BVS is responsible for controlling and renegotiating the contracts made by the THA, and by February 1995 it had concluded 2500 contracts out of a total of 3000 renegotiations registered. More and more investors are likely to ask for renegotiations owing to financial constraints. The BVS is trying to strike a balance in the case of defaulters. It does not want to sound too harsh, nor does it want to set a bad precedent. In most cases, it either grants more time or enhances the purchase price. It is easier to revise the purchase price than enforce a penalty.

Lessons to be drawn

The Treuhandanstalt provides a unique example of privatization by the state *and* market. While many western countries pursued privatization through the market (auction, vouchers, mutual funds, stockmarket floatations), the East German experience appears to be an exception. Usually the state is considered an impediment, but in East Germany, the THA, a state agency, was responsible for the restructuring of the entire economy of the GDR within a short time. It took on restructuring and privatization in a situation when East Germany was undergoing a lot of problems – social, economic and political – in the wake of reunification. It was a public agency with a supervisory board consisting of representatives from the federal government, state governments, commercial banks, trade unions, major West German firms and two European businessmen to signify the importance of non-Germans in the privatization process (Carlin and Mayer, 1994: 191).

While many marvel at the speed with which the THA was able to carry out the privatization process in East Germany, there is no dearth of scholars who look at the whole exercise as a simple contradiction in terms (Thanner, 1993: 167–86). While some experts have argued that it would have been better if THA managers had spent more time on each transaction, others have suggested that some concerted efforts by the THA towards de-mystifying the agency would have smoothed and accelerated the political process. The THA has also been blamed for the deindustrialization of East Germany; perhaps it could have exchanged properties in West Germany for assets in East Germany. Many East Germans nourish the feeling of being deprived in their own country; they were able to invest in only 6 per cent of the privatization deals. Some have even argued that the cost of German unification would have been less if financed by taxes rather than borrowing. According to Heinrich Hornef, the agency's financial advisor, it would take another generation to pay off the THA deficit (*International Management*, 6 September 1994).

The questions arise: can the Treuhandanstalt provide a model to other East European or developing economies on the threshold of active privatization? What lessons can we learn or unlearn from the East German experiences in privatization? Is it advisable to entrust the privatization process to a centralized agency or should it be left to the market? Is it preferable to follow a top-down approach or a bottom-up approach in transitional economies? Can the shift in ownership lead to economic efficiency? Could the THA succeed without access to West German markets, managerial expertise, the legal framework and financial support? Can the East German model be adopted elsewhere?

Estonia provides a rare example in Eastern Europe where a privatization strategy similar to that of the Treuhand was adopted. Preprivatization focused on splitting up large enterprises into single plant enterprises; yet sales with more than 500 employees have been rare and only two firms with more than

Table 5.3 Media focus on the THA

Main subjects	*Number of articles*	*Length in standard lines*	*Rating (1 to 5)* *
Basic discussions	255	24 167	2.9
Legal basis of the THA	197	19 408	3.1
Reports on the President	62	6 327	3.0
Organization and working	570	52 386	3.3
THA sales policy:			
Reprivatization	36	3 511	3.6
Privatization	837	58 198	2.9
Restructuring	322	26 050	3.3
Liquidation	120	8 145	3.3
Other aspects	131	8 408	3.1
Other subjects:			
Environmental pollution	10	851	3.0
Employment companies	38	2 494	3.3
Sale of special assets	54	2 075	3.4
Communication	32	2 075	3.4
East German economy	419	52 020	3.4

*1 would indicate the most positive rating.
Note: The 'rating' ranges from 1 = totally positive to 5 = totally negative
Source: H.M. Kepplinger (1996) *Treuhandanstalt: The Impossible Challenge*: 361.

1000 employees could be privatized (Nellis, 1994: 7–10). In the absence of well-functioning state agencies, domestic and foreign firms, the speed of restructuring is likely to be restricted in Eastern Europe (Grosfeld and Ronald, 1995). East Germany was lucky to have a big brother to solve most of its problems in the wake of privatization, but this is not so for East European and developing countries (Carlin and Mayer, 1995: 426–53).

Although it is premature to make an analytical, critical and evaluative study of the East German experiences in privatization, some important practical lessons can be drawn:

1. It is better to have an independent institution responsible for privatization. It can provide the necessary force, leadership, speed and credibility to the whole exercise.
2. It is advisable to fix the targets of privatization in clear terms to avoid ambiguity and to gain public support.
3. A multiple target system should also have multiple means. Both the economic and social goals should be specified and entrusted to separate institutions as far as possible. This can help in achieving legitimacy within the democratic framework.
4. Conscious and systematic efforts must be made to educate the public about the rationale of privatization in a given society. Backdoor entry can prove counterproductive (see Table 5.3).

5. There is no short-cut to success. One should be prepared to suffer hardships in order to reap benefits in the future.
6. Privatization entails not only an economic device but also a political strategy. Each country may have its own rationale for adopting privatization as its goal.
7. If privatization is seen merely as a matter of growth, economic efficiency and earning foreign exchange, to the neglect of the sociocultural dimension, it may backfire.
8. No privatization movement is free from complacency, growth of bureaucracy and a desperate pursuit of power and control.
9. Privatization may only relieve the government of its operational tasks. The conceiving, planning, goal-setting and evaluating still remain its responsibilities.
10. Privatization not only generates money but it also costs money. The East German model provides the best example.

6
Privatization in Post-Communist Societies

The opening of formerly planned economies to the world and the implementation of market-oriented reforms had profound economic, socio-cultural and political consequences in post-communist societies. Where no other alternative was available in the wake of the quick demise of communism, the resort to a market economy provided the only hope. When the state failed to produce the desired results, the market was considered the only choice left, especially when the workers' councils also could not boost the economy or bring the desired transformation in those former communist societies. 'Experts' from the west advised shock therapy and a resort to market economy to resolve the economic and political crisis as fast as possible. Their market model seemed to rely on the transcendent nature of human beings as suggested by Macpherson (1964) in his *Political Theory of Possessive Individualism*:

1. Individuals exist and it is they who initiate actions.
2. Actions are initiated rationally, with the view of attaining ends.
3. The individual is the best judge of the merits of a given end.
4. In pursuit of an end, individuals are necessarily constrained by the means available to them, as well as by the prevailing information about both the means and ends.
5. Of that which is preferred, more is preferred to less.

To liberals and the conservatives, the essence of human nature is about being oneself, and the essence of being oneself is personality development. The expression of selfhood involves the exercising of free choice. The pro-market ideology advocating a *laissez faire* approach to economic affairs has been deliberately concocted by western experts and new leaders in post-communist societies to justify what interested or suited them most.

It is generally argued that the creation of a market for a good or service will necessarily make a provision for efficiency. Secondly, it will provide wider choice through competition and it is always better to have some choice rather than no choice at all. Thirdly, markets are often judged superior to the government in gathering and communicating the necessary information rapidly. Only markets can send signals to manufacturers when demands or supplies exceed current requirements. The top officials in planning commisions just cannot do that in time. Finally, it is argued that only markets can promote the well-being of both sellers and buyers. It is assumed that enlightened self-interest operates in the public interest although the markets can never guarantee that every self-interest is always enlightened (Keynes, 1926).

Although efficiency, competition, wider choice and participation dominate the theoretical debates on privatization in advanced economies, the principal motive behind privatization in post-communist societies has invariably been the pragmatic need to find new resources for ever-increasing budget deficits incurred by past and present governments (Fraser, 1988: 144). The new watchword for these economies is, 'if it moves, privatize it' (*Business Week*, 1994: 39). It is justified on the ground that it is none of the business of government to remain in business they are not good at.

In advanced industrialized societies, the role of the state has always been limited and the private sector has been well-developed (Table 6.1). The private sector and capital markets are in a position to absorb in case the government decides to shed certain SOEs, public assets or public services. For instance, SOEs account for a mere 10 per cent of value-added in a number of countries belonging to the OECD, while only 27 per cent worked for the state sector in the UK (Lee and Nellis, 1990).

The internationalization of economies, fast means of communication and the spread of the ideology of a market economy across the world led to policy bandwagoning even in the so-called second world. While nationalization in terms of increasing the scope of government directly or indirectly through SOEs reflected a legacy of mercantist and dirigist values, privatization implied the process of increasing the role of the market in production, and the allocation of goods and services through private actions of producers and consumers (Rose, 1988).

The original impetus for privatization came from the desire to discipline the nationalized industries by subjecting them to market forces. It became common to criticize the regulatory and control mechanisms of the state and look forward to the substitution of the state for the market. The welfare state, too, came under severe attacks; privatization replaced the culture of the welfare state and nationalization at the global level.

In fact, privatization acquired a specific meaning and context in the wake of profound economic and political changes in post-communist societies – these societies rapidly changing from authoritarianism to democracy, and from command economies to market economies. Privatization became the hallmark of economic and political transformation in post-communist societies where the state had played a predominant role in production and distribution activities in the name of economic growth and development. For instance, SOEs accounted for approximately 85 per cent of total enterprises on average in former communist countries and ranged up to 97 per cent in the former Czechoslovakia (Lee and Nellis, 1990). Privatization implied the transformation of the entire economy and not only of a few SOEs. Because of the vast size involved, privatization had to be carried out on a massive scale. For instance, at one stage, East Germany had to privatize approximately 8000, Poland 7000–8500, former Czechoslovakia 4800 and Hungary 2500 enterprises (Welfeus, 1991).

Before launching the privatization drive, most post-communist societies lacked prior experience, private markets, appropriate legal structures, financial enterprise and public support. Unlike advanced economies, privatization in these societies took place in an altogether different scenario. Instead of continuing on the past track, it amounted to a break with the past, with a big jerk.

Distant history, sociocultural factors and the composition of the political elite proved to be serious impediments and roadblocks. The redistribution of income and wealth on a massive scale was bound to have political problems and popular resentment, and so the leaders in these nascent democracies and

Table 6.1 Share of the state sector in Eastern and Western Europe

	Output (%)	*Employment (%)*
Eastern Europe		
Czechoslovakia (1986)	97.0	—
East Germany (1982)	96.5	94.2
Soviet Union (1985)	96.0	—
Poland (1985)	81.7	71.5
China (1984)	73.6	—
Hungary (1984)	65.2	69.0
*Western Europe**		
France (1982)	16.5	14.6
Austria (1978–79)	14.5	13.0
Italy (1982)	14.0	15.0
Turkey (1985)	11.2	20.0
Sweden	—	10.6
Finland	—	10.0
United Kingdom (1978)	11.1	8.2
West Germany (1982)	10.7	7.8
Portugal (1976)	9.7	—
Denmark (1974)	6.3	5.0
Greece (1979)	6.1	—
Norway	—	6.0
Spain (1979)	4.1	—
Netherland (1971–73)	3.6	8.0
United States (1983)	1.3	1.8

* Excludes government services, but includes state-owned enterprises engaged in commercial services.

Source: B. Milanovic (1989) *Liberalization and Entrepreneurship.*

market economies had to sail against the wind. Privatization also acquired a different meaning and context in these societies: generally it implied turning SOEs into proprietorship or joint-stock companies with non-governmental boards of directors. It was accomplished through vouchers, direct sales or transfers to workers' councils, pension funds, mutual funds or public investment funds (Spechler, 1995: 48).

The economic heritage

It is very important to understand the economic heritage of the post-communist societies in order to understand the aims, priorities, modalities, technicalities and speed of privatization. There are significant differences between transition from non-market to market economies, and from pre-market or distorted markets to market economies (Winiecki, 1992: 72). The former lacked the requisite economic, legal and political structures prior to privatization. Even the least developed countries (LDCs) had the advantage of having at least the existence of a capitalist class, property rights and legal structures which were lacking in the post-communist societies. While the leaders of LDCs are often found unwilling to resort to privatization, the new leaders in post-communist societies had virtually no other choice but to resort to privatization (Rosa, 1992: 92). Table 6.2 shows the mass responses to privatization in various post-communist societies.

In fact, the process of economic reforms in these societies had begun much earlier, depending upon the level of attention being paid to the private sector. For instance, in Poland most agricultural land remained in the private sector

Table 6.2 Comparing mass responses to privatization in post-communist societies

	Communist regime	*Current regime (% rating positive)*	*In five years**
Bulgaria	42	55	72
Czech Republic	29	71	88
Slovak Republic	48	58	80
Hungary	68	43	72
Poland	42	56	69
Romania	35	68	82
Slovenia	46	77	87
NDB trend	44	61	79
(NDB I mean)	(35)	(59)	(82)
Belarus	60	35	46
Ukraine	55	25	49
Croatia	13	42	73
Grand mean NDB II	43	53	72

* Projection only.
Source: R. Rose and C. Haerpfer (1994) *Europe–Asia Studies*: 46(1).

and the mid-1980s Poland also saw the growth of private firms in retail trade, services and manufacturing. By the end of 1970, about 10 per cent of total production was generated by the private sector in Hungary; in 1975 there were 1.6 million small private farms. Private capital accumulation in Hungary and Poland was gradually channeled into durable consumer goods, housing and foreign currency (Inotai, 1992: 165).

However, private activities were not allowed in the former Czechoslovakia and GDR, and this explains the difference in the initiatives taken by managers in Hungary and Czechoslovakia with regard to privatization. Since Hungarian managers were exposed to private capital and managerial skills they were able to take the initiative towards privatization themselves, while their counterparts in former Czechoslovakia just waited for the government to act (*Journal of Commerce*, 16 May 1991).

The transformation in post-communist societies was generally seen as a once-and-for-all shift from one coherent order to another. (Grabher, 1994). Such a view neglected the possibilities of incoherence and turmoil before and after the hypothesized transition. Moreover, privatization was seen as the only hope to solve the economic problems inherited from the communist regime and the best way of reorganization. It was generally perceived that without privatization, better times would never come (*The Economist*, 11 May 1991: 11). Table 6.3 shows the mass responses to the changed economic systems in post-communist societies.

Privatization was expected to create the preconditions for a market economy and democracy simultaneously by creating a new middle and capitalist class.

Table 6.3 Comparing mass responses to changed economic systems in post-communist societies

	Socialist economy	*Current system (% rating positive)*	* *In five years*
Bulgaria	59	25	63
Czech Republic	44	55	83
Slovak Republic	64	34	73
Hungary	74	29	69
Poland	57	39	57
Romania	57	32	67
Slovenia	46	36	83
NDB trend	57	36	71
(NDB I mean)	(50)	(34)	(74)
Belarus	75	15	42
Ukraine	76	4	42
Croatia	28	22	71
Grand mean NDB II	58	29	65

* Projection only.

Source: R. Rose and C. Haerpfer (1994), *Europe–Asia Studies*: 46(1).

However, it is doubtful whether the middle class formed as a result of government efforts would be able to lead to the establishment of either democracy or a market economy, or a new form of interventionist economy and corporatist state (Inotai, 1992: 170).

Although the goal of privatization became embedded in the macroeconomic framework of post-communist societies, it proved to be a very tedious exercise to carry it out in practice owing to the large number of enterprises, their huge size, outdated and inefficient production patterns, huge environmental costs, economic vulnerability and the hardships involved. This explains why privatization trailed at a very low speed despite very high expectations.

For instance, in Hungary the government had to stop the programme of spontaneous privatization in the wake of rising criticism. In Poland, the macroeconomic stabilization based on shock therapy failed to create the necessary preconditions for large-scale privatization. In East Germany, the Treuhandanstalt left a debt of DM270 billion when it closed its shop on 31 December 1994, although it was expected to raise approximately DM600 billion from the sale of 13815 companies. In Poland, instead of 20, only 7 firms could be privatized by the end of 1990. Rising fears of unemployment and foreign takeovers also prevented the smooth progress of privatization in post-communist societies. Hungarian policy-makers found it easier to provide employment subsidies to SOEs than to sell them to private owners.

In Russia, the state still has a majority in one-third of approximately 9000 joint-stock firms. Although the private sector owns a 60 per cent share in terms of output and 36 per cent in terms of employment, more than 40 million stockholders in Russia during 1992–94 remained minority holders with virtually no control or influence over the corporate government. Although the private sector reached 50 to 70 per cent of the total activity in 1994, 40 per cent of the SOEs remained unprivatized in Hungary.

In fact, many privatized firms are now controlled by semi-public banks or the privatization agency itself acting as the agent of re-statization. The SPA, the agency responsible for privatization in Hungary, seems to have gained more weight in the wake of horizontal ties of cross ownership. While under communism the SOEs held judicial ownership, one or more state agencies have been able to retain ownership through shares in the wake of privatization.

In fact we find a hybrid of ownerships prevailing in most post-communist societies. For instance, in Hungary we find blurred boundaries between the state and the market; there are sectors which cannot be classified in terms of either state or market. These can be best defined as networks, strategic alliances or industrial districts. Such organizations cannot be arrayed in a continuum between markets and hierarchies, but beyond markets. Under this very complex set-up, different levels of efficiency can coexist. Nor can the inefficiencies at the local level be simply wiped out; as such they have to be tolerated by all means. In post-communist societies, dominant western technologies and organizational concepts cannot and should not be applied on a uniform basis. The institutional and economic heritage and the local forms of production and sensitivities have to be kept in mind.

Objectives of privatization

While fiscal objectives dominated the privatization drive in most advanced economies, the demise of communism propelled the privatization debate in post-communist societies. Ideologies do change; not necessarily due to their being corrupted or from reaching the end of their role, or through political opportunism, but mainly because no ideology can be fully translated into practice. New situations create the need for new explanations and emphasise new goals. Sometimes novel, unrelated or inconsistent elements creep in, fomenting changes in the basic premise.

In a society practicing the politics of incrementalism, ideology always remains an amalgam of change and continuity. It may or may not possess a logical or philosophical character, but it must have a political character. The puzzle of transition in East and Central Europe can be better explained in terms of politics rather than economics (Gupta, 1988: 13). Privatization seemed to provide a quick political solution to economic failures inherited from the communist regime (Figure 6.1).

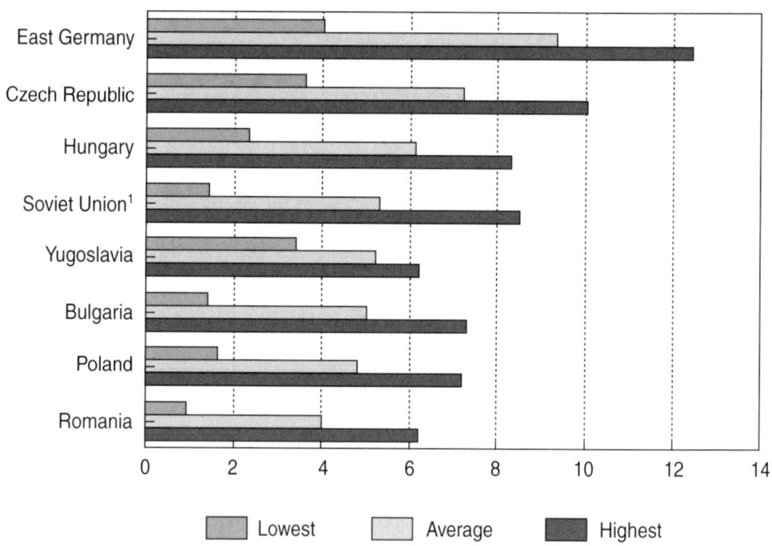

Notes: [1] erstwhile; [2] based on 10 studies.
Figure 6.1 The poverty of communism[2] (GDP per person, 1988, $000s)

At the heart of the triumph of neoliberal ideas and politics lay the inability of the planned economies in socialist countries to deliver the goods. These societies lagged far behind in terms of GDP per capita (Table 6.4). No one could really operate in a satisfactory manner under command economies in a world dominated by high-technology and diversified manufacturing. In order to save their economies from a major catastrophe, the socialist countries had already started the process of economic reforms in the late 1960s and early 1970s.

Serious attempts were made to foster the growth of private agriculture, small private businesses and small private services in the former USSR, China, Hungary and Poland. In the wake of globalization of economies in the post-oil crisis period of 1970, socialism had already begun to retreat. The rising affluence of workers along with the shift from smokestacks to high-technology had already made the political appeals to a class struggle redundant, making communism highly discredited (Roberts, 1991: 27) and 'horrendous' (Parker, 1993: 80).

However, it was soon realized that it was easier to dismantle the communist system than to build a new society atop the old. It is one thing to reform an economy or a political system, but it is quite another matter to build an altogether new system from scratch. The question before the post-communist societies was how to create capitalism in the absence of capitalists. In western societies, the top 1 or 2 per cent own approximately 30 to 40 per cent of private assets, and the top 10 per cent are estimated to hold up to 60 to 70 per cent, exclusive of housing. They can easily absorb transfers from the public to the private sector. In post-communist societies, on the other hand, people cannot afford to buy public property or invest in shares mainly because they do not own much property privately. Nor do they have private savings in surplus.

Under these adverse circumstances, western experts (Sachs, Fischer, Balcerowicz, Klaus and others) recommended shock therapy as the only remedy. The objectives of privatization were (1) to create capital markets on

Table 6.4 Economies in transition: annual growth (% per annum)

	Average 1986–89	*1990*	*1991*	*1992*
China	8.7	4.1	7.7	12.8
Russia*	2.4	–2.0	–9.0	–19.0
Bulgaria	5.2	–11.6	–22.7	–7.9
Czechoslovakia	1.6	–3.0	–15.5	–5.0
Hungary	1.4	–4.0	–10.5	–4.6
Poland	2.7	–11.4	–7.7	1.5
Romania	–0.9	–7.1	–13.4	–10.2

Notes: *erstwhile; output measure is GNP for China, net material product for Russia, and gross domestic output for other countries.
Sources: J. Sachs *et al.* (1994) *Economic Policy*: 103.

the pattern of western economies, (2) to encourage small businesses through shops and restaurants, and (3) to inject foreign capital, foreign management and foreign expertise into the domestic and national economies (Parker, 1993: 74). The former communist elites who were unable to recoup their economies also found an easy scapegoat in the form of spontaneous privatization. They were able to reap the benefits in the wake of a legal and regulatory vacuum by transferring ownership to 'themselves' through various privatization devices.

The earlier attempts towards workers' ownership did not yield the desired results under socialism. For instance, in Hungary, Yugoslavia and Poland workers' councils were authorized to exercise an owner's right to manage the public sector enterprises. These councils had the legacy of social ownership (Savas, 1992: 77). But it was unfair to treat the workers as owners mainly because the profitability of an enterprise depended on state policies rather than the performance of the workers. Secondly, these enterprises were not run on a profit motive; social objectives dominated. Moreover, the workers had no economic stakes whatsoever, and as such they lacked the necessary incentives to perform well.

Under communism prices were generally distorted through subsidiaries and administrative pricing of inputs in terms of labour, capital and natural resources. There was a preference for economics of scale. This led to the formation of giant enterprises and a concentration of production. It also insulated the economies from competition from the west by not allowing trade with the west, or by maintaining dual prices for raw materials for domestic and foreign markets. The system hardly relied on credit or debt in the western sense of these terms. The total indebtedness of corporations, individuals and government was very small in communist societies in comparison with that of western societies. In the USA, total indebtedness was almost double GNP, while in none of the post-communist societies, was it more than 10 per cent of current GNP by the end of 1992 (Parker, 1993: 79).

As such, the entire privatization debate in post-communist societies has to be seen in a different perspective. It was hoped that macrostabilization and privatization would bring not only western capital but also western management skills and an associated business culture *en bloc*. It would help in rationalizing price structures and in enhancing technical and economic efficiency. It would also help in reducing external debt. In 1992, foreign capital inflow into Hungary was supposed to cover up to 50 to 65 per cent of the country's interest payments – a major device of debt management. Foreign capital also played a crucial role in the buyouts of SOEs on a large scale; some of the lobbies even tried to woo foreign companies just to consolidate their near-monopolistic position in domestic markets.

In most post-communist societies, the problem of internal debt and the necessity to curb hyper-inflation through tougher monetary policies also gave vent to privatization. It was assumed that privatization would achieve a better allocation of resources through better investment decisions than the SOEs. In the post-communist societies, the new leadership could gain popular support from within and without only by resorting to the promise of a market economy. They could no longer cling to collectivist ideas since their political future lay in breaking ties with the past as fast as possible. They even hoped to curb the powers and influence of the old-guard through various privatization devices which aimed at guaranteeing a fair distribution of public assets among the public. Privatization also facilitated the separating of the political decision-making process from the economic sphere. This difficult task could never be accomplished under the former communist regime.

Modalities of rapid privatization

The overall objective of rapid privatization in post-communist societies was to allow the growth of the private sector relative to the state sector, rather than transfer existing firms to the private sector. As such, the leadership in these societies had to resort to a bottom-up rather than top-down approach to privatization (Table 6.5). Economic resurgence could come only through the establishment of new private enterprises and growth of the existing small units. As such, priority was given to the liberalization of real estate in order to facilitate the growth of new private firms which needed an adequate supply of land for office space. All *de jure* and *de facto* obstacles had to be removed and various new methods had to be explored to distribute public assets and activities among citizens in a free and fair manner. Since it was very difficult to sell the huge SOEs (Poland could raise a mere US$700 million by selling 180 of the strongest enterprises out of 1800 large enterprises), alternative approaches to privatization were also contemplated:

1. restitution;
2. direct sale to domestic citizens;
3. management and worker buy-outs;
4. vouchers;
5. sale to foreigners.

Restitution

In post-communist societies, the biggest problem before starting the process of privatization was to resolve the question of ownership – to whom did the state property belong? Did it belong to the workers, managers, former owners, national government, local municipality or general public? Did the collective farms belong to the state, farm-workers or owners prior to nationalization? The restoration of property to previous owners became a very sensitive issue in post-communist societies, both on moral and political grounds. Restitution as a privatization policy proved too problematic due to the absence or poor records of private property expropriated by the socialist states approximately 50 to 70 years ago.

Table 6.5 Privatization plans in Poland, Hungary and Czechoslovakia

	Poland	*Hungary*	*Czechoslovakia*
Privatization Agency	Ministry of Ownership Transformation	State Property Agency	Ministry of National Property Administration and Privatization in each republic
Period of Privatization	50% in 3–5 years	50–60% in 5 years	50% in 5 years
Methods of privatization	Free distribution	Sale primarily through stockexchange auction and tender	Free distribution on some sales
To whom	30% to general public 10% to workers 20% to pension funds 10% to banks	Any potential buyers, domestic or foreign	40–80% by vouchers; up to 20% foreign; up to 20% direct share holdings, including workers
Discount to workers	Yes	About 10% of shares at reduced prices with credit for further purchases	No
Limits on foreign holdings	Initially, 10% without holding	Excluded from retail, catering, small-scale	Only for small-scale sales
Decision to privatize belongs to	Ministry	State, enterprise, external	Enterprise, republican Ministries
Stock exchange	Being established	Yes, 8–12 now trading shares	From July, 1991

Source: S. Estrin (1991) 'Privatization in Central and Eastern Europe', *Journal of Developing Areas*: 179.

It was still feasible to settle the restitution claims in those societies where some records were maintained, but it was near impossible to resort to restitution in Russia, China and the Baltic states where the private owners were completely uprooted or exterminated. Restitution also had adverse effects on the speed of privatization in these societies; the restitution process proved to be very time-consuming. Uncertainties about the true owners also discouraged prospective investors and affected production adversely. During the second wave of privatization, some countries adopted the policy of compensating the original owners after privatization instead of restoring to physical restoration of property (Savas, 1992: 577). This policy was adopted successfully in East Germany and Czechoslovakia, and was regarded as a necessary evil by many other post-communist societies.

Divestment

In post-communist societies it was easier to resort to small privatization by shedding shops, service establishments and small production businesses than the divestment of huge SOEs. Poland, former Czechoslovakia, City of Moscow and other Baltic states resorted to small privatizations in the initial years to create a large number of domestic, legal and private entrepreneurs. It was necessary to have a capital-owning class to revitalize the entire economy and the labour markets (Kopp, 1991: 2–6). In former Czechoslovakia shops were auctioned by public bidding, while in Poland shops were leased out. Leasing was quite popular in China too. By mid-1991 all shops in East Germany had been privatized, and by the end of 1992 more than 31000 small businesses had been auctioned in Czechoslovakia. The successful buyers in post-communist societies were mostly the old *nomenklatura*. Some foreigners also purchased through domestic intermediaries (R. Parker, 1993: 395).

Divestment, in post-communist societies not only took place through the sale of an enterprise but also through free transfer, liquidation and withdrawal. An SOE could be sold to private buyers, the general public, management, employees or customers. In the case of Germany, private West German firms were even paid by the Treuhandanstalt to assume ownership of failing SOEs in East Germany in order to avoid liquidation. In many other post-communist societies, liquidation had to be carried out in those cases where a sale was out of the question due to poor prospects for survival of the enterprise concerned or a lack of adequate resources to keep them afloat.

Management and worker buy-outs

MBOs and MBIs became significant forms of privatization in post-communist societies. In an MBO, the employees of a company take over both the ownership and responsibility for managing a company or part of it. This helped in creating small and medium-sized independent companies. In the case of MBIs, managers were brought in from outside. In Germany, one out of six privatizations up to June 1993 was achieved either through an MBO or

MBI. Approximately 50 per cent of companies privatized through MBOs or MBIs had fewer than 50 employees, and only 16 per cent of them employed more than 100 at the time they were taken over by their own management. While, in the case of the MBOs, up to 93 per cent of purchasers came from inside and 7 per cent from outside, in the case of MBIs, 74 per cent came from outside (mainly from West Germany) and 26 per cent from inside (Muller, 1996: 392).

MBOs and MBIs provided a novel instrument of privatization in post-communist societies, some of which resorted to spontaneous privatization to former managers and employees mainly with the objective of getting rid of the parasitical SOEs as fast as possible. Some of the old *nomenklatura* and managers were able to reap the benefits of spontaneous privatizations, especially in Russia. During the first wave, approximately 70 per cent of the shares of the privatized companies ended up in the hand of former workers and managers (McCartny and Puffer, 1995: 58).

In Czechoslovakia, MBOs remained relatively unimportant mainly because of inadequate personal savings for the purchase of national assets. Polish citizens could acquire only 2.4 to 3.4 per cent of the total assets of companies to be privatized even if they were prepared to spend up to 30 to 40 per cent of their savings (Frydman and Rapaczynski, 1991). These managers had very little knowledge of a market economy, and most reverted to the former style of management in due course. They also had to sail against the wind. A lack of expertise and the adverse economic and political situation in the wake of the collapse of COMECON and the breakdown of the USSR also led many MBOs to bankruptcy.

Vouchers

To avoid the allegations of windfall gains on the basis of inside information to former managers and the communist elite, the new leadership preferred the voucher scheme which provided the public an opportunity to profit from privatization. Some post-communist societies preferred vouchers to workers' councils and MBOs/MBIs on the grounds of the equitable distribution of ownership and low cost to the individual (Aggarwal and Mejstrik, 1992). Voucher schemes were the major form of privatization in most post-communist societies except East Germany. Voucher privatization played a major role in Czechoslovakia, and by June 1993 approximately 61.4 per cent privatization had taken place through vouchers in the Czech republic, amounting to CSK203 billion (Czechoslovak Koruna prior to 8 February 1993). The proportion designated for voucher privatization ranged from 7 to 97 per cent of the companies' basic capital, and every Czech company was required to reserve 3 per cent of the vouchers for resolving future restitution claims (Mla'dek, 1994: 4).

Free transfers were made to employees or to their pension fund, to users or customers, or to the general public or original owners. By summer 1993, five

Table 6.6 Voucher points alloted in Czech Republic

Type of funds	*Number of funds*	*Percentage of the total no. of funds*	*Number of voucher points in billion*	*Percentage of voucher points*
IPF from 1st wave	133	37.6		
New IPF for 2nd wave	63	17.8	1.57	40
Unit trusts closed	120	33.9	1.48	38
Unit trusts open	38	10.7	0.87	22
Total	354	100.0	3.92	100

Note: IPF: Investment Privatization Fund
Source: Kuponova privatization no. 21, 2 December 1993, cited in Mla'dek, 1994: 15.

rounds of voucher privatization had been completed in Czechoslovakia. Over 270 million shares having an estimated value of US$10.5 billion, were purchased for voucher points (*Privatization Newsletter of Czechoslovakia*, 1991–92: 11). The vouchers, also known as coupons were denominated in points and used for bidding for shares in their enterprises to be privatized. The voucher holders were free to decide the number and timing of their bids. After the fifth round of voucher privatization only 7.7 per cent of the total voucher points given to the population were unused (Table 6.6).

By July 1994, the distribution of vouchers to Russian citizens during the first wave of privatization was over. Over 40 million Russians now owned stock in 19 000 out of 29 000 privatized enterprises (*The Economist*, 20 June 1994: 4). Even the most hardened skeptics were surprised by the speed and scale of privatization in Russia, but what occurred in that first phase was de-statization rather than privatization. The banks and investment funds played a very important role and controlled the voucher privatization, with the state remaining the major shareholder in most of the financial institutions and mutual funds. Instead of creating capital markets on the lines of western economies, voucher privatization led to corporative ownership in post-communist societies (Mla'dek, 1994: 10).

Involvement of foreign capital

Despite opposition to foreign ownership, it was realized that foreign capital, technology and expertise was necessary to make privatization a success in post-communist societies. In Prague and Bratislava, government agencies were established to seek foreign investments and in some cases 100 per cent foreign ownership was also allowed, though the clear preference was for joint ventures. Initially some of the fiscal benefits were also announced in the form of preferential corporate tax, tax holidays and concessionary rates to woo foreign investments. Later on, some of these privileges were withdrawn. Foreigners were encouraged to participate in privatization plans, compete in public bids and enter into joint ventures. Foreign expertise was also sought to make the privatization programme a success.

However, most western companies showed less interest in investing in post-communist societies than anticipated by the shock-therapists in general. There were the usual complaints of betrayal by the west in Poland, Hungary, Czechoslovakia and Russia, and in East Germany the total foreign investment amounted to a bare 6 per cent. Western public financing through multilateral and bilateral agreements gave more weight to political concerns than economic interests. The opening of former planned economies not only affected the Central and East European countries, but also the economies of Western Europe and North America in terms of price competition in product markets, migration and capital inflows. The western industrialized countries had three options (Holzmann, Thimann and Petz, 1993: 1):

1. allow for mass migration;
2. finance large parts of modernization and investment needs of post-communist societies;
3. allow for open trade.

All these options had to be balanced with their own political policies and budgetary constraints. Besides divestments, privatization also occurred through displacement, delegation and a combination of various divestment methods in post-communist societies. In the case of Poland, various methods of divestment were combined to shed a single SOE. For instance, 10 per cent of the shares were sold to workers at a discount, 5 per cent were sold to managers at a discount, 10 per cent was given to the pension fund, 10 per cent to the banks, 10 per cent to insurance companies, 20 per cent to adult citizens free of charge, and the remaining 35 per cent were sold directly to a single buyer either domestic or foreign (Lipton and Sachs, 1990: 293–333).

Privatization can also take place through displacement. To Savas, displacement occurs through default and withdrawal; thus, when the private sector steps in to meet public needs and demands not adequately fulfilled by the public sector, privatization occurs by default. The emergence of black markets in socialist countries can be explained in these terms. Whereas default is unintended, government can deliberately withdraw in some cases to allow the private sector to step in. This was common in former East Germany (Savas, 1992: 575). Governments can also delegate certain activities related to production or services, while retaining overall responsibility to itself. In China, contracting with a private firm to manage an SOE is not uncommon; under contract management, managers in China may agree to achieve a certain level of profitability in return for a fixed remuneration or share in the profits above the target. In China, leasing and franchising have also been used to reap the benefits of privatization.

Problems of privatization

The basic problems of privatization in post-communist societies have been aptly summarized by Janusz Lawandowski, the Polish Minister for Ownership Change in 1991. He said:

> Privatization is the sale of enterprises that no one owns, and whose value no one knows, to buyers who have no money.

The gains from mass, rapid or spontaneous privatizations in post-communist societies have been much below the high expectations. Although privatization became the hallmark of the economic reforms in these societies, the practical results have been very modest. We find a wide gap between expectations and realities. Although, small-scale privatization was a success, 'big privatization' had to face many impediments due to the insufficient purchasing power of citizens, a lack of efficient institutions and legal barriers (Inotai 1992: 171). East Germany was the only exception where a modest amount of money was available due to transfers from Western Germany. In all other societies, private savings proved to be quite inadequate.

Moreover, economic and political instability, often aggravated due to lack of proper policies or inadequate policies, put the prospective domestic and foreign investors at bay. Domestic citizens could not switch over to risk-taking behaviour appropriate to a market economy automatically; nor were they willing to part with their assets for unpredictable future gains. Foreigners also moved in a very cautious manner, taking a long time to appraise themselves of the local norms and culture. The valuation process in itself was also lengthy. Since proper records were not maintained by most of the SOEs, it proved a herculean task to assess the correct value of an enterprise. For instance, in 1990, the Gorbachev government offered De Beers an exclusive five-year concession on all Soviet diamond production in return for US$1 billion. The most conservative estimates put the real value of Russian diamond production at five times that amount. Due to the lack of proper stockmarkets, valuations of national assets were either too erroneous or subjective (Sandberg, 1994: 15).

It also proved a very costly affair to value these public assets. The prolonging of the valuation process in order to get the best price, or to prevent corruption, resulted in high economic and social costs. It required a large bureaucracy to handle the business of privatization. Sometimes the domestic or foreign partners joined the process to serve their vested interests. For instance, in Poland, the foreign companies responsible for privatization of the first five Polish firms were able to reap a dividend of approximately 25 per cent of the total value of these companies (Sachs, 1991). There were also many reports of widespread corruption in post-communist societies in the wake of privatization. For instance, in Hungary, the number of companies dealing in foreign trade rose from 2000 to 10 000 in just one year (1990), while in Czechoslovakia approximately 1500 joint ventures were created just to obtain the real estate; these companies stopped operating after attaining the desired property. We find similar reports about MBOs in East Germany.

With foreign capital not forthcoming at the right time and of the right amount, post-communist societies had to resort to the transfer of national assets in the form of vouchers. Ideological preferences for equity and social service collided with the notion of economic efficiency. Nor could the restitution claims be reconciled with economic and political stability. Similarly, the free distribution of vouchers could not be supported on sound economic grounds since these could neither prove useful in generating the much needed capital resources at the critical juncture of historical transformation, nor prove useful in monitoring or adequately checking on the newly-privatized enterprises. Most enterprises required restructuring before they could be privatized, while most post-communist societies lacked the financial resources to do that. These societies also had to face many other dilemmas.

Privatization proved to be no less than political dynamite. In post-communist societies, it involved redistribution of property rights, wealth and opportunities at a time of great political and economic turbulence – at a time when capital market institutions and expertise were lacking and the new democratic institutions were untested (Schmieding, 1992: 99). There was an urgent need for rapid and spontaneous privatization, even if it was found to be corruption-prone. Due to the paucity of adequate information, necessary infrastructure, lack of any past experience and the impossibility of judging future prospects correctly in the prevailing turmoil, all those engaged in the privatization process were bound to make mistakes. They were prone to make major blunders by following the British-style of privatization without giving due consideration to their own circumstances and requirements. It was equally wrong on the part of the new leadership to expect quick or automatic gains from privatization.

Instead of enhancing the popularity of new leaders, privatization in the form of vouchers, MBOs and spontaneous privatization marred their popularity. Widespread ownership through vouchers impeded the effective control of the private owners. The general public could not tolerate the rise of the few at the cost of many through the sale of public assets; nor could they enjoy holding the vouchers if the companies quickly became bankrupt. In some instances, the ex-socialists, discredited nomenclatura and foreigners were able to take maximum advantage of various privatization devices in post-communist societies by finding easy ways of converting their financial assets or powers into real assets. Consequently, the egalitarianism of the communist era gave way to capitalist exploitation.

Mass response to transformations

It is premature to analyse the outcome of various privatization experiences in post-communist societies where the sequence of events cannot yet be predicted. Nor can we ensure whether these societies would be able to follow precisely the democratic system or the market model as understood by advanced western economies (Miller *et al.*, 1993). These societies are on the road to market economy and full-fledged democracy, but have not yet been able to reach their destinations.

These societies are not only in transition but also in metamorphosis – undergoing political, economic and social transformation simultaneously. They are undergoing an altogether different transformation than that followed by Europe after 1945 in terms of economic reconstruction or transformation from an authoritarian to a democratic regime (Pereira, *et al.*, 1993). The problems of post-communist societies are political, economic, social as well as cultural, and as such their economic transformation cannot be understood without understanding the political and sociocultural context.

Moreover, we find wide disparities among the post-communist societies themselves. These societies differ from one another in terms of the 'distance travelled' by each away from the communist regime. The Czech Republic and Hungary have been far ahead of the former USSR or Bulgaria. We can also make comparisons across time, both within and between these societies. Within them divisions may occur among the new democrats, old communists or new authoritarians along ethnic and class lines or simply on the basis of winners and losers in the wake of economic and political transition form the communist regime to a market economy; these divisions may be so sharp and deep as to disrupt the very fibre of the new regimes.

At present we find a lot of ambivalence among the people with regard to the economic and political transformation. According to a survey (Figure 6.2), the dynamics of the change at the individual level can be explained in four ways:

1. Individuals who disapproved of the communist system and approved of the present system as the only possible alternative comprised approximately 32 per cent;
2. Individuals who endorsed the former communist regime and disapproved the present system comprised 23 per cent;
3. Individuals who disapproved of both the old and the new regime comprised approximately 25 per cent;
4. Individuals who voiced approval of both the old and the new regime comprised approximately 20 per cent.

However, while reactionaries rate the current regimes as worse than the communist regimes, sceptics are slowly moving in the direction of approving the new regimes. In fact, while the collapse of the communist regime helped in removing certain problems, it has also created new problems in the wake of transformation. The communist regime appeared modern as it could send rockets to the moon, build high-rise buildings and guarantee full employment (Winiecki, 1988). Four decades of life under the communist regime rejected the use of markets to direct the economy, and allowed the communist party to become totalitarian in its aims and design.

Many activities were restricted on political grounds, such as ordering a book from abroad or travelling abroad. People had to stand in long queues just to get the bare necessities of life. In the wake of transformation, intensive queuing dropped by 9 per cent from the autumn of 1991 to autumn 1992. Only in Belarus and Ukraine had a majority of households to spend at least an hour per day queuing (Rose and Haerpfer, 1994).

But in the wake of the regime change, the masses had to face acute problems of unemployment and hyper-inflation. Since most people did not understand the intrigues of macroeconomics, they blamed the new political and economic system for their woes. The introduction of a market economy led to unemployment on a massive scale, and even if such unemployment were transitional, people were still scared because they were not used to changing jobs so frequently.

Inflation proved yet another major obstacle causing social distress. Just as unemployment was necessary to increase productivity, inflation was also inevitable in the wake of transformation from the non-market to the market economy. Prices were bound to increase with the demise of state subsidies, and the expansion of the money supply by the governments led to

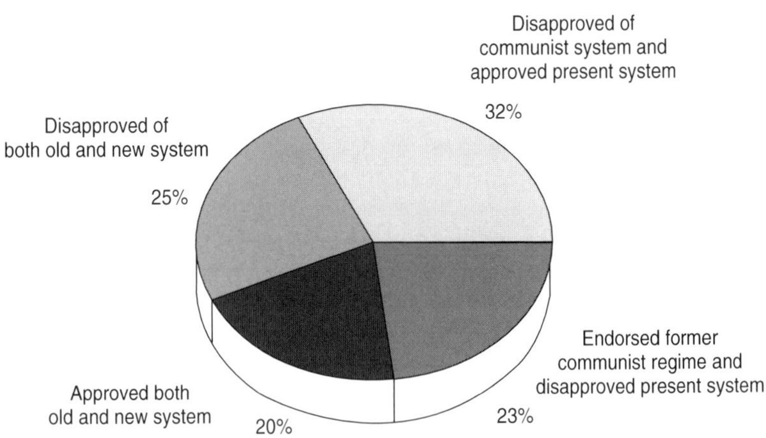

Figure 6.2 Dynamics of change in post-communist societies
Source: Rose and Mishler (1994).

Table 6.7 Trust in institutions in post-communist societies

	Czech Rep.	*Slovakia*	*Hungary*	*Poland*	*Mean*
			(*% expressing trust*)		
State institutions					
Army	42	52	40	63	49
Courts	38	37	40	46	40
Police	36	35	34	46	38
Government	48	49	19	22	34
Public authorities, officials	27	30	24	23	26
Parliament	19	24	20	12	19
Representative institutions					
Churches	33	45	42	41	40
Media	40	39	34	35	37
Trade Unions	24	31	20	21	24
Parties, political movements	20	20	10	8	14

Source: Plasser and Ularam (1993): table 4, in R. Rose and C. Haerpfer (1994), *Europe–Asia Studies*: 46(1).

escalating inflation. For instance, in Czechoslovakia the official exchange rate declined by 300 per cent during 1989 to 1991. Since the prices had depressed below market level, there was a sudden leap in inflation. In January 1991, prices rose by 25.8 per cent in Czechoslovakia (Parker, 1993: 393). However, it was brought under control by summer 1991 (Charap, Dyba and Kupka, 1992: 7). Many saw inflation as a 'greater threat' than 'unemployment'. Those with positivist attitude envisaged the economic reforms in post-communist society in terms of 'J. shaped' reforms – a big dip down and then a speedy recovery.

The transformation of the political systems has also created new asymmetries in these societies. While under communism the citizens showed trust in traditional institutions of state authority (army, courts, police, government and public authorities), they viewed the new leaders and new institutions in the wake of emerging market economies with serious doubts. In East and Central Europe the civil society is comparatively weak and the citizens generally lack democratic culture (Table 6.7).

Under communism people took very little part in politics, and as such they were not good at articulating demands for public action and had no bargaining power. It was a misnomer to describe them as voters. In post-communist societies, while the political movements against the communist regime have lost their *raison d'etre*, the new parties have not yet become strong enough to carry out the necessary economic and political reforms in an undeterred way. These societies seem to be divided on the basis of individual versus collective values (Rose and Haerpfer, 1994) and the future remains very uncertain (Table 6.8).

Table 6.8 Shift in values in post-communist societies

	Equal income	*State responsible for welfare*	*State-owned enterprises*	*Secure job first*
		(% housing collective provision of welfare)		
Bulgaria	41	63	47	65
Czech Republic	10	46	17	48
Slovak Republic	13	57	27	37
Hungary	31	60	24	73
Poland	23	85	31	67
Romania	22	54	48	69
Slovenia	30	55	20	85
Belarus	22	52	46	65
Ukraine	28	57	52	39
Croatia	29	40	15	47
Mean, NDB II	25	57	33	60

Source: R. Rose and C. Haerpfer (1994), *Europe–Asia Studies*: 46(1).

Lessons from post-communist societies

The issue of privatization gained momentum in post-communist societies primarily due to events in the advanced economies, especially the United Kingdom. The limited extent of friction, the ease and the speed with which the political and economic changes have been introduced in these societies since 1989 are simply marvelous. The politicians who aimed at rapid transformation of these societies hoped that most of the SOEs would survive after getting a dose of privatization (Bös, 1991).

In fact, the privatization movement needs to be seen in an altogether different context in post-communist societies where till recently central planning dominated and the SOEs had virtually no financial or decision-making autonomy (Milanovic, 1990). The first step towards privatization involved commercialization – transformation of public enterprises into joint-stock companies. Under planned economies, the enterprises operated on the basis of orders form central planners; prices virtually played no role in resource-allocation and were usually irrational. As such, the move from command economies to market economies involved something more than mere privatization.

Since long-term solutions were required to remove the problems faced by the SOEs, it was decided to privatize them first and restructure them later under private control. It was argued that by privatizing rapidly, the onus on the government for restructuring would be greatly reduced and pressures for subsidies and protection would be easier to resist. Moreover, the private owners were supposed to do a better job than the government in saving the viable parts and sloughing off the unviable ones. It was just the reverse of

British-style privatization where an enterprise was first restructured to make it more attractive for privatization purposes. While in advanced economies privatization served only as a means towards economic reconstruction, in post-communist societies it became an end in itself.

The experiences of post-communist societies in privatization suggest that there are no short-cuts to success. No country can hope to return to the mainstream of a market economy without passing through a valley of tears during the transitional stage. The post-communist societies will have to find out their own devices to invigorate their economies, but they can learn from the wider, longer and versatile experiences in privatization from the first world and the third world; what they cannot do is simply xerox or duplicate them.

The most prudent course for these societies would be to accept the mixed forms of ownership and a gradual approach towards privatization to ensure political support from all sections of society; rapid privatization can threaten social and political stability (Spechler, 1995: 51). On the basis of the limited experience of the 27 post-communist societies in privatization, it can be inferred that:

1. It is one thing to privatize the state-owned enterprises, public goods or services, but it is quite another thing to privatize the entire economy.
2. Privatization can be either the cause or consequence of democratization. It is very difficult, if not impossible to carry out political and economic reforms simultaneously.
3. It is easier to dismantle a structure than rebuild it. It is easier to indulge in small privatizations in post-communist societies than big ones, especially when the appropriate legal, economic and political structures are either lacking or underdeveloped.
4. There are big gaps between expectations and realities in terms of actual privatizations that have taken place in post-communist societies. While the state still controls approximately 40 per cent of the SOEs in the Czech Republic and Hungary; Romania, Slovakia, Slovenia and Bulgaria are far behind on the road to privatization. Some post-communist societies have yet to start the process of privatization.
5. In most post-communist societies privatization agencies, semi-public banks and investment funds have gained from the privatization process. Lack of ready buyers has resulted in the transfer of the majority of shares to judiciaries and semi-public authorities free of government control. The motive of abortive voucher privatization in Poland and Russia seems to defer ownership rights to workers' councils. It can only be called sham privatization.
6. Privatization in post-communist societies has been imposed from above, but privatization can be successful only when it occurs from below. Privatization from below can help in creating favourable socioeconomic conditions necessary for privatization from above. It can also help in

reducing sociopolitical conflicts generally accompanying mass privatization on the one hand, and enhance the speed of privatization on the other.

7. The post-communist societies simply cannot emulate western-style privatization; they have to find their own solutions. Privatization has been an outcome of economic prosperity and democracy in advanced economies and not necessarily a precondition for both. As such, their experiences in privatization cannot be copied rapidly or deliberately.
8. Privatization programmes cannot succeed in post-communist societies without involving foreign capital, foreign management and foreign expertise. It is essential to foster public support for the involvement of foreigners in order to avoid the dangers of xenophobia.
9. Rapid or spontaneous privatization in post-communist societies can be corruption-prone. It is necessary to take adequate precautionary steps and establish regulatory bodies to keep proper checks on the nascent privatized bodies.
10. Where private capital markets are thin and foreign ownership is not tolerated, it is better to transfer SOEs to a privatization agency on the lines of Treuhand, or to investment companies or mutual funds. Although mutual funds emerging in the wake of spontaneous privatizations can be fraud-prone, under strict state supervision they can only amount to a change of label. It is better to set the deadline date by law, by which time the state assets and shares should be sold to other interested parties. This step can eventually lead to privatization.

For the sake of better distributional results, privatization may be organized in tranches and the proceeds distributed after each round. Asset prices are likely to be depressed by the shortage of domestic liquidity if the property were to be sold for money instead of vouchers. Vouchers can be preferred only if the major part of the state-owned assets are to be distributed in one go. Transparency in distribution should be given priority over economic efficiency, and one should not be dogmatic about the privatization modalities. Privatization should be seen as one of the devices of economic transformation and certainly not the only one.

In fact, privatization policies cannot be separated from other economic policies such as liberalization, deregulation and demonopolization. Nor can the economic, sociocultural and political goals attached to privatization be achieved simultaneously. Rapid privatization can cause deterioration of the macroeconomic environment, while too slow privatization might become a victim of a deteriorating sociopolitical environment. As such, the need of the hour is to strike the right balance between the size and speed of privatization in post-communist societies.

7
Privatization in the Developing World

The spread of privatization within liberal democracies, post-communist societies, authoritarian or military regimes alike is really remarkable, and more surprising is the rapidity with which this phenomenon has unfolded across the world. It is rare in history for any economic and monetary policy to catch up so quickly in the developed and the developing world alike, as has privatization (*Financial Times*, 16 September 1987). But it remains a puzzle as to why so many countries took to nationalization prior to 1980, and why they took a somersault only during the 1980s and 1990s? Privatization policies and practices cannot be explained simply in terms of domestic politics or requirements. The dynamics of privatization have to be explained in terms of the international context – political, economic and sociological.

The international context

Although each country occupies a distinct position in the international arena, and its patterns of behaviour and outcomes are affected by domestic politics and economics, the widespread and rapid programmes and policies such as privatization cannot be explained without analysing the comparative behaviour of various other countries across the world (Keohane, 1984: 15). To John Ikenberry, there can be three ways of understanding an international phenomenon:

1. Different countries may react to different kinds of problems and the policy outcomes may have a common appearance by chance. We cannot call it a movement.
2. There may be common factors responsible for certain economic and political changes, but various countries may not interact with, learn from or induce change in other countries, they may simply react to a common underlying set of stimuli.

3. Different countries may or may not face similar problems but they may try to copy certain policies through interaction with other countries (Suleiman and Waterbury, 1990: 90).

The privatization phenomenon cannot be explained in terms of a unidimensional movement. Different countries may have different reasons for adopting the privatization policy. Although the decline in economic growth and increase in expenditures, the expansion of the welfare state in general and the public sector in particular, necessitated a shift in economic management in favour of privatization in most countries belonging to the developed world, yet the fiscal crisis cannot be termed as the main cause of the single policy response in terms of privatization. Technological changes also played a major role in providing an impetus to the privatization drive in advanced economies functioning on a competitive basis at the international level. For instance, the fall in costs of advanced technology in telecommunications forced the three industrial giants (United States, United Kingdom and Japan) to seek opportunities across borders by putting pressure on various governments to deregulate their economies (Vickers and Wright, 1989).

Besides fiscal and technological pressures, political interests also propelled the debate on privatization in advanced economies. With changing circumstances at the national and international level, the mechanisms of state policy towards the public sector also changed. Not long ago, Keynesian social democracy became the vantage point and the Keynesian policy of state management had important influences on the US bureaucracy. During 1945–70, Keynesian ideas dominated the economic and political policies of industrial nations; they influenced the agreements reached at Bretton Woods, and were soon transmitted to the developing world. While Turkey adopted the concept of import substitution industrialization (ISI) long before the Economic Commission on Latin America (ECLA) came into being, many other developing countries adopted the same under the influence of Soviet industrialization. As long as it suited the elite, nationalization remained in vogue. When the leaders found it difficult or unadvantageous to continue with the old model, they were indulged into new coalition building.

Even if coalition building is not regarded as one of the goals of privatization, it became the necessary ingredient for its implementation (Ikenberry, 1992: 94). The most obvious mechanism of coalition building can be seen in British privatization in the form of people's capitalism. Serious efforts were also made to engage voters, workers and domestic investors in the privatization programmes in advanced economies. In the developing world, on the other hand, the threats from privileged groups (politicians, businessmen and bureaucrats) created major obstacles, making it imperative to create new bases of support to make privatization programmes a success.

As such, from the point of view of the political elites both nationalization and privatization can be seen as necessary political strategies to gain popular support. Both the expansion and contraction of the state's role in economic management in general, and the public sector in particular, involved coalition building. While nationalization involved government employees and beneficiaries of state-subsidies and public services, privatization involves capitalist entrepreneurs and technocrats. Various organizations have also played a crucial role in popularizing the very idea of privatizatizon as a cherished goal.

From the developed to the developing world

Primarily because of the media focus and close attention being paid to privatization as an instrument of economic and political management in the developed world, the developing world has also tried to emulate privatization despite having an altogether different sociocultural and economic millieu than that prevailing in advanced economies (Table 7.1). Three models can be advanced for the diffusion of privatization policies in the developing world, (1) external inducement, (2) emulation or policy bandwagoning and (3) social learning. External inducement refers to the role of external pressures from international aid-donors and lending agencies such as the World Bank, IMF and the US Agency for International Development to pursue privatization as a national goal. Such external pressures can be implicit or explicit and vary from overt coercion to trade sanctions.

In the Philippines, for instance, external agencies played a crucial role in creating a consensus around the goals of privatization and market-oriented policies. The IMF, World Bank and Asian Development Bank played an important role in collecting information on the poor performance of SOEs and in developing reform programmes in terms of ceilings on public borrowings and transfers to the public sector (Haggard, 1988: 103). Privatization served the political purpose of the varied interests by severing ties with the Marcos' supporters and strengthening ties with those of Aquino. A nexus was formed among the external agencies, state officials and private groups. Sometimes the national elite actually welcomed external pressures to strengthen their domestic position.

Mostly, the developing economies emulated the privatization policies and programmes of the advanced economies hoping for quick political and economic dividends. Usually innovations from the core nations find an easy breakthrough into nations belonging to the periphery in the wake of international competition (Hall, 1988: 139), under which political and economic policy innovations prompt other nations to emulate them at the earliest opportunity. Those policies are likely to be emulated more that have a direct or immediate bearing on international standing. Some countries may adopt a policy of wait and see before joining the bandwagon. While Canada adopted the privatization policy in early 1980s fascinated by the electoral successes of the Conservative Party in the UK, Thailand on the

Table 7.1 Sharp increases in privatization activity: major worldwide sales of state-owned enterprises and state participations

	1988		*1989*		*1990*		*1991*		*1992*	
	Number of transactions	*$millions*	*Number of transactions*	*$millions*	*Number of transactions*	*$millions*	*Number of transactions*	*$millions*	*Number of transactions*	*$millions*
Developed world	...	36 773	39	20 945	...	17 997	...	31 058	...	24 398
Australia	...	1450	2	87	–	–	2	1620	2	1297
Austria	3	569	3	315	1	55	1	35	1	162
Canada	...	1962	3	824	4	990	3	713	5	1217
Denmark	–	–	–	–	1	700	–	–	–	–
Finland	2	303	1	107	–	–	–	–	–	–
France	1	360	–	–	–	–	1	376	2	1353
Germany	3	1333	1	237	*	1340	*	8075	*	16 350
Italy	1	840	2	987	–	–	–	–	2	1566
Ireland	–	–	–	–	–	–	2	489	–	–
Japan	1	22 800	–	–	–	–	–	–	–	–
Netherlands	–	–	4	2100	–	–	2	150	1	100
New Zealand	6	1846	3	869	7	3803	–	–	5	1052
Norway	–	–	–	–	2	127	–	–	–	–
South Africa	–	–	3	1435	–	–	–	–	–	–
Spain	2	810	2	1465	2	132	2	252	–	–
Sweden	–	–	1	3820	–	–	–	–	1	263
United Kingdom	1	4500	14	8699	...	10 850	7	19 348	5	1038
Developing world	...	2457	20	3817	35	7337	...	17 424	...	23 260
Argentina	–	–	–	–	4	2119	2	1022	8	6200
Brazil	*	250	1	8	1	44	4	2189	8	2150
Chile	1	170	4	295	–	–	–	–	–	–
China	–	–	–	–	–	–	–	–	9	543
Colombia	–	–	–	–	–	–	1	52	–	–
Czech Republic	–	–	–	–	–	–	–	–	7	361
Greece	–	–	–	–	1	42	4	232	2	648

Table 7.1 (continued)

Hungary	–	–	3	130	1	32	97	180	*	845
India	–	–	–	–	–	–	–	–	*	261
Israel	1	95	1	53	1	74	–	–	1	235
Jamaica	1	19	1	42	1	42	1	42	1	23
Kenya	1	8	–	–	1	12	–	–	–	–
Malaysia	–	–	–	–	2	928	1	190	5	1619
Mexico	4	1915	1	140	4	2410	12	9400	10	6374
Nigeria	–	–	–	–	3	13	–	–	–	–
Pakistan	–	–	–	–	–	–	–	–	1	82
Panama	–	–	–	–	–	–	1	23	–	–
Peru	–	–	–	–	–	–	–	–	1	120
Philippines	–	–	1	80	1	325	4	190	1	368
Poland	–	–	–	–	1	32	*	350	*	309
Portugal	–	–	4	494	5	796	5	1014	4	1023
Puerto Rico	–	–	–	–	–	–	–	–	1	142
Russian Federation	–	–	–	–	–	–	–	–	1	50
Singapore	–	–	–	–	3	177	3	67	–	–
South Korea	–	–	1	2100	–	–	–	–	–	–
Sri Lanka	–	–	–	–	–	–	1	13	–	–
Taiwan	–	–	1	285	–	–	2	405	2	1363
Thailand	–	–	1	85	–	–	–	–	1	240
Turkey	–	–	1	105	4	267	–	–	2	304
Uruguay	–	–	–	–	1	15	–	–	–	–
Venezuela	–	–	–	–	1	9	3	2055	–	–
Total Worldwide	...	39 230	59	24 762	...	25 334	...	48 482	...	47 658

Source: *Privatization International* (Special Issue).

Notes: * Number not available because of block sales of small enterprises or government participations.

... Indicates data not available.

– Indicates no privatizations occurred.

other hand preferred to adopt a cautious approach (*Financial Times*, 16 September 1987: 8).

Emulation is an important process through which economic and political policies spread across the world. Technological innovations and fast communications seem to have electrified the speed of emulation in the current era. US hegemony has also played a crucial role in spreading the ideology of privatization across the world in the name of ending other ideologies. The idea of privatization has spread to different parts of the world in the same way as the philosophy of Keynes became diffused. In fact, the US exercised direct influence on the economic policies of other major countries not because of its intellectual superiority but because of its hegemonic position.

The fiscal crisis in most advanced economies and developing countries following the oil-crisis of 1971 provided the right opportunity for experiments with privatization in the developed world. Leaders found their own pretexts for pursuing privatization policies in their own national frameworks. Local elites were generally found susceptible to demonstrative effects of successful economic and political policies abroad.

Surprisingly, there is very little social learning involved in the adaptation of privatization programmes and policies in the developing world. Social learning amounts to the spread of new knowledge that underlies policy-making at the international level. Social learning does not amount to a mere spread of knowledge among intellectuals or technocrats, but in addition include the spread of knowledge among policy-makers and other influential groups. Keynesian ideas were widely spread among policy-makers and politicians in the industrialized nations although this diffusion was never straightforward. Nor could we predict what innovations in socioeconomic and political policies would click in secondary countries and what would not. Nor can the patterns of diffusion or the processes through which the spread of innovation takes place be predecided (Ikenberry, 1990: 99).

Divergent expectations

Undoubtedly, the scope for privatization in a given society is set by socioeconomic conditions, the political culture and the management expertise available therein. It may be easier for those countries to reduce the role of the state in the public sector which have accorded considerable legitimacy to the private sector. But it may be difficult to reduce state intervention in those countries which have been emphasizing the redistributive role of the state in pursuit of social justice. Privatization becomes difficult in LDCs because it substantially alters the very means through which the state intervenes in an economy. It would not be inappropriate to say that in advanced economies, the state did not have to indulge in the business of privatization under pressures from abroad. Nor was privatization an outcome of structural adjustments. In these economies, privatization was guided more by sociopolitical constraints than economic ones. It was an outcome of the new consensus formed in favour of reducing the role of the state by taking as much load off the government as possible.

The most important factor which inspired the process of privatization in advanced economies was the question of the welfare state (Suleiman and Waterbury, 1990: 8). During 1945–70, the conservative and the socialist governments in the UK, France, Greece, Spain, Portugal and Japan were equally committed to a positive role of the state in the market. A welfare state, in the sense of government committed to certain minimum standards of well-being became the bulwark of political stability. During the era of sustained economic growth it was possible to treat the welfare state as an appendage of economic growth. At that time, the focus used to be on resource inputs as symbols of progress and commitment, to the neglect of outputs.

However, by the end of 1970 it became clear to the leaders and policy-makers in advanced economies that the social policy commitments made during the decades of economic growth could no longer be sustained. Growth prospects and competitiveness seemed to suffer on account of excessive costs and rigidities imposed by state provision of the market. Soon the public sector became the easy scapegoat for the economic ills confronting the industrialized countries and privatization seemed to provide a ready-made solution. Shaken by the crisis of confidence in view of the economic decline, leaders found it difficult to fulfil their obligations towards public well-being. They found it advantageous to shift some of the responsibilities and, if possible, costs too, to the private and non-governmental sector in order to escape from public criticism of poor performance. They hoped to find some relief in a retreat of the state in the form of privatization.

In the case of the developing world, privatization does not necessarily symbolize the triumph of the market. At the most it can be seen as a harbinger of the new phase in which the state has to redefine the scope and modalities of its intervention in the economy. Quite paradoxically, liberalization, deregulation and privatization simply cannot be carried out successfully in developing economies in the absence of a strong state. Privatization as a goal is accepted mainly with a motive of strengthening the state in financial terms. Governments may resort to liquidation of public enterprises and public assets primarily with an objective of reaping quick gains and once-and-for-all resource transfer to the national exchequer.

While the long-term goals of privatization in developing countries could be improving productivity, increasing economic wealth and shedding the redistributive role of the state, the short-term impetus towards economic reforms is often derived from the compulsion to reduce external debt and deficits in the public budget in order to maintain creditworthiness, access to foreign capital and foreign investments. Governments in the developing world have only two options, (1) improve public enterprise performance through economic and administrative reform, or (2) reduce public enterprise debts through liquidation and privatization (Table 7.2).

In most developing countries the approach towards privatization has been primarily negative (Bienen and Waterbury, 1989: 619); it is generally seen as unloading loss-making SOEs rather than building viable enterprises for a more vibrant economy. Surprisingly, only a few decades ago, public enterprises in the developing world were intended to achieve similar motives which underlie the privatization movement now – reduction in fiscal drain, replenishment of exchequer, attraction of private investment, response to pressures from international donors and lending agencies, ideological commitments, economic development and general well-being of the public (Humphrey, 1990: 8). These also aimed at achieving the goals of economic sovereignty, industrial catching up, income redistribution and enhancing the national strength. The short-term and pragmative goals included controlling inflation and improving credibility at the international level.

In developing countries it is not easy to reverse the trend of state-retrenchment which took place through explicit or implicit social pacts. Here, too, the Keynesian entente took the form of various strategies in terms of alliances with politicians, industrialists, civil servants, organized labour, military and trade unions. The policies of liberalization, devaluation and privatization can threaten the existence of these very coalitions. Even military and authoritarian regimes are not free from such coalitions. As such, it is not easy to break with the past in order to promote economic reforms, nor can developing countries bear the legalization of the activities of black markets or parallel economies. Privatization in these countries, therefore, especially in the LDCs, may increase when the economy contracts, but the state sector may expand when the economy expands (Wilson, 1988: 27).

In LDCs, privatization aims at promoting export-led growth, but whether private capital markets are thin or wide economic disparities prevail, and privatization can prove advantageous only to the very few at the cost of the many. These few may attempt to learn how to compete and survive in international markets if they are provided support by the state in terms of cheap credit, export subsidies and lucrative dividends. But their efforts may be highly vulnerable to the rapid shifts in international markets, failure to protect or expand one's niche and changes in interest rates. Some of the newly-privatized firms may even become bankrupt in their attempts to sail the ocean in a small boat and no prior experience. In such situations, governments will soon have to involve themselves in rescue operations, whether they like it or not. For instance, the Chilean government had to face such an experience.

But once a government takes an enterprise into its fold, it may become very difficult to dislodge it. As such, we can only expect cyclic patterns in terms of expansion or contraction of state ownership in the developing world. The extent of these cycles may be smaller and over longer periods in the developed

Table 7.2 Balance of payments developments, 1985–92

Year	*Balance of current account excluding official transfers*			*Balance of capital account* & net errors and omissions (US$ billions)*			*Changes in reserves***		
	Lt. Am.	*Asia*	*C.E.R.C.*	*Lt. Am.*	*Asia*	*C.E.R.C.*	*Lt. Am.*	*Asia*	*C.E.R.C.*
1985	–5.5	–18.7	–1.2	6.5	22.7	–0.6	–1.0	–4.0	–0.6
1986	–19.8	–1.1	–0.1	13.2	25.5	1.6	6.6	–24.4	–1.7
1987	–11.8	–14.8	–2.1	15.0	24.7	–2.2	–3.2	–39.5	0.1
1988	–13.4	–2.6	–5.9	5.7	8.7	–2.7	7.7	–11.3	–3.2
1989	–10.1	–8.1	–2.7	12.7	17.1	1.9	–2.6	–9.0	–4.6
1990	–8.5	–10.0	–0.2	23.6	31.7	–0.5	–15.1	–21.7	0.7
1991	–20.5	–10.2	–6.6	38.9	48.9	8.7	–18.4	–38.7	–2.1
1992	–34.6	–25.2	–1.2	53.4	46.3	3.3	–18.8	–21.1	–2.1

Notes: * A negative sign indicates a deficit in the pertinent account; ** a negative sign indicates an increase; Lt. Am. = Latin America; C.E.R.C. = Central European Reform Countries (Croatia, Czech Republic, Hungary, Poland, Slovak Republic, Slovenia, Estonia, Latvia, Lithuania, Albania, Bosnia-Herzegovina, Bulgaria, Macedonia, Romania, Serbia & Montenegro, Belarus, Russian Federation and Ukraine).

Source: *World Economic Outlook*, IMF (1993a), May; in R. Holzmann and C. Thimann (1993), 'Pressure to Adjust: Consequences for the OECD Countries from Reforms in Eastern Europe', Vienna, 18 October, annexure I, table A1.

world in comparison with the developing world, keeping in view the prevalence of SOEs on a massive scale in the latter.

Contrast with post-communist societies

We find fundamental differences in the context, rationale, modalities, priorities, problems and speed of privatization experiences in post-communist societies – the so-called second world – and countries belonging to the developing world – the so called third world (now also known as the 'majority world'). While privatization involved the transformation of the entire economy in post-communist societies, it involved only substantial parts of the economies in Asia, Africa and Latin America. The role of the state sector in agriculture in the developing world amounted to a mere 0.5 per cent (United Nations, *World Development Report*, 1983: 50), though it varied from 5.25 per cent in mining, manufacturing, transports and communication to 75–100 per cent in electricity, gas and water. We also find significant differences in the transition from non-market to market economies and from a pre- or distorted market to a market economy. Developing countries had an edge over post-communist societies mainly because the former had at least some experience, institutions and legal structures related to a market economy (Table 7.3).

It is easier to liberalize or deregulate economies in the developing world by decontrolling interest rates and eliminating credit charges where proper banking systems prevail. But it was very difficult to do so in the communist societies where banks happened to be only cashiers' windows for the SOEs; they had virtually no control over their lending policies. In the post-communist societies, banks still continued lending to SOEs, without consideration of their creditworthiness. Although we find banks' behaviour changing in developing countries in the wake of economic reforms and

Table 7.3 Growth of the world economy, 1988–92

	1988	*1989*	*1990*	*1991*	*1992*
World output	4.3	3.0	1.0	0.0	2.1
Developed market economies	4.3	3.3	2.4	1.4	3.0
Eastern Europe and former Soviet Union	3.7	1.4	6.3	9.5	4.5
Developing countries	5.0	3.0	2.9	3.5	5.0
Western Conglomerate	0.8	1.1	0.7	7.5	3.0
Africa	2.1	3.3	3.4	3.0	3.0
West Asia	1.1	2.4	0.0	0.5	0.7
South and East Asia	8.7	6.0	6.1	5.5	6.0
China	11.33	3.3	4.8	5.5	6.0
Mediterranean	1.4	1.0	0.7	2.0	4.0

Source: United Nations (1991) *World Economic Survey*: 1.

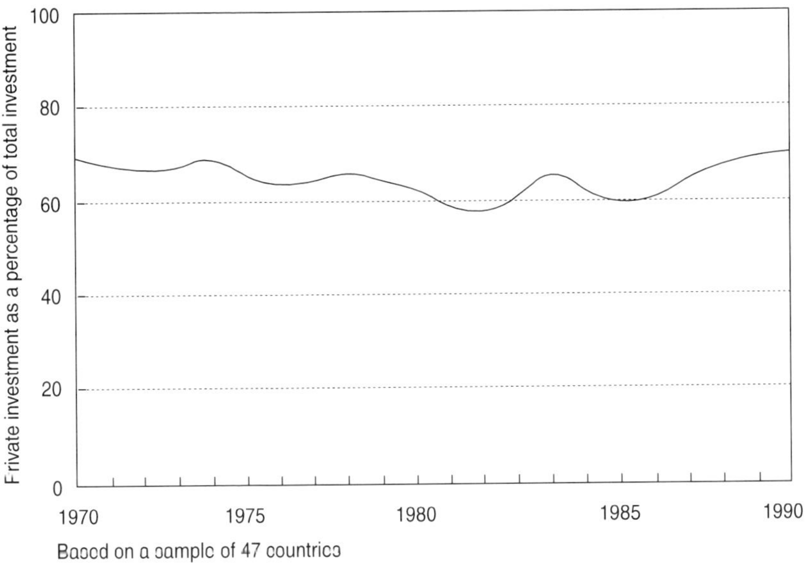

Figure 7.1 Private investment in developing countries, 1970–91
Source: United Nations (1993) *Human Development Report*: 52.

structural adjustments, in some post-communist societies the old patterns of behaviour still prevail between state-owned banks and their old state-owned clients (Winiecki, 1992: 72).

In the developing world, SOEs behaved in a distorted way owing to policy constraints. Quite interestingly, we find the principles of the market economy prevailing in the black markets or parallel economies, and we also find the existence of both private capital and capitalists (Figure 7.1). We find people or groups experienced, competent and wealthy enough to take control of the small and medium-sized SOEs if privatized, but it was just not possible to find such people or groups in the open market except the communist *nomenklatura*, which were usually discredited and no longer tolerated by the masses.

Yet, the post-communist societies also had certain advantages in terms of political economy over developing countries. Their economic and political actors were keen to resort to privatization, while most of leaders in developing countries have found it hard to accept the privatization option at the mental level, even if they are found propogating it themselves under domestic or international pressure. The interests of such self-seeking leaders in a predatory state do not reconcile easily with those of the masses, so they adopt privatization as a last resort only when they realize that the costs of not privatizing can be greater than the costs of privatizing and liberalizing the economy under their control. Deepak Lal tried to explain this with the help of the 'Laffer curve' of intervention. To him, at a certain stage, intervention diminishes the extent of state control instead of increasing it (Lal, 1992: 135–55).

While the new leaders in the post-communist societies had no other choice but to resort to rapid privatization, leaders in developing countries could afford to go slow or adopt a policy of wait and see. Usually there was a consensus in post-communist societies for a shift to a market economy and rapid privatization. In most developing countries, however, leaders had to confront ideological onslaughts both from their party members averse to the risks involved and opposition parties and pressure groups alike. They became entrenched because of the great risks involved in either case – adopting or not adopting a privatization policy.

In developing countries, nationalist feelings were also mixed with ideological ones, and the private sector was also found ambivalent in most cases. They neither wanted to face competition from abroad, nor were they prepared to forego the advantages enjoyed by them from state contracts. Privatization could lead to feuds among leaders, businessmen and bureaucrats in developing countries, while it proved to be a unifying factor in the case of post-communist societies.

State-owned enterprises in developing countries

During the 1950s–1970s, nationalization was the rage in some developing countries. International aid donors, such as the IMF and the World Bank encouraged the setting up of public enterprises in these countries, and their establishment and expansion became a major characteristic of the developing economies. Both left and right-wing regimes, poor and rich, liberal and military regimes intervened in the national economy.

The state turned entrepreneur not for ideological reasons but for promoting growth, and planning and state-owned enterprises were considered to be the main pillars of development. Most developing countries were ill-equipped to operate in the modern and competitive economic scenario that emerged after the Second World War. They had inherited an economic system that had served the interests of colonial powers. Moreover, the tradition of direct governmental participation and control of the economy also prevailed in these developing societies.

The economies in these developing countries were quite elementary and fragile, heavily agricultural and oriented towards the production and processing of raw materials (Table 7.4); hardly suitable to meet the demands of economic development on a rapid scale. The private sector was either undeveloped or underdeveloped, and few indigenous persons with an aptitude for management were usually absorbed by the bureaucracy itself.

Furthermore, the private sector was essentially commercial and not entrepreneural in its approach. As such, it was either unable or unwilling to

Table 7.4 National income accounts in the developed and developing world, 1993

	GDP (US$ billions)	Agriculture (as % of GDP)	Industry (as % of GDP)	Services (as % of GDP)	Consumption		Gross domestic investments (as % of GNP)	Gross domestic savings (as % of GNP)	Central govt. expenditure (as % of GNP)	Human development index rank
					Private (as % of GDP)	Govt. (as % of GDP)				
Developed world										
Australia	289.4	3	29	67	63	18	20	19	28	11
Austria	182.1	2	35	62	55	19	25	26	40	13
Canada	477.5	...	...	...	61	22	18	18	26	1
Denmark	117.6	4	27	69	52	26	14	21	46	17
Finland	74.1	5	31	64	57	23	14	20	45	6
France	1251.7	3	29	69	61	19	18	20	46	7
Germany	1910.8	1	38	61	58	20	22	22	34	18
Italy	991.4	3	32	65	62	18	17	20	53	20
Ireland	43.0	8	10	82	56	16	14	28	47	19
Japan	4214.2	2	41	57	58	10	30	33	...	3
Netherlands	309.2	4	28	68	61	15	19	24	54	4
New Zealand	43.7	...	...	...	60	15	21	24	37	14
Norway	103.4	3	35	62	52	22	20	26	...	5
South Africa	...	...	...	...	...	...	...	...	...	...
Spain	478.6	...	...	...	63	18	20	19	35	10
Sweden	166.7	2	31	67	55	28	13	17	54	9
United Kingdom	819.0	2	33	65	64	22	15	14	43	16
Developing world										
Argentina	255.6	6	31	63	84	...	18	...	...	30
Brazil	444.2	11	37	52	79	...	19	21	26	58
Chile	43.7	...	...	...	66	10	26	24	23	33
China	425.6	19	48	33	51	9	41	40	9	108
Colombia	54.1	16	35	50	70	12	22	18	...	49

Table 7.4 (continued)

Czech Republic	31.6	6	40	54	54	26	17	20	41	37
Greece	63.2	18	32	50	71	19	20	10	13	21
Hungary	38.1	6	28	66	62	27	20	11	...	46
India	225.4	31	27	41	66	11	24	24	17	135
Israel	...	...	...	...	...	...	...	...	...	...
Jamaica	3.8	8	41	51	61	13	35	26	...	86
Kenya	4.7	29	18	54	66	13	16	21	29	128
Malaysia	64.4	...	...	...	49	13	33	38	27	53
Mexico	343.5	8	28	63	75	9	22	16	...	48
Nigeria	31.3	34	43	24	63	18	15	19	...	137
Pakistan	46.4	25	25	50	74	14	21	12	24	134
Panama	6.6	10	18	92	59	17	25	24	32	43
Peru	41.1	11	43	46	76	8	19	16	14	91
Philippines	54.1	22	33	45	76	9	24	16	18	95
Poland	85.9	6	39	55	65	22	16	13	...	56
Portugal	85.7	...	...	...	65	17	27	18	42	35
Puerto Rico	...	...	...	...	...	...	...	...	...	...
Russian Federation	329.4	9	51	39	52	15	26	32	...	57
Singapore	55.2	...	37	63	43	9	44	47	20	34
South Korea	330.8	7	43	50	54	11	34	35	17	29
Sri Lanka	9.4	25	26	50	75	9	25	16	27	89
Taiwan	...	...	...	...	...	...	...	...	...	...
Thailand	124.9	10	39	81	54	10	40	36	16	52
Turkey	156.4	15	30	55	65	13	27	22	26	84
Uruguay	13.1	9	27	64	72	14	16	14	29	32
Venezuela	60.0	5	42	53	73	9	19	18	19	44

Source: United nations (1996) *Human Development Report*: 184–5, 207.
Notes: ... Indicates data not available.

meet the challenges of a modern economy. The business sector was also regarded with distrust and disdain in most traditional societies; they were at the lower edge of the social hierarchy and often looked down upon for being exploitative and profit-seeking.

Under these circumstances, public interests were best served by placing the economy in the hands of the government. Therefore, a number of public enterprises were purposefully created to generate revenues, redistribute income, create jobs, promote regional development, collect monopoly rents, develop infrastructure, fill the gaps where the private sector was either unwilling or unable to enter, take over sick units from the private sector, counter capitalist monopolies, nationalize foreign or indigenous enterprises in the public interest, strengthen economic sovereignty against multinationals, or protect national security through direct intervention in areas of strategic importance (Bienen and Waterbury, 1989: 618).

Most developing countries set up public enterprises to fulfil as many of these objectives as possible, although in some cases the objectives were either ambivalent or conflicting. Some of the enterprises were specially created to provide particular goods and services or to serve particular regions or people. As such, they were used as instruments of social and economic policy. The all-pervasive and widespread SOEs were supposed to reach commanding heights in due course.

It is now being held that the era of wholesale expansion of public enterprises has come to an end; there is instead a drive towards privatization and globalization of the economy. But very few governments seem to have taken this drive willingly. Rather, they are forced to do so because of the dismal performance of the state-owned enterprises in general. They could neither generate sufficient resources for future development nor fulfil their social obligations efficiently. Most often, there were conflicts within their assigned roles and prevailing socioeconomic conditions (Bremer, 1986: 7–8).

Their ability to perform efficiently was affected further when they were manipulated for political purposes – to weaken the opposition, pay off political cronies or take as much personal advantage as possible. A state-owned enterprise offered ample opportunities for in-house corruption owing to the highly bureaucratic set-up in most developing countries. Sometimes, very ambitious plans were launched during the first euphoric years following independence. Many governments indulged in tasks beyond their capacities; they made extravagant promises which could not be met. The challenges were big and the resources were meagre or inadequate. Political and economic instability also inhibited private investment, both domestic and foreign, a situation bound to result in underachievement, with consequent disillusionment and cynicism.

Gradually, the SOEs became a substantial drain on the exchequer. Even if they were able to satisfy the needs of those for whom they were created, the costs involved were monumental. In fact there are already well-documented stories of gross inefficiency, huge losses, overblown bureaucracies, unimaginative management and widespread corruption pervading the public sectors and the SOEs. Though some SOEs operated efficiently and generated profits, most lost money and the entire system created a tremendous drain on already tight national budgets and scarce resources.

In those cases, where the state took over sick units from the private sector, it only increased the problems by institutionalizing inefficiency, compounding the losses and adding corruption to the list (Wortzel and Wortzel, 1989: 633). Faced with the poor performance of the SOEs and beset by the burgeoning need for more and more funds, many governments began looking for alternatives. They found a timely solution in privatization.

Rationale for privatization

Liberalization, deregulation and privatization, in the context of the developing world, amount to the transformation of the economy rather than the simple establishment of a balance of payment equilibrium by curbing domestic demand and stimulating exports. Slashing government spending, coupled with increases in taxation and controls over the supply of credit to investing bodies and consumers, were some of the measures adopted towards structural adjustment with a definite motive to promote market-based forces on the one hand, and to reduce state intervention in the economy on the other. The agricultural sector was expected to play a major role in the structural adjustment process by boosting output and foreign exchange.

The shift towards a market economy took place only during the late 1970s and 1980s against a background of global recession and a severe external debt crisis which began to emerge during 1979–81. The fundamental changes in the economic and political strategies adopted by developing countries in the last ten to fifteen years amount to a greater reliance on market forces, a progressive withdrawal of the government form economic decision-making in general and productive activities in particular, and an increased openness towards direct foreign investment and strengthened efforts towards promoting exports (Economic and Social Commission for Asia and Pacific, UNO, 1995: 1).

With the swing of the pendulum, the developing countries started competing with one another in rejecting the past. Policy reforms leading to a more liberalized economy in the CIS, China and Eastern Europe, which were ideologically committed to public ownership of the means of production and distribution, also provided a fillip to the privatization drive in the developing countries. It became quite common to argue that development could be best achieved in these societies by freeing the market and letting invisible hands do their work (Olson, 1984: 39–40).

In the course of political and economic debates, the Asian Tigers were usually referred to as symbols of remarkable economic growth achieved essentially through large and active private sectors. In contrast to Japan, Singapore, Taiwan, South Korea, Hong Kong and Malaysia, countries like India and Tanzania were viewed as heavily statist and slow-moving (Shackleton, 1986: 434). Soon yesterday's truth became today's heresy. In the past, pervasive public control of the economy was thought to be essential for social progress and decentralization of power, it also aimed to keep foreign domination out. Now the recipe prescribed was just the reverse (Cardos, 1991: 35).

During the 1950s, development economists viewed state intervention in the economy as essential. The intellectual tradition of Keynes, Prebisch and Rosenstein Rodan encouraged the belief that government coordination of economic activities led to successful economic development. But the new models of increasing returns and endogenous growth reject earlier beliefs (Short, 1984: 110–14).

In an interesting econometric study of 73 developing countries, it was pointed out that state intervention significantly reduced a country's economic growth, other factors being constant (Singh, 1986: 434–5). The most important factor for the poor performance of public enterprises was less-efficient resource allocation associated with over-protective regulation on the part of governments, especially in matters related to trade and exports.

When regulations and barriers to trade distorted the price mechanism, artificial political advantages guided the economic policies. When profits depended upon government policy and not on market forces, positive returns could only be achieved by devoting more efforts towards interacting with policy-makers, bureaucrats and local elites than by resorting to efficient production. When economic policies allocated resources at less than their actual price, the resources were often merely withheld. This was bound to lead to a system of patronage allowing governments to extend economic favours to the few in exchange for wider political allegiance. The situation was found to be more or less similar in most developing countries.

In the 1990s, privatization came to be recommended on the grounds that private ownership is more efficient in terms of resource allocation than public ownership, owing to the different incentive structures. The case for privatization in developing countries is two-fold: (1) it allows governments to offload loss-making enterprises and bolster efforts towards rationalization of economic relations, and (2) dissatisfaction with the performance of the SOEs. Governments are no longer seen as factory managers, they are seen as watchdogs.

The growth of the private sector in many developing countries over the last four decades has also provided a necessary boost to the privatization drive. In many developing countries the private sector has now acquired greater capacities for handling a wide range of sophisticated economic activities than ever before; financial and human resources, though still in short-supply, are better than before. Moreover, bilateral and multilateral donor agencies have also put subtle pressures on developing countries to adopt privatization as an economic policy. In most cases the donors have been more ideological in their inclinations than the recipients, who tend to wrestle with economic problems on more pragmatic terms.

In fact, the increasing pressures within developing countries from the rising middle class for consumer goods and higher living standards also accelerated the interests of the leaders in economic reforms in general and privatization in particular. While the examples of East and Southeast Asia boosted their morale, the disintegration of the former USSR and turmoil in Eastern Europe eroded their confidence in central planning as the principal tool of economic development (Economic and Social Commission for Asia and Pacific, 1995: 17). During the 1960s and 1970s, the average annual growth rate of countries like Sri Lanka, Nepal and Bangladesh was much lower than those of East and Southeast Asian countries. After undertaking the tedious exercise of economic liberalization, the gap between East and Southeast Asian countries on the one hand, and South Asian countries on the other, has narrowed to some extent.

Techniques of privatization

The general norm prevailing in developing economies seem to be, 'when the going gets tough privatize it'. Privatization, in the present context, refers not only to the transfer of ownership of public assets but also the abandonment of some of the functions that the government had taken upon itself in the recent past. Reduction in the size and role of the public sector and an emphasis on price and markets as allocative mechanisms also amount to privatization. In fact, developing countries are resorting to various techniques of privatization ranging from divestiture to marginalization.

Usually the discussion on privatization has been restricted to the transfer of ownership of public enterprises from the private sector. But this amounts to mere explicit privatization. In the context of developing countries, implicit privatization can be perhaps more important and relevant. Implicit privatization may be defined as yielding a larger place in economic space to the private sector than before, without transforming the ownership of the public assets as such. This includes handing over some of the government's functions and activities to the private sector or market.

The usual practice of implicit privatization involves allowing the private sector into areas hitherto considered the domain of the public sector, such as generating electricity, building roads and bridges, making steel, and so on. Another area could be handing over some of the responsibilities to the private sector that are directly linked to the government's finances earlier. It implies not only the transfer of certain responsibilities, but also potential revenues to private agents.

Implicit privatization can take some other forms also. For example, the state may decide to scrap cash subsidies to promote exports and introduce freely tradeable exim scrips, the premiums on which would serve as an incentive to exporters. By exim scrip we imply an import licence issued to an exporter for part value of his exports as a prize. The exporter can hawk this in the market and pocket the premium. It replaces the former cash compensatory support which was a drain on the budget; now it is the importer who pays the subsidy to the exporter. In addition, it keeps imports tied to the growth in exports (Kalra, 1992: 17).

A further incentive to exporters could be provided through devaluation. As such, the government can abdicate its role in boosting exports through macro adjustments and pave the way for the private sector to come forward. Withdrawal of subsidies could provide another example. It is possible to attract private investment either by providing guarantees of returns or letting the pricing system take care of returns (Ramana, 1991: 14).

The experiences in privatization in developing countries indicate that transfer of ownership is neither necessary nor sufficient for achieving efficient allocation and utilization of resources. In most developing countries the enhancing freedom of entry and intensity of competition do not prevail. Furthermore, there are multiple constraints ranging from profitability to capital market limitations that continue to impede the implementation of divestiture – the most common variant of privatization (Killick and Commander, 1989: 1465). Many public enterprises in developing countries are, in fact, loss-making, and divestiture in such cases is only a remote possibility unless and until it is accompanied by market and tax concessions (Table 7.5).

Where ownership transfer remains a problematic option, two other less-visible methods are likely to be employed, the most common of which is liquidation or closing down. Liquidation may prove difficult for a government because it involves admitting failure. It may also involve establishing alternatives. Selling public assets at throw away prices may also invite severe public criticism, but, nevertheless, liquidation helps in putting an end to the continuing losses while adding something to the exchequer.

Marginalization, on the other hand, may prove to be politically less volatile than divestiture or liquidation. It involves freezing or reducing the budget operations of a public sector enterprise, while slowly building up the private sector as a replacement. It may be effective in the long term but costly in the short term, since two entities need to be supported simultaneously during the early stages.

The techniques of privatization may vary from case to case and country to country. They may take the form of partial divestiture involving the sale of a particular unit of a particular public sector enterprise, or the sale of a limited percentage of shares. In some cases, the commercial and the administrative functions may be split and the marketing activities privatized. Other arrangements could be contract management, franchising or leasing. Leasing or franchising shift the focus of an enterprise towards a market-driven mode because the lessee or franchise holder is given a free hand to run the enterprise on a commercial basis, even though the government maintains a modicum of influence and certain residual rights.

Although, such mechanisms can enhance the efficiency and profitability of public sector enterprises to some extent, depending upon the degree of autonomy given to the management contractor, the results are nevertheless likely to be limited because of the prevailing bureaucratic environment. Privatization cannot shift the bureaucratic model of public enterprises prevailing in developing countries into a market model *ipso facto*.

Table 7.5 Favourable and unfavourable effects of divestiture

Favourable effects	*Unfavourable effects*
1. Where the enterprises concerned had been loss-making, and where there are no redeeming extra-enterprise(s) circumstances to justify it, taxpayers will benefit from the divestiture	1. If profit-making PSEs are transferred to the private sector, that will have the effect of transferring profit incomes without the corresponding interest charges to private investors
2. Where employees extract high benefits at the expenses of consumers and the government (who is the shareholder), privatization will benefit both the consumer and taxpayers	2. There will in most cases be a loss in employment when the privatized enterprise retrenches labour. Consequently there will be reductions in wage incomes for certain groups of people. On the other hand, in some or in several cases, privatization leads to an increase in employment due to expansion of output
3. Privatization can nullify the subsidies going towards consumers (perhaps in the form of low prices) who do not really deserve them. In fact, it can even lead to the elimination of cross subsidies which may have existed or which could have existed in the future	3. In most cases, the programme of divestiture involves the sale of profit-making enterprises while the loss-making enterprises remain with the government
	4. If a public sector monopoly is converted into a private sector monopoly, the imperfections in pricing and in the distribution of revenues that existed before can and may persist. So can the losses arising form the reform

Source: V.V. Ramanadham (1991) *The Economies of Public Enterprises*: 404–5.

The techniques of privatization vary from country to country and enterprise to enterprise, depending upon the local economy in general and the private sector in particular. A variety of financial methods may be employed to carry out privatization transactions, including loans from official banks or development finance institutions, establishing loan-guarantee programmes in cooperation with private commercial banks, floating shares, converting bonds, creating debt-equity swaps, writing off liabilities, allowing flexibility in the valuation of public sector assets, making the regulatory framework more flexible, encouraging private investment, setting up joint ventures, obtaining binational or multinational financing, and so forth.

Quick versus slow

The rationale for privatization in developing countries implies a model of ecological adaptation by enterprises in response to external stimuli, greater access to private capital, discipline exercised through stockmarkets, the threat or reality of competition in the product market, and so on (Woodward, 1990: 267). It is assumed that the privatization process will automatically lead to financial viability, but the process has revealed some anomalies in this rationale – these may be called the paradoxes of privatization.

The first paradox relates to the speed and process of transformation of an organization and its staff. The second paradox relates to the welcome to be accorded to privatization by the supposed victims, and the third paradox relates to pre-privatization transformation of some of the organizations through restructuring, deregulation and liberalization. The biggest paradox is to find buyers for the loss-making-enterprises in an underdeveloped economy, with a thin capital market and underdeveloped private sector. Yet another paradox lies in privatizing the agricultural sector in traditional societies.

It is generally assumed that public enterprises are staffed with bureaucrats who are more concerned with building empires than economic efficiency. Divorced from market discipline, industrial managers are not sensitive to customers' needs. Under privatization, conditions automatically change, including the change in attitudes towards the work culture. But the rhetoric of privatization may prove to be yet another fashion, rather than a lasting solution to the deep rooted problems of an organization.

The question remains unresolved: should the approach towards privatization be gradual or do the public enterprises need shock therapy. The extent of friction, the ease and speed with which privatization is introduced can be pivotal in making it a grand success or a total failure. Neoclassical economists tend to assume that human adjustments to new situations can be swift; they advocate shock therapy for the command economies if they wish to reap quick economic benefits. They believe that it is impossible to cross over a chasm in two leaps (Sachs, 1991: 4). Some experts, belonging to the Chicago School, also assert that the duration of the pain of transition can be lessened and benefits increased if the essentials of a market system are put into practice quickly (Becker, 1990: 11).

Neoclassical economists tend to assume that people are the same in all societies, cultures and historical situations. As rational beings, they seek to maximize their self-interest, and scrapping undue restrictions can free their entrepreneural spirit and quickly lead to a free economy. But it is one thing to have mercentalism, and quite another to have entrepreneural skills.

Far from having fixed self-interests, individuals are penetrated by institutions and cultures in which they spend their formative years. Besides the quest for profit, there can also be the quest for affection, self-respect and self-expression. People in developing countries may lack the professional spirit depicted by their western counterparts; or they may have formed certain work habits which cannot be easily or quickly modified. These might include working slowly, avoiding undue exertion, avoiding initiative or extra responsibilities, stressing quantity over quality, feather-bedding, using office time for personal activities, bartering office time and materials to gain favours, adopting low-technology approaches, and so on. The transition to a western style of work and competition is unlikely to develop quickly. Rather, all such attempts are likely to be resisted vigorously instead of being incorporated wholeheartedly.

A comparison between Chile and Mexico might lead to a gradualist approach towards privatization. Chile had, in fact, two waves of privatization. The first one was by all accounts a disaster: the government adopted a massive deregulation of the economy accompanied by an equally massive privatization in the first phase. In a few years, the entire Chilean economy collapsed with the banking system leading to disaster. In fact, the lax regulation of the banking sector resulted in an oligopolistic banking system and the concentration of credit in a few hands. The banks provided easy credit to financially weak enterprises under the increasingly leveraged conglomerates owned by these very banks. When these enterprises collapsed, they took the banks with them. This necessitated a second round of privatization, ensuring that government regulatory agencies were in place and all markets were transparent.

The Mexican government, on the other hand, adopted a gradualist approach towards privatization. It closed down unviable enterprises during 1983–85; it adopted a policy of privatizing small and medium-sized enterprises during 1986–88; it undertook the privatization of large-scale enterprises only after 1988. As such, it resorted to privatization in a phased manner.

There is a general tendency among politicians to gain instant credit by announcing all-pervasive, far-reaching and quick reforms. But haste in such matters may lead to breakdown. In fact, the timing of privatization also matters. Privatization involves a lengthy and tedious process, and is beset with technological, financial and legal problems. As such, it is unwise to announce privatization on a massive scale in a hurry. For instance, the Nawaj Sharif government in Pakistan announced a far-reaching programme of privatizing 115 SOEs as quickly as possible. These included 14 chemical manufacturing plants, 7 fertiliser plants, 8 textile mills, 24 vegetable oil plants and 16 bakeries. In all, the government aimed to spin off SOEs yielding revenues worth US$6.5 billion with a total employment of over 100 000 people (Goldstein, 1991: 12). But the privatization movement in Pakistan was hobbled right form the beginning. The industrialists who were expected to be the prime beneficiaries did not turn up when sales were announced. Nor has there been much interest from multinationals. Pakistan's government also failed to lure money out of the huge black economy. In fact, the reserve price was set too high by the bureaucrats who did not want to relinquish their hold on big chunks of the economy, the accompanying patronage and money-making opportunities. Resistance also came from the trade unions against the retrenchment policy; state enterprises in Pakistan employ approximately 2.5 per cent of the total industrial workforce.

This explains the slow pace of privatization in most developing countries. In fact there is more rhetoric than actual implementation of privatization policies and programmes: we find big gaps between policy statements and actual implementation. For instance, in Argentina the Carlos government failed to fulfil its promise of privatizing one company per month. Even under the aggressive programme adopted by the Thatcher government, the UK could not privatize more than five firms per annum on average during the 1980s (Sachs, 1991: 26). The British government followed a pattern in which an enterprise was first prepared for privatization through internal restructuring, followed by valuation by an appropriate authority to get the best price before finally offering it for sale. The whole episode took about a year or so.

In developing countries, where the public sector plays a dominant role, it may take still longer time to privatize an enterprise, and resistance may come from various sections of the society. Developing countries simply cannot privatize as many state-owned enterprises as they would like. Nor can they achieve an extensive privatization programme within the short time periods they would often like. Even after 16 years following the introduction of private pension in Chile, citizens do not understand its meaning fully. Nor can they comprehend the outcomes and consequences (*The Economist*, 14 December 1996: 52).

Before launching a privatization drive formally, governments in developing countries have to cross various hurdles. This requires a gamut of policies – sorting out legal and constitutional hurdles, providing a regulatory framework for the privatized industries, providing a safety net for retrenched workers, finding an alternative for the social obligations of the public enterprises to be privatized, providing adequate incentives to domestic and international investors, setting standards for accounting and disclosure, paving the way for multinational corporations, and gaining public confidence (Bienen and Waterbury, 1989: 623).

Privatization, therefore, involves a tedious process, and resistance can come both at the policy-making stage and at the implementational stage. Ambivalent attitude of government towards privatization may further reduce its pace. As such, privatization can by no means serve as a quick fix to resolve the economic problems of developing countries.

Impediments to privatization

The politics of privatization involve holding out future gains to the general public as well as to the immediate beneficiaries. The gains are to be weighed against the immediate costs of those who are likely to lose either jobs or influence, or both (Mosley, 1988). The beneficiaries of the *status quo* may succeed in sabotaging the whole move before the future beneficiaries get a chance to organize themselves or vice versa.

There is a dilemma involved in privatizing public enterprises in the developing world. They are enmeshed in state bureaucracy and in dire need of benefits brought by privatization, yet by their very nature they are the least likely candidates for divestiture. Similarly, governments in these countries may be willing to get rid of chronically sick units in the public sector, yet find it impossible to liquidate a few of them. Even if a government announce the divestiture of some of the loss-making parasatals, they may fail to find buyers for them. Domestic investors may not find them attractive enough. To attract potential buyers the government may have to grant monopoly powers to the private sector in some cases, at the cost of microeconomic efficiency gains to be derived from the transfer of ownership.

Moreover, the public in general perceives the structural reforms and privatization policies to be warranted by international aid-donors, but such prescriptions from above are likely to meet opposition at the domestic level. The strong advocacy of economic reforms by the US government has been particularly important, and has percolated not only through USAID but also through multilateral and other bilateral donors. For instance, George Schultz, a former Secretary of State in the USA, sent a telegram to USAID missions 'to encourage the LDC to follow free market principles' and 'move away from government intervention in the economy' (Schultz, 1986). Privatization was an explicit condition for loans by multinational agencies in the cases of Senegal, Jamaica and Pakistan. And it was opposed by various political parties for selling economic sovereignty to international aid-donors in India.

In a society infested with ethnic, religious or regional tensions, under the dominance of particular groups, privatization is likely to pose serious problems. It may not be feasible to allow certain groups to gain economic and political ascendancy at the cost of others. For instance, Asians or Middle Easterners are not tolerated in Nigeria. Similarly, indigenous Kikuyus are not tolerated in Kenya. Such difficulties can be aggravated where the public sector harms are the greatest (Austin and Cobum, 1986: 56–7).

Privatization is likely to cause immediate hardship by adopting hiring and salary freezes, de-indexing wages, cuts in social services, reduction in the workforce, and so on. These economic measures are usually necessary to make an enterprise viable in the now competitive market, but they may lead to turmoil among both the managerial and operational employees. People may lose their jobs on a massive scale; entire divisions, plants or levels of management may be cut; the measures may cause short-term pain, loss of purchasing power and disruption of the domestic economy. The promise of a brighter future may not be acceptable to the present sufferers.

The reform process and privatization are usually regarded with understandable apprehension by the trade unions. Few workers can be persuaded to change their jobs from the secure public sector to an uncertain private sector. Job-creation has, in fact, been a crucial part of the social pact in many developing countries. While governments are under pressure to maintain high levels of employment, the deteriorating economy may warrant freezes on fresh appointments and a substantial reduction in already bloated payrolls. Furthermore, there are limits to which workers can be pushed in a given set up. In the absence of adequate employment opportunities and entrepreneural skills, the tradition of mobility may be found lacking. Unlike the US or British examples, managers and middle-rank employees may also resist the privatization effort. Once a public enterprise has been in public hands for a significant period of time, there develops a strong inertia that tends to maintain the status quo (Haggard and Kaufman, 1988: 25–6).

Surprisingly, resistance may also come from the private sector itself. In many developing countries, the private sector is the real beneficiary of government loans and subsidies. It would very much like to continue reaping the benefits from public enterprises without actually contributing anything towards the public well-being. Owing to high enforcement costs, the private sectors may not be willing to enter certain areas. For instance, the agricultural sector by its very nature is least likely to be privatized; there is a relative lack of profitability in agricultural activities in comparison to the trading sector. Governments can persuade private participation and private investment only by offering a combination of subsidies and preferential market conditions, thereby sacrificing some of the benefits of privatization.

There may also be significant resistance from vested interest groups. In most developing countries we find individuals or groups who, while remaining outside government, are able to influence the national policies to suit their interests. These groups may resist all such attempts which are likely to affect them adversely. For instance, in Argentina the sale of Aerolines Aircraft could not take place owing to resistance from certain vested interests

In military regimes, the military itself may have vested interests in running public enterprises, and they may not tolerate a move towards privatization. For instance, when a leasing arrangement between General Motors and Nast Automobile could not materialize in Egypt, the Military Industrial Organization came forward with a new project to manufacture a people's car in collaboration with a South Korean firm. The military had definite interests in controlling the economy directly or indirectly (Bienen and Waterbury, 1989: 626).

Yet it may not be easy to privatize in a democracy either; a government may not be able to gather enough courage to do away with a sacred cow. On the contrary, the performance of an enterprise may be tainted by using it as an instrument of public policy, rather than an instrument of economic growth. Where an enterprise has been used to meet social and non-commercial objectives, it is unlikely to be privatized without sacrificing some of the more compelling social objectives (Hemming and Mansoor, 1988: 19–20). Privatization would be criticized by intellectuals and workers alike.

The prospects for privatization are further marred by political and economic instability. It is an error to assume that a nation that has had a long-lasting but non-responsive government is stable. The success of a privatization programme depends on the popular support enjoyed by government. If a privatization programme enjoys a high level of acceptance within all the major political parties, or among the people, it may succeed. If it is seen as a favourite programme of the ruling head of the government or the finance minister, with little political or popular support, the smallest change in the political situation may erode the support base needed for a sustained privatization programme.

The media can also play an important role in making a privatization programme a success or a failure. The proponents of privatization include the business community, including the chamber of commerce and other trade associations, economic policy-makers and political leaders. Opponents may include intellecutals, academics, bureaucrats, workers, trade unions, well-placed members belonging to the economic oligarchy, and so on. The battle lines are already drawn and only a consistent, long-term effort with measurable results, can tip the scales one way or the other (Humphrey, 1990: 74).

To be able to assess the constraints and prospects of privatization, one must have a clear picture of the economic sectors that are likely to gain or lose, the amount of gains or losses that are likely to be sustained by the dominant sections, including economic as well as political coalitions, organized labour, the indigenous private sector, managers, civil servants and the armed forces. However, these may constitute a very small proportion of the entire population in predominantly agricultural societies. Larger sections may still remain outside the domain of privatization.

The role of multinational corporations

To overcome some of the impediments faced by developing countries during their privatization drive, multinational corporations (MNCs) may be involved in the economic transformation. Such corporations have already taken an active role in the privatization of various industries: for example, Boeing aircraft acquired De Havilland in Canada; Hospital Corporation of America is operating some hospitals in Singapore; New Zealand's Carter Holt Holdings bought Copec, a forest product in Chile; Volkswagen purchased Spain's SEAT; and British Telecom attained ownership and operational interests in telephone companies in Belize and Saudi Arabia.

MNCs can bring capital, specialized industrial knowledge and managerial skills to an enterprise to be privatized. Many enterprises in developing countries suffer from an inadequate infusion of capital, and, furthermore, most state enterprises may be technologically backward and lack modern managerial techniques. A steel mill in Togo, a forestry operation in Chile and a telephone company in Belize are now contributing to their governments, rather than being drains on the national coffers, only because of the efficient control of foreign multinational corporations (Molz, 1990: 17).

Most public enterprises in developing countries lack the most rudimentary forms of cost control, standardized accounting practices, knowledge of marketing techniques, systematic approach to human resource management, and so forth. The knowledge and application of modern management techniques can greatly facilitate the economic growth and viability of an enterprise, since management skills count more than raw materials in modern technology. For instance, Citosan, a cement manufacturing consortium in Turkey, posed a lot of problems before privatization because of its poor management system and idiosyncratic accounting practices (Erginsoy, 1990: 18).

Multinationals can come to the rescue in such cases where nations are under pressure from international aid-donors to reduce debt and public sector deficits, while the governments are not in a position to opt for hard options. Under these circumstances, governments may pass on the responsibility of running the loss-making enterprises to multinational corporations, whereupon the MNC can use its unique competence in rehabilitating an enterprise that may have been floundering under governmental control. For instance, the state-owned enterprise Anabib, manufacturer of steel sheeting, steel tubes and waterpipes in Algeria, suffered heavy losses; it never operated at full capacity and its finished goods were of such low quality as to be unusable. Such an enterprise could be rehabilitated by competent multinationals (Revzin, 1988: 1).

MNCs can gain from a privatized enterprise by converting it into a profitable venture. The MNC can provide an opportunity to expand its activities abroad, and may also use its interests in the privatized enterprise to import its other products and services to the host nation. For example, the privatization of Spain's Grenade Telephone Company provided an opportunity to import telephone equipment manufactured by the British Cable & Wireless.

Privatization also provides an opportunity to MNCs to acquire an established trade name in the host nation; for instance, Volkswagen's acquisition of SEAT, a Spanish auto-manufacturer. Another favourable condition could be an equitable regulatory environment. For instance, competitive protection was offered by the regulatory system before British Telecom acquired a part-interest in the Belize telephone system. Host countries may also negotiate a price favourable to the multinational corporations, in return for being able to shed responsibility on the one hand, and putting an end to the cash drain on the national exchequer on the other.

Sometimes, the change from a bureaucratic model to a market model can also create problems for multinationals. If an enterprise is not depoliticized in the process of privatization, the multinationals may simply find themselves embroiled in third-world politics. In some cases governments may continue to enjoy control over the new board of directors or managers. Under the threat of invoking new legislation, renationalization or a direct appeal to influential employee-leaders, the government may continue to exert pressures indirectly. Since many privatized enterprises were used to achieve public policy objectives earlier, the government may wish to continue this situation even after privatization. Governments may also use multinationals as a foil to dispose of loss-making parasatals without involving public criticism. Economic pitfalls may also plague the multinationals; the host country may restrict them from repatriating profits out of the country, preferring them to reinvest in the host country itself, or the host country may allow repatriation of profits only at an artificial exchange rate. This may amount, in practice, to a virtual additional tax. Multinationals may also suffer on account of hyperinflation following privatization in some developing countries. For example, Brazil experienced inflation at an annual rate of 700 per cent in the early 1990s. Furthermore, multinationals may find themselves functioning in a political world of high-stake financing, owing to massive foreign debts, and may be viewed as wealthy partners able to absorb some of the debts.

The MNCs may also face problems owing to weak production operations, tumultuous financing, lack of documentation, a bloated pay roll, and a lack of standardized accounting and control system. Such enterprises may require a complete overhaul to make privatization successful. Mexico's effort to privatize state-owned sugar mills in Costa Rica provides one such example. The limited availability of qualified local managers, technicians and workers may further aggravate the situation; and if they are available they may not be able to adopt easily the new work culture, work norms and work values of the multinationals. The MNCs may also have to provide formal training to workers and technicians barely above a basic level of literacy (Laux and Molot, 1988).

Just as the MNCs may experience either positive or negative results by acquiring privatized enterprises in developing countries, the host country may also experience the transaction as an opportunity for revamping the economy, or as a pitfall. The main opportunities accruing to the host country include: inflow of resources; access to new technology and know-how; access to new markets; and general improvement in the domestic market. It may result in better customer services, new goods and a robost economy.

On the other hand, the host country may suffer from a loss of autonomy and political dissent. For example, Chile sold its ownership of vast forest holdings to the New Zealand companies Carter Holt Holdings and Fletcher Challenge Ltd. These companies may have an altogether different approach to the use of these forests within a global economy, whereas the Chilean government would have made decisions with regard to the forests to serve domestic interests if left to itself.

This loss of autonomy creates the possibility that collaborations with multinationals may not be politically acceptable, despite potential economic benefits. Fears may be exaggerated if the MNCs have to resort to drastic cuts in the workforce to make an enterprise commercially viable, and such changes may be resented by workers, trade unions and the public alike. As such, involvement of MNCs in the privatization effort should be given deep thought and consideration; the goals, objectives and motivations should be clear to both parties. MNCs should be prepared to work in an altogether different culture and economic background, and failure to bring appropriate management skills, techniques and resources to suit the requirements and capabilities of the host country may lead to non-acceptability and political dissent. The transition cannot take place at the same speed that is considered normal in advanced industrialized countries.

Can privatization lead to economic growth and development?

Of late, we notice a definite change of mood and change of perception at the level of policy-making. There is a widespread view that the private sector can be more efficient and productive than the public sector. Proponents of privatization include important multilateral institutions such as the IMF, the World Bank, the United States Agency for Development and so on, who point to the experiences of the Asian tigers, and more recently Turkey and Chile. Furthermore, there is a substantial body of literature indicating that economic liberalization encourages faster economic growth.

However, on the basis of the few empirical studies made on some aspects of economic growth and development, it cannot be argued effectively that the promotion of private sector initiatives and reductions in the role of the public sector would necessarily lead to an overall growth of the economy. The marginal productiveness of public and private sectors differs from country to country, having different effects on the long-term rate of economic growth. But, at any rate, the value added by the public industrial enterprises in developing countries is such a small proportion of GDP that not many growth points can be added on account of privatization (Short, 1984).

Some other empirical studies have found a negative relationship between public sector spending and economic growth. Nunnenkamp, for instance, analysed the role of state enterprises by correlating four indicators of economic performance – real growth in GDP; gross fixed investment; the industrialization level; and growth in employment – with the share of GDP contributed by the state enterprises and their investment shares. None of the 16 coefficients estimated showed any significant relationship between state enterprises and general economic performance. In fact, the coefficients for growth in real GDP and gross fixed investment were found to be negative.

Marsden, on the other hand, used tax revenues as an indicator of the relative size of the non-market sector and regressed the real average growth rate in 20 developing countries during the 1970s on the basis of their corresponding ratios of tax revenues to GDP. The result was a statistically significant negative relationship between growth rates and tax shares. A RAND study, based on 27 countries during 1972–82, also found a statistically significant negative relationship between central government spending and average annual growth (Yoder, 1991: 430).

Although it is widely held that the public sector has become too large in the developing countries and consequently needs rolling back, some analysts such as Cook and Kirkpatrick, have found such an argument empirically unsubstantiated. On the basis of a sample study of 23 LDCs, Kirkpatrick found no relationship between the share of public enterprise output in GDP and growth in income during 1970s (Cook and Kirkpatrick, 1988: 10). Olson, too, found no significant relationship between the size of the public sector and economic growth (Olson, 1984: 93–4). Pryor compared growth rates of the OECD (Organisation for Economic Cooperation and Development) and CMEA (Council for Mutual Economic Assistance) and found no difference in their respective growth rates during the 1950s to the 1980s (Pryor, 1985).

Other researchers, at the macroeconomic level, have found similar results. For instance, Jonathan Aylen compared the publicly-owned steel companies of South Korea with those of India and found no difference in labour productivity (Aylen, 1987: 19–20). Similarly, a comparison between the technical efficiency of publicly-owned, privately-owned and joint-ventures in plastic manufacturing in Brazil showed no significant differences (Tyler, 1988: 477–95). Millward and Parker in their review of the existing literature have concluded that there is no evidence of a statistically satisfactory kind to suggest that public enterprises in LDCs have a lower technical efficiency than private firms operating at the same scale of operations (Millward and Parker, 1983).

On the basis of the existing literature and empirical studies, the relationship between privatization and development cannot be established. Neither GNP nor GDP can be taken as an accurate measure of development. Most development analysts now recognize the need to go beyond economic growth in assessing development, and it is argued that development should also be measured in terms of a Human Development Index, including variables such as literacy, life expectancy and freedom.

Viewed in these terms, the claims of privatization appear to be overstated and unsubstantiated (Khathate, 1991). If there is any lesson to be learnt from the experiences of the developing countries and Eastern Europe, it is quite contrary to what is generally argued. For instance, the success in some Asian countries is not the result of liberalization, but of societal coherence, the literacy rate, land reforms, a better income distribution, a balance between agricultural and industrial growth, complementary roles of the public and private sectors, government regulation, national will and a general awareness among the people (Yoder, Borknolder and Friesen, 1991: 432). Collective endeavour rather than privatization *per se* can lead to economic development and general well-being (Kothari, 1991: 23).

Lessons from the developing world

Many countries in the developing world initiated the process of privatization, liberalization and deregulation much before Eastern Europe saw the ascendancy of free-market democrats over authoritarian protectionists (*The Economist*, 30 November 1996: 17). In Latin America, Argentina and Mexico, free-marketeers were in charge of the political economy during the 1980s–90s, while gradualists had an upper hand in Brazil and Chile in recent years. But as in most countries in Eastern and Central Europe, the market economy failed to triumph. We even find U-turns in some cases and public resentment against public reforms. While the first wave of privatization succeeded in gaining popular support in some countries such as Mexico, Chile, Peru and Argentina, it could not be sustained during the second wave of privatization, mainly because the popularity of the reforms was based on unrealistic expectations.

What was not revealed during the first phase of economic liberalization during the 1970s–80s became more visible during the 1990s. In Mexico and Venezuela, short-lived booms ended in banking crises, and in most countries which resorted to privatization, unemployment, economic disparities and regional disparities increased in real terms. Privatization and deregulation caused too much strain on the weak sociopolitical structures. In Mexico, the middle class joined the backlash against economic reforms by the poor, voting against privatization. 'Down with neoliberalism' became the popular slogan of the rebels; in Venezuela, Rafael Caldera, known for his anti-reform stance, was elected in 1993. And we find a spiral of violence in Mexico, Columbia and Ecuador. In these countries, the state is likely to play a stronger role than ever before in order to promote institutional democracy and economic growth.

We should not forget that the state played a catalytic role in promoting privatization in East and Southeast Asia. Their experiences point to a very carefully crafted synergy between macroeconomic fundamentals and industrial policy and a strategic proactive role of the state. The usual commitment for privatization came from the government instead of coming from the orthodox free market paradigms (Economic and Social Commission for Asia and Pacific, 1995, development paper no. 17: 52). Malaysia, for instance, provides the first case of a national privatization programme in the developing world. The government was committed to coordinate privatization programmes and policies to maximize overall efficiency, to utilize external resources of finance, managerial skills, new forms of technology and marketing expertise. The Malaysian government used privatization as a policy instrument (Hensley and White, 1993: 72).

In all of these countries, privatization has been politically-driven, highly structured and well-planned. The governments tried to reap benefits by enhancing competition at the international level, and they tried to imbibe the Japanese culture of economic reforms in terms of the '3 Cs' – consistency, competence and commitment. The Newly Industrialized Economies (NIEs) had the benefit of a huge reservoir of skilled manpower, the availability of natural resources in abundance, adequate infrastructural facilities and a very strong desire to catch-up with their role-models. They also had close links between the state and society. The governments had flexible attitudes towards business, and businessmen and entrepreneurs were outward-oriented. They succeeded in reaping quick benefits by starting the privatization process early, and their geo-political position also helped them in obtaining foreign capital, foreign technology and foreign expertise.

In fact, the economies in the Asia-Pacific region were able to reap the benefits of post-Fordist practices. The Asian nations (Thailand, Malaysia, Indonesia, Singapore and Philippines) are now exploring the possibilities of extending their free trade zone eastward to Taiwan and North Korea, and westward to India and Sri Lanka. Myanmar and India may join soon. Unlike the private efforts in North America and the European Union, the state has played an important role in shaping the development of the economy in the Asia-Pacific region (Japan, South Korea, Taiwan, Hong Kong, Singapore, Malaysia and Thailand). The building of networks helped these economies to grow at a rapid speed, and privatization was just one of the factors responsible for the economic miracle. Even if other developing countries try hard to replicate their high-growth economic performance, they simply cannot succeed. For instance, the innovative privatization strategies of build–own–operate (BOO) and build–operate–transfer (BOT) adopted by Malaysia cannot be successfully adopted by the Philippines, Indonesia, Mexico, Chile, Sri Lanka or India.

In the same way, privatization efforts cannot yield similar results in Africa as those achieved by Asia or Latin America. SOEs played the predominant role in Africa in the 1960s, 1970s and early 1980s more than in any other region in the developing world. A great deal of human capital, time and financial resources in Africa were diverted to marginally productive activities, and the enthusiasm of private entrepreneurs was marred due to inappropriate political policies. In order to restructure their economies, many countries in Africa started looking eastward and westward. These countries could neither afford to carry on with the loss-making parasatals nor could they attract enough investments from abroad. They had no other option but to resort to structural adjustments. Although Nigeria, Senegal and Togo adopted very ambitious privatization programmes, they had varied results.

Nigeria adopted its privatization programme in late 1988. The main objectives were to reduce the level of unproductive public sector investment, improve the viability and performance of enterprises, encourage recourse to capital markets in lieu of the treasury, create a favourable atmosphere for foreign and local investment, and to reduce debt by debt–equity swaps (Drum, 1993: 146). It hoped to divest 70 out of 100 enterprises either through shares or liquidation. These included enterprises in textiles, food, beverages, agro-processing and insurance. The government anticipated raising approximately US$325 million through privatization proceeds by the end of 1992, but it had to face many problems ranging from political opposition to a lack of adequate resources on the part of small investors.

Senegal created a new unit on privatization in the Presidency in 1989, although the programme had its origin in the mid-1980s; in 1987, 26 SOEs were slated for privatization. Under the London Club agreements, some debt–equity swaps were also announced for Senegal. In Togo, a privatization programme was launched as early as 1982, and by the end of 1988 the Togonese government had been able to raise approximately US$25 million for privatization. Approximately US$48 million were invested in the newly-privatized firms (Drum, 1993: 147). The programme was implemented by the Ministry of Industry and State Enterprise but the process slowed down after 1991 owing to the lack of a stock exchange and well-developed capital market. Lack of a requisite fiscal and accounting enterprise also delayed the entire process.

Lessons to be drawn

1. The first lesson to be learnt from the various examples of privatization in the developing world is that each country needs a tailor-made privatization strategy to suit its particular requirements, capabilities and learning skills.
2. The economic miracles achieved by the NICs cannot be repeated by other developing countries. There have been many factors responsible for their success, and privatization happens to be just one of the many ingredients used. It is also doubtful whether the Asian tigers or the Asian dragons will still remain in the front row even at the dawn of the twenty-first century. The strike by workers on a massive scale in January 1997 in South Korea points to the impending socioeconomic crisis ahead.
3. A high level of political support is needed to make privatization a success; it is necessary to mobilize sufficient political concensus, will and commitment. Every privatization plan must include well-defined

objectives and well-thought out strategies both for short-term and long-term goals.

4. Privatization can be a means to an end, but not an end in itself. It should not be seen as a panacea for general economic sickness. All economic activities should be seen as socially constructed; it is by means of social construction of market systems that capital is accumulated, its formation controlled and labour exploited.
5. It is very important to have transparency in the privatization process, especially in those countries where corruption prevails and political and democratic institutions are weak. Only transparency can ensure fairness and integrity.
6. The process of privatization is fraught with tremendous legal, political, and socioeconomic problems. It is usually characterized by controversies and uncertainities, and a strong state is needed to implement the privatization programme successfully. The political, social and economic costs can be unsurmountable if the privatization programme is dropped midway.
7. Privatization can lead to disastrous consequences in those countries where either adequate or efficient free market institutions do not prevail, or a social security system is lacking. Where most people remain outside the mainstream of the economy, the state cannot absolve its role as sole provider of social welfare to large sections of the deprived population solely dependent on the state. The state has to provide a safety network to those public-sector employees who become retrenched in the privatization process.
8. It is very important in the context of the developing world to create a favourable environment in which privatization can take place. It would be beneficial to initiate campaigns aiming at public education and dialogue with groups that are likely to be affected by privatization favourably or unfavourably.
9. Privatization is an art. Policy-makers and various other actors involved in the privatization drama should not hesitate in seeking direction from economic, legal, technical or other experts.
10. Each country should evolve its own paradigm of development and economic or political strategy in a manner that best serves its short-term and long-term national interests. It should not try to copy another country or attempt a quick fix. It should keep in mind the feasibility of privatization in its given set-up.

8
The Indian Scenario

India provides a typical example of a developing country where privatization has provided both options and challenges in a big way (Mohnot, 1991). It has polarized policy-makers, economists, politicians, academicians, journalists, intellectuals and the general public into two camps: (1) those who support the New Economic Policy based on globalization, liberalization and privatization, and (2) those who oppose full-fledged privatization on the grounds that market forces based on dirigiste dogma (Lal, 1983) cannot be suitable for a country like India where the whole debate about privatization is concerned merely with minority 150 to 200 million people comprising the better-off sections of society. The domestic sector – corporate and non-corporate – or the MNCs and TNCs are simply not concerned with the rest of the 750 to 700 million people in the country (Table 8.1).

Such polarization is bound to occur in any third-world country where apparently contradictory characteristics and structures exist simultaneously. We find development and underdevelopment at the same time; we find very rich and very poor people coexisting; and similarly we find feudal and capitalist structures coexisting in an uneasy harmony. Or we may find mixed political cultures, structures, functions and processes amounting to the coexistence of mutually opposing forces. Because their is no single enduring synthesis, it is impossible to speak of any correct economic or perfect political solution, and it is very difficult to arrive at a consensus or attain legitimacy in such a complex situation. India is no exception to this scenario (Patel, 1994).

India can be considered a microcosm of global-level diversities. In terms of social complexities and cultural diversities, India cannot be compared with any other country except perhaps China and the former USSR. India is more than a state, larger than a nation and bigger than a country. It is the second most populous and territorially the world's seventh largest country. Its population is more than the total population of the three continents combined – Latin America, Africa and Australia. India's continental dimension, survival and continuity for more than 3000 years of recorded history and perhaps 1000–2000 years of pre-history, together with its social complexities

Table 8.1 Dynamics of human resources in India

Sectors	*Public*	*Private*	*Total*	*Unorganized sector*	*Total*
Agriculture	0.56	0.85	1.41	114.09	115.50
Mining and quarrying	0.94	0.09	1.03	1.49	2.52
Manufacturing	1.86	4.41	6.27	33.47	39.74
Construction	1.18	0.06	1.24	12.62	13.86
Electricity, gas and water supply	0.80	0.04	0.84	1.50	2.34
Transport, storage and communication	2.97	0.05	3.02	14.72	17.74
Other services	9.72	1.87	11.59	49.17	60.76
Total	18.03	7.37	25.40	227.06	252.46

Source: K.P. Ganesan (1991).

and cultural diversities, makes it the world's oldest, largest and most tenacious pluralistic society, perhaps unique in human history (Gupta, 1996).

In theory, India has all the prerequisites necessary for launching the privatization debate. It has a relatively strong parliamentary democracy with deep-rooted cultural and social traditions, a free and open society with sufficient courage to face adversity, and a volatile polity. There is a firmly based private sector, stockmarkets, human resources, a free and fair judiciary, strong media and an appropriate legal structure. India is at an advantage because English remains the main language of government and business, yet it has not been able to attract much foreign direct investment so far, despite opening up its economy as early as 1991. It suffers from a bad image at the international level for being unpredictable, ambivalent and unreliable. Politicians, businessmen and bureaucrats also lack confidence to stand up to global competition, in case India decides to privatize on a massive or rapid scale (Table 8.2).

The context

The declaration of the New Economic Policy on 24 July 1991 by the Narasimha Rao government signified the end of the 'licence raj' in India. The NEP aimed at stabilizing the economy which had started crumbling in the wake of the fiscal crisis (Hopper, 1995: 25); India had become the world's third most indebted nation with a fiscal deficit claiming 8.4 per cent of GDP. Its foreign reserves fell to a mere US$1 billion, while inflation rose to a peak of 17 per cent. Its overall position fell to 134th out of 173 countries in 1994. According to the *Economic Survey of India*, the external debt which stood at US$63.4 billion at the end of 1990–91 rose to US$71.11 billion in September 1992. The situation became so alarming that India had to mortgage its gold to get fresh loans from

Table 8.2 Key financial indicators on India (selected accounts, US$ millions)

	1988–89	*1989–90*	*1990–91*	*1991–92*	*1992–93*	*1993–94*	*1994–95*
GDP	243 547.9	245 457.4	266 286.0	225 557.0	204 781.2	225 449.5	257 012.0*
Fiscal deficit (as % of GDP)	7.80	7.80	8.30	5.90	5.70	7.40	6.70
CPI	163.0	173.0	193.0	219.0	240.0	258.0	n/a
WPI	154.2	165.7	182.7	207.8	228.7	247.1	n/a
Foreign investment	n/a	n/a	n/a	150.0	341.0	620.0	756.0
Foreign portfolio investment	n/a	n/a	n/a	8.0	92.0	3493.0	3141.0
Trade balance	(5526.0)	(4607.0)	(5932.0)	(1546.0)	(3345.0)	(1068.0)	(2011.0)
Foreign exchange rate/US$	14 482	16 649	17 943	24 474	30 649	31 366	31 388
NRI deposits	7896.0	9183.0	10 372.0	10 144.0	11 141.0	12 665.0	13 365.0
Foreign exchange reserve	4226.0	3368.0	2236.0	5631.0	6434.0	15 068.0	20 000.0*

Notes: * Estimates. CPI = Consumer Price Index; WPI = Wholesale Price Index; NRI = Non Resident Indian.
Source: S. Kaushik (1996): 57.

abroad. All this had a negative effect on the Indian psyche; the average Indian felt ashamed and dishonoured.

For the first time since independence, economic issues took the edge over political ones. Although India enjoys the position of being the seventh largest country in the world with the fourth largest reserves of iron ore, the third largest of manganese and the third largest pool of scientific manpower, it is still castigated as a developing economy. There are many deficiencies and distortions in the structures and functioning of the Indian economy which are reflected in the form of fiscal and trade imbalances, economic and social disparities, inefficiency in production, black marketing, oligopolistic tendencies, corruption and malpractices in business. Huge investments in the public sector failed to bring either economic growth or social justice (Table 8.3), and the old consensus on the Nehru model of a socialist pattern of society also lost credibility.

We find a definite change in the popular mood towards the role of the government in general and to the public sector in particular. The terms privatization, deregulation and liberalization are no longer looked at askance. The media, bureaucratic cliques, World Bank loyalists, certain vested interests and business groups played a very important role in shifting the focus from a planned economy to a market economy. The genesis of the New Economic Policy (NEP) and Structural Adjustment Programme (SAP) can be traced back to the political rise of Rajiv Gandhi in 1984. A technocrat by profession and immature in politics, Rajiv Gandhi and his mentors thought it advantageous for the Congress party to break from the Nehruvian–Mahalanobis model of economic development which led to civic discontent and a crisis of ungovernability.

Rajiv Gandhi adopted a policy of economic liberalization and reliance on the private corporate sector as an effective step towards India's move into the twenty-first century with dignity. He sought to achieve rapid economic growth by associating the private sector in the process of liberalization. He considered technological progress as fundamental to India's economic growth and development on the one hand, and competitiveness of Indian industries at the global level on the other. Making his perspectives clear in his very first broadcast to the nation, he said:

> The public sector has spread into too many areas where it should not be. We will be developing our public sector to undertake jobs that private sector

Table 8.3 Analysis of public sector undertakings (PSUs): gross profit to capital employed, 1989–90

	Range of profit	*Industry group*	*Rate of return*	*Capital employed*	*% of total*
A	Negative rate of return	Consumer goods	–6.38	972	
		Textiles	–6.96	859	
		Contract and construction services	–2.40	569	
		Industrial development & technology Consultancy	–3.90	377	
		Sub-total (A)		*2777*	*(3.3)*
B	0–4%	Fertilisers	1.88	2692	(3.2)
C	4–8%	Steel	5.93	7054	
		Agro-based Industries	7.02	64	
		Tourist Services	7.60	178	
		Sub-Total (C)		*7296*	*(8.6)*
D	8–12%	Coal	8.95	7097	
		Power	9.76	10 490	
		Transport equipment	9.76	2415	
		Trading & marketing	10.29	6589	
		Transport services	9.95	5198	
		Financing services	8.17	9894	
		Mineral & metals	11.88	5068	
		Sub-total(D)		*46 751*	*(55.4)*
E	12% or more	Petroleum	27.76	15 513	
		Chemicals & pharmaceuticals	13.24	1409	
		Heavy engineering	15.04	1975	
		Medium & light engineering	13.05	2914	
		Telecommunications	19.79	3077	
		Section-25 companies	22.65	32	
		Sub-total (E)		*24 920*	*(29.5)*
Grand total		*A to E*		*84 436*	*(100.0)*

Source: Reclassified and calculated from data provided in Government of India, *Public Enterprises Survey, 1989–90*, Vol. 1; R. Dutt (1991) 'Public Sector Performance: Turning from Black to Grey', *Mainstream*, July 21: 22.

> cannot do. But we will be opening up more to private sector so that it can expand and the economy can grow freely. (November, 1984)

The blame for rising unemployment, higher inflation, large current account deficits, soaring international debts and balance of payment crisis was put on the poor performance of the public sector. It became fashionable to argue in academic circles and business forums that public sector enterprises were highly inefficient, bureaucratic and corrupt: instead of generating resources for future growth, they had become a drain on the national exchequer. The role played by the public sector in providing infrastructure and technical advancement during the last four decades, besides providing employment and social justice to millions of people in India, was easily forgotten. The sole concern was with the poor rate of return and paramount losses incurred by the PSUs. According to one report, the reinvestible surplus or net profit of the public sector over the last three decades averaged to just 1 per cent of the huge investments made (Table 8.4). The average opportunity cost varied from Rs 9000 to Rs 12 000 crore per annum at existing prices (Thakore, 1991: 12).

Besides domestic economic constraints, pressures from international lending agencies also provided a fillip to the privatization debate in India (Table 8.5). In the 1980s the economic situation had become so critical that the World Bank and IMF refused to grant further loans unless and until the government decided to do something about the leaking buckets – the PSUs. But for the pressures from these external bodies, the minority government in India would not have gathered enough courage to open Pandora's box. As such, the prescription from the IMF and the World Bank need not be castigated on dictatorial outright; in view of the tremendous problems faced by the country on both economic as well as political fronts, the time was ripe to axe the 'drumstick tree' (Joshi, 1991: 8).

On 24 July 1991 Manmohan Singh, the Finance Minister in the Rao government (and a former Professor in Economics at the University of Delhi) presented his first budget to parliament based on the New Industrial Policy. He stressed the need for fiscal adjustment and macroeconomic stabilization during 1991–92, to be followed by fiscal consolidation thereafter. The New Industrial Policy contained four important decisions which had a bearing on the privatization of public sector enterprises in India directly or indirectly:

1. Reduction in the list of industries reserved for the public sector from 17 to eight;
2. Disinvestment of shares in PSEs in order to encourage participation of the general public and workers in managing and controlling the economy;
3. Uniform policy for sick enterprises whether in the public or private sectors;
4. Recourse to contract management through memoranda of understanding in order to ensure better performance and accountability.

Table 8.4 Patterns of investment in public enterprises (Rs hundred thousands)

	Group		As of 31 March 1985 Total	%	As of 31 March 1990 Total	%
1	Enterprises under construction		3597	8.43	6224	6.27
2	Enterprises producing goods		32 726	76.69	72 059	72.55
	(i)	Power	3811	8.93	17 253	17.37
	(ii)	Coal and water	4742	11.11	11 997	12.08
	(iii)	Petroleum	4706	11.03	10 005	10.07
	(iv)	Steel	6329	14.83	8300	8.36
	(v)	Minerals and metals	3330	7.80	5778	5.82
	(vi)	Fertilisers	3381	7.92	5271	5.31
	(vii)	Engineering	2444	5.73	3981	4.01
	(viii)	Transportation equipment	1492	3.50	2541	2.56
	(ix)	Chemicals and pharmaceuticals	1023	2.40	2011	2.02
	(x)	Textiles	1093	2.56	2316	2.33
	(xi)	Consumer goods	335	0.79	2534	2.55
	(xii)	Agro-based	40	0.09	72	0.07
3	Enterprises producing services		6350	14.88	21 032	21.18
	(i)	Financial services	2072	4.86	9646	9.71
	(ii)	Transportation services	2583	6.05	4712	4.75
	(iii)	Trading & marketing services	937	2.20	2454	2.47
	(iv)	Telecomunication servises	–	–	2804	2.82
	(v)	Other services	758	1.77	1416	1.43
	Total (1+2+3)		42 673	100.00	99 315	100.00

Source: Compiled from Government of India, *Public Enterprises Survey, 1989–90,* Vol. 1; R. Dutt (1991): 22.

In the 1992–93 budget few exemptions and deductions in indirect taxes were announced on the basis of Raja Chelliah's report on tax reforms. A new liberated exchange rate management system (LERMS) was also introduced to promote partial convertibility of the rupee and a market-determined rate for foreign exchange up to 60 per cent. Various other measures towards

Table 8.5 External and internal pressures for privatization

External pressures	*Internal pressures*
International aid donors (IMF and World Bank)	Financial crunch, balance of payments crisis and budget deficits
Foreign investors and NRIs	Allocative and distributive efficiency; prevalence of sick units
Market ideology	Shift in ideology and emergence of new beneficiaries
Demands for globalization of economy	Demands for globalization of economy

Source: G. Gouri (ed.) (1991): 116.

decontrol, delicensing, disinvestment and deregulation during the past five or six years have paved the way for privatization in India, though in a limited way (Table 8.6).

Despite criticizing the damaging effects on liberalization, deregulation and privatization on the masses, the opposition parties in India failed to come out with an alternative to globalization and privatization. Even the shortest-lived government formed by the Bhartiya Janta Party (BJP) under Atal Bihari Vajpayee in May 1996 (the government lasted for just 13 days) had to announce its desire of retaining the New Economic Policy because it could not afford to lose foreign support at the critical juncture when India's external debt stood at US$91.78 billion and its fiscal deficit at 5.9 per cent of GDP (1995–96).

Under the leadership of Deva Gowda in 1996, the United Front government had to face an acute dilemma. It could neither carry on with the New Economic Policy launched by the Congress Government on 24 July 1991, nor drop it midway. Realizing the ground realities of specific socioeconomic milieu of India, the United Front government took the initiative of doubling the size of rural credit for the next five years (beginning June 1996), doubling the share of NABARD (State Level Development Financial Institutions) and setting up the private local area banks (LABs) to promote investment in commercial and high tech agriculture (Mujumdar, 1996: 3237). Contrary to the popular view, public sector investment plays a dominant role in the agricultural sector in India.

As such, the government's approach towards privatization in India remained *ad hoc*. It proved highly costly both in fiscal and political terms. Instead of relying on the domestic and global markets, the government adopted the policy of 'wait and see'. It was a mistake to assume that the partial disinvestment of our prime PSUs (the navratanas – nine jewels) could take the economy out of fiscal crisis at a time when in the geo-political scenario, the value migration was steadily taking place from the 'tangible' to 'non-tangible'.

Table 8.6 Privatization efforts in India

Year	*Base investment (Rs bn)*	*Incremental investment (Rs bn)*	*Divestment (Rs bn)*	*Cumulative investment (Rs bn)*
1991–2	2.000	400	40	2360
1992–3	2.360	300	150	2510
1994–5	2.510	250	250	2510
1995–6	2.510	200	350	2360
2000	2.360	500	1200	1660

Source: S.R Mohnot in V.V. Ramananadham (ed.) (1993): 274.

Moreover, the political leaders and economic analysts constantly kept the pressure on the country to emulate the experiences of the 'Asian tigers' (which later on turned out to be mere cats), despite the vast differences in sociocultural backgrounds in the two cases. Besides South Korea, Singapore, Taiwan, Malaysia and Philippines, privatization was also resorted to on a massive scale in some of the neighbouring countries such as Bangladesh, Pakistan, Sri Lanka and Nepal. The stress was on the quantity rather than the quality of privatization in the media. Moreover, developments in the former Soviet Union and Eastern Europe also created an environment favourable for launching the privatization movement in India.

The privatization debate

A decade ago, the concept of privatization as a catalyst was hardly acknowledged in India. Not long ago it was nationalization that was in vogue. Even international aid-donors such as the IMF and the World Bank had recommended a larger role for the public sector during the 1950s and 1960s, and they refused to grant loans to those countries which did not have government-sponsored development programmes. Now it is just the other way round. The prescription of privatization is being sold, rather over-sold, as a panacea to cure our economic ills.

The New Economic Policy reflects political expediency. It is difficult to say whether ideological shifts from the left-of-centre position to the extreme right, or practical constraints, are more responsible for the oscillation on the part of the leadership in India. Nevertheless, the privatization debate is open now. One school, which is more vociferous at the moment, is of the view that the only solution to the present impasse lies in a drastic contraction of the government's role in the economy.

This view is based on the assumption that inefficiencies, corruption and nepotism in the public sector and the government's attempts to impose upon itself too many obligations, has brought the financial situation to its present critical state. And it is time for the country to abandon the path of a centrally planned economy, allowing market forces to operate more freely. The government, on the other hand, should concentrate on those areas which rightfully belong to it. Instead of running bakeries, hotels and restaurants, it should look after public health, education and general well-being.

Those who are ideologically opposed to this view still agree that the public sector in India needs to improve its efficiency; they blame the stronghold of the wealthy and articulate class for the current impasse (Bagchi, 1991: 19). To them, despite industrial production increasing a thousand fold and actual GNP by at least a factor of 25, the country has become engulfed in an alarming economic crisis pushing it on the brink of disaster primarily because of the misdoings of the politician–bureaucratic–businessman nexus (Kaul, 1991: 9–14).

According to this school, salvation lies in either compelling the better-off sections of society to contribute more, commensurately, for all the advantages they have been taking from the present system, or cutting down their share in future growth and development and opting for a strategy that is likely to exacerbate the inequalities and further immiserize the poor.

This school advocates drastic cuts in government expenditure, and is in favour of restructuring the public sector rather than its abolition. It has supported the government's policy of freeing industry from the licence permit raj, and discretionary controls followed by lower protection to domestic industry from foreign competitors. Such a new approach to industrial and trade policy can lead to a vibrant and competitive economy in the coming years without resorting to privatization *per se*. Further, the stress is laid on all-round human development rather than mere economic growth. To them, the future of 700 million people cannot be put at stake for the betterment of 200 million Indians, comprising only the better-off sections of society.

The case for privatization

Privatization is very much in vogue these days; it has been a source of public debate, seminars and workshops all over the country. The resource crunch has provided the necessary impetus to the privatization debate in India. Even if it is difficult to prove on ideological grounds that the public sector is usually inefficient, wasteful and slow-growing, a case for privatization can certainly be made on pragmatic grounds. Where is the money to invest for future development and growth? Can we ignore this simple truth? What is the fun of keeping those enterprises under the public sector which should not have been in the public sector at all and which have become financially non-viable?

Many have invoked privatization as a result of fiscal compulsions; some are motivated ideologically and others are led by the cold logic of productivity. Some have suggested privatization just for the sake of change, and others because everybody else is doing it. Privatization has become the fashion of the day and the general mood is – 'let's privatize'. The affluent class is more active in propagating privatization in India; the middle class remains sceptical. The common man in India can be easily led to the path of privatization in the wake of disillusionment with the public sector; he has to face a lot of problems in his day-to-day life owing to rising corruption, nepotism, inefficiency, insensitivity and high-handedness on the part of public officials, especially at the lower level (Mohnot, 1991: 9).

The media, too, has played a crucial role in setting the stage by highlighting the losses incurred by public sector enterprises year after year, without bothering to inform the readers about the inefficiencies prevailing in the private sector. The case for privatization in India is primarily based upon the dismal performance by the public sector in terms of profits and sustained growth. There is indeed an interesting relationship between comparative advantage and privatization. Generally speaking, privatization is supposed to lead to efficiency, competition and additional resources on the one hand, and to help in getting rid of loss-making enterprises on the other. The myth prevails – what the public sector can do, the private sector can do better.

The wave of privatization may be seen in the form of countering the previous wave of nationalization. It is now being held that the performance of the public sector can be improved only by exposing it to a market discipline, and it is asserted that the best use of resources comes from opening up new areas to market forces wherever feasible. This can be accomplished by returning industries and activities to the private sector where managers can choose their strategy unhindered by government interference and reap the benefits of success or face the consequences of failure. Consumers can also benefit from wide choices available in the wake of globalization and privatization.

Competitiveness and not ownership is supposed to be the guiding spirit behind privatization in India. As a policy prescription it has been successfully applied in countries like the UK, Japan, Malaysia, Philippines, Chile, Mexico, Australia, Thailand, Singapore, Hong Kong and South Korea. The general feeling is that in a changed world scenario, if India does not want to be left out of the mainstream of the global economy, both its public and private sectors should emerge from the protective cocoon. In a society where industries are unwilling to enter into a highly competitive international market, it is argued that indigenous industries need to be forced to export (Chelliah, 1991: 17).

In the fast changing scenario, Indian enterprises cannot remain independent of economic developments and trends worldwide. A survey conducted by the World Bank on 41 developing economies suggests that the economic performances of the outward-looking economies are far better than those of the inward-looking economies, though the links between trade strategies and macroeconomic performance cannot be established. It is difficult to say whether it is the outward orientation that leads to better economic performance or vice versa; but one thing is certain, privatization is likely to increase the international competitiveness and allocative efficiency of an enterprise (Ramchandran, 1991: 8).

Privatization can play an important role in recapitalizing capitalism both by reducing the size of the public sector and by providing ready-made markets for the private sector. Privatization also implies freedom to produce, choose, innovate and prosper. It can help in getting rid of loss-making entities which cannot be revamped any more. While private management can close down non-viable economic activities, the government cannot do so, especially, in a democratic set up. Privatization thus helps in shifting the responsibility of taking harsh and unpopular decisions from the government to a select few, who might have vested interests in a given enterprise, without imposing any direct accountability towards the public (Goyal, 1987: 230).

Moreover, privatization is supposed to lead to better allocation of resources. Privately-owned companies are found to be making better use of labour, capital and other resources; and management is dictated by market forces, rather than a bureaucratic set-up. They are in a better position to redeploy assets than management in the public sector. In fact, the whole ethos and cultural environment of the two sectors differ altogether. That is why privatization has been recommended by many. A public sector enterprise is usually over-administered while a modern enterprise needs to be professionally managed. In this context, privatization has acquired special significance (Patted, 1991: 7).

Pressures from the stockmarket can also help in improving the performance of management. Some ownership by the public is supposed to act as a pressure on overall performance. As markets become more competitive and the equity base is enlarged, companies become more and more efficient. In recent years, the equity culture is growing in India as the household savings rate is quite high in comparison with other developing countries. A substantial part of shareholding in private enterprises is held by the financial institutions, insurance companies and banks.

It is now being held that privatization through equity shares can herald economic democracy in India (Singhvi, 1991: 7). Just as universal franchise heralds political democracy, equity shares can herald economic democracy, runs the argument. Those who own equity shares have the right to vote at general meetings, while debenture and deposit holders have no such right. While in political democracy each citizen has one vote, in an economic democracy a share's weight commensurates with the number of shares held by the owner. Whereas the number of voters runs into hundreds and millions in a political democracy, it is confined to a few millions in economic democracy in the case of India. Nevertheless, privatization can also lead to democratization of the economic process, where both workers and consumers have a say in management (Sathe, 1991: 11).

As indicated earlier, a major objective behind privatization has been the desire to reduce the role of the state in economic activities, which has grown to incredible heights and which has resulted in the politicization of the economy and distraction from the domain basically assigned to the state. In the name of social obligations, huge funds have been misappropriated by those in power. Instead of transferring wealth from the rich to the poor, the state in India has only succeeded in redistributing it from the very rich to the dishonest rich (Palkhiwala, 1991: 11).

Besides its poor financial performance, the state in India has failed to evolve an egalitarian society. Services provided by the state on a subsidized basis were used more by the better off sections of society than by the poor and needy. Whereas the private sector used public money for private gain, the public sector used public money for public loss only. Whereas the private sector remains highly private, the public sector could not remain public.

In the name of social obligations, the public sector can no longer be allowed to conceal its inefficiencies. It is now being argued that privatization can help in reducing the wasteful use of scarce resources both by employees and the public. And savings from reducing subsidies can be used in a better way for the upliftment of those who are in dire need of state support (Gupta, 1989: 17). The proponents of privatization justify any scheme which improves the national economy and enhances its productivity.

Case against privatization

The opponents of privatization have expressed fears that the transition from a paternalistic to a free market form of government will inflict severe hardships on those who are least prepared to face such a situation. For instance, in the Indian situation approximately 85 per cent of the people are not in a position to participate in the privatization of public sector enterprises in any case (Nankani, 1990: 149). The whole debate about nationalization versus privatization is focused on 150 to 200 million people in India comprising the better-off sections of the society.

The first phase of financial reforms in India covered the period 1969–91; the second phase 1991–96; and third phase began with the emergence of the United Front government in June 1996. During 1991–96, the credit policy pursued even by the public sector banks gave priority to consumer goods. For instance, M.S. Shoes got cheap credit, while the production of sugar in Maharashtra suffered. Instead of supporting the priority sectors, banks and financial institutions in the third phase of economic liberalization (1996) onwards) are likely to pose a serious threat to growth-enhancing credit policies (Mujumdar, 1996: 3238).

In fact, demand for good quality consumer goods from the emerging middle class was one of the factors responsible for opening up the Indian economy to MNCs; the collaborations approved during the 1980s were meant for elite consumption (Shekhar, 1992: 8). Foreign direct investments from companies such as Pepsi, Coca-Cola, McDonalds, IBM, Hewlett-Packard, Texas Instruments, Enron, GM, GE, Black & Decker, AT&T, NYNEX and Ranbaxy began to flow at the rate of approximately US$200 million a month (Kaushik, 1996: 60).

Moreover, supporters of the public sector have argued quite effectively that the performance of these bodies is not as bad as made out by the media and vested interests. In fact, the public sector has played to role of a catalyst in the rapid economic and industrial development of the nation. Prior to independence, India had to import even needles; whereas today it is engaged in shipbuilding. Some public sector enterprises are highly efficient, and in fact the number of profit-making enterprises increased from 117 to 131, while loss-making enterprises decreased from 106 to 98 during 1989–90 (*Financial Express*, 28 February 1991: 12). Most of the loss-making enterprises comprised the sick units taken over from the private sector itself. Out of 20 000 sick units, 90 per cent belonged to the private sector. While the inefficiencies in the public sector are condemned by one and all, the micro-level inefficiencies in the private sector remain concealed. That is why it is said that the private sector is very private, while the public sector is highly public (Mitra, 1991: 11).

Nor can the performance of the public sector enterprises be judged in terms of profits only. Generating profits was never the target behind setting up these enterprises; rather, they were adopted as an instrument for rapid socio-economic transformation based on pragmatic considerations. The public enterprises (PEs) were left free to formulate their own micro-objectives, the setting up of which should be seen as an end result of a process requiring participation of both the government and the enterprise managements. The Bureau of Public Enterprises in India listed the macro-objectives of PEs as follows (Beesley and Littlechild, 1987: 6–7):

1. To help in the rapid industrialization of the country and to create the necessary infrastructure for economic growth and development;
2. To earn returns on investment and generate resources for development;
3. To promote the redistribution of income and wealth;
4. To create employment opportunities;
5. To promote balanced regional development;
6. To assist in the development of small-scale and auxiliary industries;
7. To promote import substitution, and save and earn foreign exchange for the economy, and so forth.

As such, the poor performance of the public sector enterprises cannot be attributed to state ownership or managerial inefficiency alone. Many factors are responsible – a lack of clear objectives, unsound investment decisions, bad decisions in terms of location and technology, over-capitalization in terms of time and cost overruns, delay in decision-making, over-staffing, under utilization of capacity, lack of incentives, too much political interference, too many rules and regulations, lack of autonomy, lack of adequate resources, constraints on raising capital from the market, inappropriate pricing policies, poor and obsolete technology, corruption and nepotism, and so on (Jatar, 1990: 10).

Moreover, it should be kept in mind that the public sector in India does not constitute a single entity. A large return in the petroleum sector cannot be compared with a small return in the steel sector. In the absence of autonomy or an appropriate pricing policy, a highly efficient unit can also be loss-making. Financial profitability can be an index of efficiency only if an enterprise is run on commercial lines. If the goals of the public and private sector vary, the tools to measure their performance must also vary. All the activities of public sector enterprises cannot be converted into quantitative terms, nor can the results be uniform, having long, medium or short-term spans.

As such, privatization as a proposition has to be examined in the context of various dimensions of an enterprise – be it public, private or hybrid. Hybridization can take various forms such as cooperatives, joint sector units, privately-owned and publicly managed or publicly-owned and privately managed organizations. While public enterprises may be required to be in constant touch with private undertakings, the private companies can go public to raise the additional capital. Many big private companies also have investments from public financial institutions. In the context of India, public sector enterprises may take different forms in terms of their structures such as departmental undertakings, public corporations and companies incorporated under the control of both central and state governments, or companies embracing both sectors.

As such, no uniform solutions can be found for these enterprises. The departmental undertakings being extensions of the government may operate on a no-profit-no-loss basis and may not have a market other than the government. Nor do the public corporations work on commercial lines. There are also divergencies in the modes of functioning adopted by these public corporations; while the Damodar Valley Corporation does not have any share capital, for example, the IFCI may have.

Nor is the distinction very clear between a public and a private limited company. The government has within its fold companies which are the largest in the country, yet continue to be private limited companies. Surprisingly, though, in the government corporate sector some companies are privately held. By the end of March 1988, out of 1104 government companies, 630 were private limited companies, and 474 were public limited companies. Out of 154 415 non-government companies, 136 430 were private limited and 17 985 were public limited. Under this situation the whole thrust towards privatization seems to be misdirected (Chattopadhyay, 1991: 4).

As such, there is no hard evidence to support the thesis that the private sector is more efficient than the public sector. If a public enterprise becomes more efficient after privatization, it does not mean that the managers had become suddenly more efficient; rather, the environment becomes more flexible. The induction of a few private individuals into the public sector may not bring an iota of privatization. For instance, the appointment of Rahul Bajaj and Ratan Tata on the Boards of Air India and Indian Airlines could not revamp them.

Moreover, the privatized enterprises appear prone to exploitation by vested interests in lieu of genuine gains in overall economic prosperity. The move to hand over the management of UPSCC (UP State Cement Corporation) provides one such example: contrary to the well-established practice of fixing the asset-value at its market value, the valuation of UPSCC's assets were fixed at Rs68.28 crore on the basis of the paid up capital of the corporation. This amount was further adjusted downwards by 75 per cent to Rs51.21 crore in view of the depreciation of the corporations' fixed assets. The amount of the Dalmias' 51 per cent share was fixed at Rs26.12 crore (Swamy, 1991: 12–13). In return, the Dalmias were to get 1.5 square kilometres of land, 5000 residential units and factory buildings, and three limestone mines covering 30 square kilometres with mining rights for another 40 years. The value of the land was estimated at Rs135 crore, of residential units at Rs55 crore and the capitalization value of the limestone mines at Rs24.83 crore. Moreover, there were other advantages in terms of tax concessions. The deal was highly favourable to the Dalmias, besides making them a dominant manufacturer in the cement industry. However, due to political pressures the deal could not materialize (Table 8.7).

To opponents of privatization, if we adopt deregulation, liberalization and privatization merely to woo international aid donors we may succeed in fulfilling short-term goals but fail miserably in the long run (Gupta, 1991: 15–16). Even the report-cards of the USA and the UK on the one hand, and developing economies on the other, are far from satisfactory. Privatization has lost momentum in the UK; it has slowed down in the USA, France, Australia, Indonesia, Philippines and elsewhere. There has been more rhetoric than actual implementation of privatization across the world.

Impediments to privatization

In India, pragmatism and expediency rather than a well-thought-out and well-debated ideology seem to be behind propelling the privatization debate all over the country. The adjustment programme ordained by India's foreign creditors was started by the minority government led by Narasimba Rao without any political sanction or mass support, and in a reckless manner. In a democracy it is futile to hope that the electorate will put up with inflation, a slowdown of growth, retrenchment of surplus staff and cuts in subsidies for farmers that the IMF loan conditionalities entail.

The biggest impediment to privatization in India remains the lack of a determined effort on the part of government. The party in power has so

Table 8.7 A balance sheet of UPSCC's privatization

Value assessed by auditors	*Rs crore*	*Actual value*	*Rs crore*
A (i) Value of fixed assets (based on a combination of balance of life method and capitalization of operating earnings method)	83.9	A (i) Value of fixed assets at current market prices	190.00
		(ii) Capitalized value of mining rights	55.00
(ii) The present value of tax concessions	48.9	(iii) Present value of sales tax and other liabilities deferment (discounted at 12% per annum)	200.00
(iii) Shareholders fund	68.28	(iv) Value of machines, spares, fixtures etc.	170.00
Total	201.08		615.00
B (i) Accumulated losses (without taking into account equity funds of Rs 68.28 crore)	(163.6)		
(ii) Expected losses till 1994	(24.4)		
	(188.00)	B (i) Liabilities of UPSCC	(115.00)
C The net equity funds	13.1	(ii) Negative current assets, approximately	(40.00)
			(155.00)
		C Net value of assets	460.00

Source: G.V. Ramana (1991): 7.

transformed itself over the years that it has now become a party with no principled commitments or ideology. When Rajiv Gandhi became prime minister after his party won an overwhelming majority, the nation was filled with hope. He took an uncompromising stand towards public sector enterprises by asking them either to mend or end in a short time-span. But his party soon dragged him down to their level and inculcated in him the harsh realities of Indian politics.

Because of the nexus of the politician–bureaucrat–businessman, no party in India is in a position to privatize the public sector. The task is gigantic and the obstacles mind-boggling (Hariharan, 1991: 10). The major obstacle comes from the politicians themselves. The public sector, with an investment of Rs100 000 crore provides the biggest source of power to an Indian politician. Power gives him immense satisfaction, makes others run to him for succour, and helps him dispense favours that eventually fortify his vote-bank. He does not mind misusing the resources and facilities of the public sector to serve his vested interests. As such, he is unlikely to relinquish his stronghold over the public sector by letting go of this *kamadhenu* (Pennathun, 1991: 6).

Bureaucrats, too, have their reasons for not favouring privatization. They have to toe the political line for the advancement of their careers. Those nearing retirement look forward to post-retirement sinecures in the public sector for which the politicians' help is needed. They also know very well how to get the most out of the public sector during their tenure. Most of them have an 'itchy palm'. Aspects like indiscipline, absenteeism and the general lack of a work ethos are common. The smartness of the staff lies in making more money without having to work for it. They are bound to oppose any move to privatize tooth and nail.

Employees are also opposed to privatization. Any loss of control by the government could bring about an upheaval in industrial relations; workers feel safe and secure under government control. They consider it their birthright to do whatever they like without any repercussions, and they also take undue advantage of their rights in a parliamentary democracy. In the Indian scenario it is difficult to turn out an inefficient, good-for-nothing and work-shy fellow in the public sector due to very strong reactions from the trade unions.

The National Campaign Committee of Trade Unions (CCTU) has already become active in providing stiff resistance to privatization moves, especially with regard to retrenchment (Guha, 1991: 7). There was vehement opposition from trade unions for moves towards privatizing Scooters India and the UP Cement Corporation. The CCTU dubbed it a total sell-out of the country's sovereignty under pressures from the IMF. A Bharat Bandh was also organized on 29 November 1991 against the politics of retrenchment (*The Times of India*, 18 October 1991: 5).

Of the many hurdles faced by the governments on the way to privatization, none looms larger than the exit policy. While it has become imperative to close down sick units if the country wants to follow a path of liberalization and privatization, it is most difficult to do so in practice. The government has failed to convince workers and their trade unions that far from reducing employment, a free industrial exit can actually increase the job opportunities in the long run (Aiyar, 1991: 8).

Interestingly, industrialists, traders, organized and unorganized sections of society, and the farmers too, have opposed privatization moves in India. In fact, insulated from the perils of corporate life such as competition, natural death, accountability and global competition, the big industrialists, in particular the large houses, have benefited from the licence raj in India. State actions favoured big business, and big business favoured the states in return. They still prefer continued protection from the state, and are not in a mood to face competition from abroad (Table 8.8).

Even small industrialists are not in favour of competitive imports, since they are behind in reaping the benefits of government subsidies and tax concessions. Big traders, particularly in foreign trade, have close links with ministers and bureaucrats alike. They also have access to 'scarcity-rent' (Reddy, 1989: 40). Furthermore, the general attitude of the private sector in India has been commercial rather than entrepreneurial; they have a love–hate relationship with multinationals and their so-called professional management (Rangnekar, 1992: 21).

Under strong pressure from the indigenous, well-entrenched and well-organized interest groups, the privatization movement can never succeed in India. Unionized labour is considered the most powerful interest; and huge amounts are incurred every year to protect employment in the public sector. The unions enjoy recognition and statutory protection, and they have vested interests in maintaining the status quo. They are bound to resist any move towards retrenchment or liquidation, with full force (Tendulkar, 1991: 9).

Table 8.8 Holdings by financial institutions in select Tata companies

Company	*Equity base (in Rs crore)*	*Financial institution's holding %*	*Market value of 20 per cent disinvestment (in Rs crore)*
TISCO	229.43	45	1068
TELCO	103.67	47	532
ACC	55.96	45	290
TATA Tea	17.09	35	90
TATA Chemicals	73.75	36	90
TOMCO	19.74	40	30
VOLTAS	19.84	35	36.5
TATA Power	20.84	25	14
Indian Hotels	14.78	40	31.5
Total	555.1		2182.0

Source: S. Guru (1991): 22.

The farmers' lobby also exerts pressure on the government, and although not so well-organized they too carry power and influence. Rich farmers enjoy greater benefits from government policies, such as subsidies on food, fertilizers, water and power. But these benefits are enjoyed only by the rich few, while the majority in rural areas attract neither public investment nor subsidies. But they are unorganized, and the organized group is able to mobilize themselves and reap benefits disproportionate to their number. Instead of explaining, arguing and persuading the various interest groups, the government has often yielded to their protests or threats.

The Left also form an integral part of these organized interest groups. They are, in fact, most vociferous in opposing privatization and liberalization moves in India, and some of them have come out with an alternative thesis of privatizing the private sector first (Guru, 1991: 11). A mere shift of ownership from public to private hands is no solution, as it would only amount to replacement of one monopoly with another. With the financial markets in the hands of public enterprises, the private sector remains the handmaiden of the public sector. It is, therefore, necessary to free the private sector from the apron strings of the public sector, financial institutions and mutual funds. Only when India is able to build up a modern and dynamic financial system, can we hope to see the emergence of a strong private sector that can compete on the global front (G.V. Rao, 1991: 9–10).

Reeling under the shock and confusion following the collapse of communism in the former USSR and Eastern Europe, the left in India have not been able to provide any concrete solution to the economic problems faced by the country as a whole; nor are they prepared to accept a market mechanism. By opposing luxury consumption by the affluent class, they are in effect acting as unwilling lobbyists for the inefficient domestic capitalist producing the same luxury goods. The other group for which they act as lobbyists knowingly is the working class. By supporting inefficient companies or workers, they are doing long-term harm to the economy as a whole. Those who will ultimately bear the brunt are the unorganized poor who remain outside the system (Bardhan, 1991: 2408). The affluent class is already seceding from the social and pubic institutions by forming a parallel state system, putting the very concept of nationhood in danger (Gupta, 1995).

Even if the national mind may accept the drive towards privatization, the national heart still remains unreconciled. The general perception is that current efforts towards liberalization, deregulation and privatization are all motivated. The experience and profile of the private sector, too, fails to induce sufficient confidence among the public; it is feared that privatization may enlarge the number of sick units, requiring further support from the government. Nor does the public have full confidence in politicians, who are too busy pursuing their private interests in the name of the public interest. Even Rajiv Gandhi, the late Prime Minister of India, admitted that out of every one rupee meant for development purposes, only 15 paise reached the intended beneficiaries. While the new economic policies demand rationality in approach, the politician–bureaucrat–business nexus wants to maintain the status quo, however irrational it may be (Khare, 1991: 8).

Besides, under IMF pressures and economic constraints the government seems to have launched its privatization move in haste. It has neither clarified its objectives nor worked out the modalities in detail. Rather its approach seems to be 'one step forward, two steps back'. Nor has it sorted out the constitutional and legal hurdles. The privatization efforts by the government require a thorough revision of the constitution itself. V.K. Krishna Iyer, a former judge of the Supreme Court in India, blamed the Narasimha Rao government for giving up the very spirit of the constitution. Citing as an example Kamani Tubes, which was on the verge of being declared sick and was to be managed by its employees with profit, he emphasized the need for giving meaningful participation to employees in management (*The Times of India*, 12 December 1991: 11).

In fact, Article 43A of the Indian Constitution prescribes for participation of workers in management. Under the Directive Principles, the state is still under an obligation to foster workers' participation, and as such workers should be given the first option to run an enterprise on its being privatized. Without amending the Preamble first, which declares India to be a sovereign socialistic democratic republic, the proponents of privatization cannot practise unbridled forms of it. Similarly, privatization cannot be implemented without amending Articles 38, 39 and 43A of the Indian Constitution. Pending such changes, privatization is fraught with serious legal and constitutional improprieties. The Indian Constitution clearly forbids elected oligarchies from emulating a merchantalist state (Baxi, 1991: 33).

It seems, therefore, that there are too many hurdles to be crossed simultaneously. The question arises: is India ready or not? If we privatize in haste, we may have to repent at leisure. Although, privatization is creeping into the economic consciousness of the people, the conditions to make it a success are yet to be designed and implemented. The country is facing a cruel dilemma. Owing to the poor state of the economy with its huge debt and inadequate foreign exchange resources, privatization seems to be the need of the hour. But industries cannot be privatized or globalized all of a sudden, and we have no time to wait either. Even if we succeed in fulfilling the short-term goals, the long-term consequences could be grave. It would amount to having economics without history and politics without sociology (Das, 1992: 10). Therefore, privatization provides both a challenge and an opportunity. One should not commit the mistake of overemphasizing the gains from privatization and underestimating the obstacles (Dhameja, 1991: 133).

Scope for privatization

In view of the various constraints to privatization, the scope appears to be quite limited as far as India is concerned; those advocating privatization have been guilty of oversimplification. Privatization involves a very tedious, time-taking and complex process. On the other hand, those who have ideological commitments, or stakes in the public sector, have exaggerated the difficulties of moving to the private sector. Diametrically opposite views have been expressed during the privatization debate:

- Privatization holds the key, therefore privatize most of the public sector, especially the non-core sector; or it is better to mend the public sector rather than end it.
- All profit-making public enterprises should be privatized; or only loss-making public enterprises should be privatized.
- Why should the government lose revenues by privatizing profit-making enterprises; or who will buy the loss-making enterprises at all.
- Public-sector enterprises need shock therapy; or privatization should be resorted to in a phased manner.
- Part privatization through the sale of equity is sufficient for the time being; or part privatization does not amount to privatization at all.
- There is no need to change ownership to achieve the objectives of efficiency and competition; or privatization without change in ownership is meaningless.

Unfortunately, the new economic policy enunciated on 24 July 1991 did not advocate any specific objectives of privatization. It opened up certain areas hitherto reserved for the public sector for private investment, including percentage levels of foreign investment. It also decided to unload 20 per cent of equity investment in select central public enterprises and to refer sick units to the Board for Industrial and Financial Reconstruction, and so on.

The 1992–93 budget provided a boost to the liberalization policy adopted during 1991–92 by opening up the Indian economy to the world. The Narasimha government decided to make the rupee partially convertible, and to abolish import licenses and reduce custom tariffs from 150 to 110 per cent in order to globalize the Indian economy. It allowed foreign investment in power, gas and oil, the three most capital-intensive industries in India. Foreign investment from reputable institutions like pension funds was also allowed in the share market. The government also decided to further disinvest equities in public sector to raise additional revenues of Rs3500 crore during 1992–93. Out of this, Rs1000 crore were set aside for a National Renewal Fund. The government also decided to expand the National Renewal Fund to provide relief to those affected adversely by the new economic policies. While paving the way for the private sector to come forward in an outward-looking economy, the government chose to forgo its control pricing and premiums.

For the first time in the history of independent India, the budget provided a definite policy thrust to the Indian economy. Earlier, the government's attitude used to be ambivalent, yet during debates on privatization the terms public sector and public enterprise are still confused by many. While the public sector refers to various government activities related to public administration, public utilities, public services, public enterprises, public finances and commercial activities, public enterprise refers to only those activities that are carried out by entities legally separate from the government. Moreover, no public sector activities are financed by the budget, while public enterprises are not fully dependent upon budgetory support (Gouri, 1991: 547–8).

Surprisingly, in the growing debate on privatization in India the state-level public enterprises (SLPEs) are generally ignored. The SLPEs account for almost 35 per cent of the total investment in the public sector which was Rs130 000 crore by 31 March 1989, the SLPEs taking Rs46 000 crore of that. There were nearly 1000 SLPEs on 31 March 1989, while the number of central PEs stood at 230. The SLPEs employ nearly half of the total executive personnel employed in the public sector, and these are engaged in a wide range of activities – commercial, developmental-promotional and social welfare. Compared with their counterparts at the centre, their operational profile is more variegated (Sankar, Mishra and Nandgopal, 1990: 169–74).

On the basis of the performance of the SLPEs with reference to the public purpose served by them, the extent of resources mobilized outside the state budget and profitability, it was found that approximately 300 SLPEs need drastic action in terms of liquidation or other devices of privatization. Other SLPEs are also in dire need of restructuring if they are to be retained in the public sector (Table 8.9).

The state of Maharashtra took the lead by inviting the private sector to put up a Rs10 000 crore package of public utilities including roads, ports and power stations to meet the state's infrastructural needs. Other states are gearing up, interacting with big business and competing with each other in bringing in more and more investments. With the economy being divested of many controls, the various states have to compete for their share of investment. While Gujarat and Maharashtra, with just 14 per cent of India's population, have succeeded in capturing more than 35 per cent of proposed new investment, Assam, Bihar, West Bengal and Orrisa with a combined population of 25 per cent have only been able to manage 5.43 per cent (Mohanty, 1997: 159).

In view of state-level competition, Kerala has turned to Tata Consultancy for professional advice, while West Bengal is working extra hard to break its image of a state with inadequate infrastructure and on intractable workforce. It is now trying to associate the private sector with power sector in the wake of 'parallelization'. Gujarat has painstakingly built itself up as an important competitor to Maharashtra; it has learnt how to create attractive packages of incentives and put together nuclei of infrastructure. It has already invited the private sector's direct intervention in port-development, and is forging a profitable partnership with private companies to develop 11 medium and 28 minor ports in the state (Bhatt, 1991: 7).

Table 8.9 Privatization of state level private enterprises

Category	*Public purpose*	*Resource mobility*	*Profitability*	*No. of SLPEs*	*Policy option*
1	H_1	H_2	H_3	75	Continue in the state sector
2	L_1	L_2	L_3	200	Closure or liquidation
3	H_1	L_2	L_3	360	Accent on resource mobilization and profitability
4	H_1	L_1	H_3	75	ditto
5	H_1	H_2	L_3	–	Reorganise internal management
6	L_1	H_2	H_3	55	Disinvest
7	L_1	L_2	H_3	49	Introduce financial adjustments before disinvesting
8	L_1	H_2	H_3	–	Disinvest

Key: H = high; L = low.
Source: R.K. Mishra and R. Nandgopal (1991): 11.

By contrast, Tamil Nadu is struggling to find its feet; there are proposals to privatize the joint sector power-cum-lignite mining projects and chemical laboratories. On the northern front, Haryana is trying to emulate Maharashtra and Gujarat, but, so far, efforts at privatization by the Haryana state government are negligible. While public authorities want to wash their hands of the whole business and let someone else clear the mess, private enterprises contend that loss-making activities should be left to the public sector. Until the issue is resolved, citizens will continue to go public to meet their private needs.

It has been argued that public enterprises which provide essential goods and services should be retained by the public sector, although international practice does not warrant it. All those activities which are considered strategic or sacroscant or beyond the capacity of the private sector are also to be retained by the public sector. Privatization is generally recommended in those cases which are chronically sick or where the private sector already exists. Private enterprises are not allowed to reap benefits out of the long efforts of the public sector. At the most, small amounts of equity capital can be divested in select public enterprises.

While it has been universally accepted that the provision of infrastructure facilities like roads, bridges and power is a public function to be administered by appropriate government bodies, persisting constraints on available resources have made it imperative for the government to seriously consider the commercialization of infrastructure projects. The implementation of infrastructure projects in association with the private sector has been in vogue in many developed economies such as the USA, the UK, Japan and France, but it is a relatively new concept in India.

The government of India is now willing to throw open certain areas hitherto exclusively reserved for the public sector, such as railways, civil aviation, telecommunications, power, gas, oil exploration, minerals and mines, arms and ammunition, and so on. The underlying feature of infrastructure privatization is that the investment made by private sector financiers is recovered through the levy on users. For instance, in the case of roads and bridges such recovery can be made by levying a toll tax. The infrastructure can include a wide spectrum of industries: (1) roads, highways and bridges, (2) power projects and pollution control and (3) development of industrial estates with attendant infrastructure (Pherwani, 1991: 6).

In the context of power, the government has encouraged private sector participation in power generation, transmission and distribution. In September 1991, the Lok Sabha passed the Electricity Laws (Amendment) Bill to this effect. The private sector can set up coal, lignite or gas-based thermal, hydro, wind and solar energy projects. It can also set up units as licensee companies to supply and distribute energy in specified areas. Even investments from NRIs and foreign sources are acceptable. Although some proposals have already been received, only about half of 30 000MW Eighth Plan targets are likely to be met (Bidwai, 1996: 13). After much controversy, Enron and the Maharashtra government agreed to a new contract involving US$300 million, but the deal had to be renegotiated on grounds that proper bidding had not taken place. It involved a political fight between the central and the state government (Kaushik, 1996: 60).

Similarly, very heavy investments are needed for surface transport, and it has become imperative to invite private capital. A road construction and maintenance company can be promoted under an institutional format with private sector participation, and the cash generated from the initial projects can be deployed into road segments. Of late, Infrastructure Leasing and Financial Services Ltd. has been emphasizing the need for commercialization of the roads sector by associating with private capital. For instance, the Maharashtra government signed a memorandum of understanding with Infrastructure Leasing and Financial Services Ltd. for construction of a toll bridge and flyover network connecting Bandra and Worli. The project is expected to cost around Rs175 crore. The ambitious project envisages an integrated traffic system with sophisticated toll collection on an international design. In the USA, those who are willing to pay a little extra can use road privately maintained. In return they can save petrol and time because these roads are less crowded, better maintained and short in distance.

Like power and road, telecommunications also plays an important role in the development of an industrial economy. The benefits of an improved telecommunication system can be stunning in the modern era. Improved telecommunications can lead to reductions in energy costs and a lessening of pressures on the already over-burdened transport sector. Although tremendous progress has been made in the telecommunications sector in India, much remains to be done to render the Indian economy globally competitive. Parallel telecommunications networks can be installed for this purpose. The government has already decided to open switching, equipment and value-added services such as car phones, paging, videotext and other services for foreign investment. Many companies including multinational telecom giants are interested in investing in this core area. However, the Department of Telecommunications is reluctant to give away the high-earning sector of car telephones to the private sector. Cellular phones have already become a status symbol in India and the C. Dot and MTNL are doing good business.

In view of serious resource limitations, the government is now planning to open other areas to the private sector. There are also pressures from the World Bank to allow the oil, gas, coal and power industries to be run on commercial lines (Chakravorty, 1991: 1), and the resulting growth of internally generated resources would make them less dependent on budgetary support. For instance, the working group on coal and lignite for the Eighth Plan has projected a total investment of Rs16 552 crore for a production level of 295.46 million tonnes of coal and 23.50 million tonnes of lignite in 1994–95. The likely availability of plan outlay is Rs11 000 crore from the coal and lignite sector, leaving a shortfall of Rs5500 crore. Private sector investment can thus play an important role in relieving the public sector of financial constraints.

There is an indication that a few coal mines may be provided as captive mines to the power plants sanctioned in the private sector. Out of a total of 398 coal mines, 97 made a profit of Rs991.50 crore employing 25 per cent of the workforce and producing 3.74 lakh tonnes per day; while 63 per cent of the workforce in 251 coal mines produced only 28 per cent of coal, incurring a loss of Rs1117 crore. With a total investment of Rs99 315 crore in 244 units in heavy industries, only 131 made profits of Rs5741 crore up to 31 March 1990. Out of them, 50 are chronic loss-makers (Kirpekar, 1991: 9).

Like coal, the steel industry had also been incurring heavy losses. Despite the availability of rich raw materials, India remains dependent on imports in steel, while countries like South Korea and Brazil are doing far better; in both of these countries steel has been privatized. The government of India has now deregulated steel, and on 16 January 1992 it abolished price controls on iron and steel to make them competitive in international markets. In the case of other minerals and metals the government is exploring the prospects of involving private participation to meet the growing demands of the country. However, it has ruled out the privatization of profit-making oil companies altogether. Similarly, the government has ruled out privatization of LIC and GIC, the two insurance companies in India.

However, the government is actively engaged in part privatization of railways. A high-power internal committee constituted by the Railway Board has recommended privatization of several sectors of Indian Railways for proper, efficient and profitable management (*The Pioneer*, 6 December 1991). These include building of locomotives, wagons, coaches, rails and a large number of components presently being imported. In a bid to attract resources and the latest technology, proposals from foreign companies and NRIs are also acceptable. An investment of Rs45 000 crore was needed during the Eighth Plan by Indian Railways (*The Economic Times*, 7 December 1991).

The Railways are planning massive privatization, and private promoters are even being invited to develop the real estate sector. The Railways have 4.35 lakh hectares of land, out of which 88 000 hectares fall under existing rail lines (*The Economic Times*, 25 September 1991). It is planning to lease out land to mop up additional funds for providing better amenities to commuters, and is planning to set up a Level Management Corporation to manage its vacant land for commercial purposes. Over the years, the real estate of Railways has appreciated a great deal but has not been fully taken advantage of.

Out of Rs1000 crore allotted for construction work, Rs150–200 crore are to be given to the private sector for trade-laying. This will help in expanding and upgrading existing rail lines, while adding more new lines (*The Financial Express*, 16 October 1991). Another area where the help of the private sector is sought is catering, and proposals have been received from ITDC and Annapoorna of Chennai. This will help the Railways to offload some responsibilities and allow them to concentrate on certain areas on a priority basis, such as electrification, indigenization of components, and conversion of metre gauge into broad gauge and laying of new tracks.

The privatization debate has also been triggered in the civil aviation sector. Both Air India and Indian Airlines may go private with a certain percentage of their shares being disinvested. Privatization of airlines would mean a larger shareholding by the public in these organizations, and would help in widening the capital base while making these organizations more accountable. Indian Airlines has already plunged into the red and was estimated to have suffered a loss of Rs82 crore before tax during 1990–91, against Rs15 crore during 1989–90. One of the main factors responsible for the heavy loss was the prolonged grounding of the entire fleet of Airbus A-320 following the crash in Bangalore in February 1990, killing all the passengers. Air India also suffered heavy losses owing to suspension of its flights to the Gulf during 1991. Prior to the Gulf war it operated 47 flights to the Gulf per week (Table 8.10).

While there is a good chance for part privatization of Air India and Indian Airlines, the chances for Vayudoot, the third-local feeder airline in India, are quite dim. Vayudoot has been incurring heavy losses ever since its inception;

Table 8.10 Should Indian Airlines be split: passengers' responses

Airport	*Total number of passengers surveyed*	*Yes*	*No*	*Can't say*
Santa Cruz (Bombay)	343	295	41	7
Dum Dum (Calcutta)	239	177	45	17
Indira Gandhi (New Delhi)	350	283	53	14
Total	932	755	139	38

Source: *Business India*, 5–18 March 1990: 50–3.

amounting to Rs2.7 crore per month in early 1990s. Even its monthly income was down from an average of Rs3.5 crore during 1989–90 to Rs1.5 crore during 1990–91. No private buyer is willing to take over Vayudoot with liabilities of over Rs80 crore, and the government has ruled out of its closure. However, in the late 1990s, Modiluft and Sahara airlines were doing good business on certain sectors.

The government is now encouraging the private sector to build aviation infrastructure. The country has major plans for the expansion of its airline fleets, development of airports and other ground infrastructure, and there are moves to deregulate the Indian skies (Sen, 1991: 8) by removing all constraints on private air-taxi operations. The air-taxi plan took off with the government granting licences to three private firms and 'No Objection Certificates' to another 18 firms (*The Times of India*, 20 August 1990: 8). An inaugural flight took place from Bombay to New Delhi in July 1991.

However, public opinion is divided in the case of road transport. The experience of associating private operators with Delhi Transport Corporation has not been satisfactory. Commuters have to face a lot of problems owing to rash driving, overcrowding and overcharging, and, lacking all norms, their buses are more prone to accidents. During the 1950s, the stress was on a public transport system, and by 31 March 1990 there were 68 nationalized state transport undertakings with a fleet of 102 067 passenger buses and an investment of approximately Rs3700 crore. They employed more than 7 lakh persons and carried approximately 60 million passengers per day. Even if the private sector is actively involved in public transport, the state will have to play an active role in enforcing the regulations.

Besides transport, privatization has been recommended in several other areas such as hotels, textiles, tourism, oil refinement and exploration, and bread-manufacturing industries by the Standing Conference of Public Enterprise (SCOPE) and the Managing Committee of Associated Chambers of Commerce and Industry. SCOPE has also recommended that an amendment be made to Article 12 of the Constitution to exclude government-owned corporations and companies under the jurisdiction of Committee on Public Undertakings (COPU). There are talks of privatizing Hotels and Tourism,

ITDC, Duty-Free Shopping, Banks, Pesticides Lab, Life Insurance, Social Housing, and so on (Sharma, 1989: 16).

The company Maruti Udyog has already been privatized, and the parent Japanese Company, Suzuki, has now been allowed to raise its equity from 49 to 51 per cent and is now eligible for loans from International Finance Corporation, the private lending arm of the World Bank. It can also expand to manufacture cars for export. India has held road-shows in London, Singapore, Hong Kong and Bombay to promote Global Depository Receipts (GDR) of Steel Authority of India (SAIL), Mahanagar Telephone Nigam Limited (MTNL), Oil and Natural Gas Commission (ONGC) and Container Corporation of India. The shares of many public sector enterprises are now listed on domestic and international stockmarkets. Attempts are also being made to associate the private sector both at the planning and implementation stages.

Interestingly, the whole debate about the prospects of privatization has concentrated on a few industries only in an agrarian economy. These industries, including the public sector, account for approximately 10 per cent of India's net GDP, so that even an unusual annual increase of 10 per cent would affect the whole economy by barely 1 per cent. As such, no economic miracles can be expected unless the winds of change reach the rural sector also. Widespread and sustainable agricultural growth is an important precondition for industrial development. In fact, a 10 per cent increase in agricultural productivity is equivalent to a threefold increase in industrial productivity (Baig, 1991: 8).

Contrary to the popular view, public sector investment plays a dominant role in the agricultural sector in India. The state's role is reflected in the government's control over agricultural activities through administered prices and distribution, investments, subsidies and the supply of inputs like fertilizers, seeds and support to research and extension services. Realizing the realities of the specific socioeconomic milieu of India, the United Front government in June 1996 took the initiative of doubling rural credit over the next five years, doubling the share of NABARD (state level development financial institutions), and setting up private local area banks (LABS) to promote investments in commercial and high-tech agriculture.

To provide a boost to the agricultural sector, private intervention can be allowed in the seeds sector and in providing extension services. If the Rs15 000 crore annual levies on fertilizer and food subsidies, poverty eradication programmes, interest on defaulting rural credit and financing of matching grants by the state government were eliminated, there could be a budget surplus and an immediate reduction in inflation, as well as a lowering of the administered prices of essentials like oil, power and steel, with a real possibility of reducing taxation. These measures alone could make India a vibrant member of the global economy, rather than the dismantling of controls and investments by NRIs or foreign nationals (Baig, 1991: 8).

Modalities of privatization

The privatization programme as it stands today is geared to four major directions: (1) capital disinvestment, (2) liquidation of sick and unavailable units, (3) *ad hoc* privatization, and (4) incremental privatization. The National Democratic Alliance (NDA) government allotted 42 PSUs to a newly-formed Disinvestment Commission to look after various issues and problems related to restructuring prior to disinvestment of equities in select public sector enterprises in India (*Business Standard*, 18 December 1999). There is also a Bureau of Industrial and Financial Regulation (BIFR) to aid and advise on sick units in the public sector. Instead of divestiture, India has opted for divestment of shares through direct offers to the public and open auctions (Table 8.11).

The Rangarajan Committee on PSE recommended divestment of 49 per cent of equities in industries reserved for the public sector, and 74 per cent in other cases. However, during 1996–97, the government succeeded in mobilizing only Rs168 crore against an ambitious target of Rs7000 crore due to adverse market conditions (*The Times of India*, 15 January 1997:15).

Depending upon the motivation, privatization can take different forms. Various modalities can be worked out to obtain the best results from public, private or hybrid organizations. A large number of public sector enterprises need to be mended, rather than ended: in some cases, private investment can be injected; other enterprises can be publicly-owned but privately managed by

Table 8.11 Stocks disinvested and listed

S. No.	*Name of PSU*	*Share capital (rupees crores)*	*Price**	*Govt. of India holding (%)*	*Other major share holders*
1	FACT	354.77	NA	87.35	
2	ONGC	1525.92	175	96.13	
3	NALCO	1288.62	38	87.15	FIs
4	SAIL	4130.4	22.25	85.82	UTI
5	SCI	282.3	32	80.12	UTI
6	CONCOR	64.99	375	76.92	M. Stanley
7	ITI	88	NA	76.67	FIs
8	HZL	422.53	15.85	75.92	FIs
9	BEL	80	NA	75.86	FIs
10	MTNL	600	237	65.73	FIs & FIIs
11	IPCL	248.95	131.5	62.4	FIs
12	BEML	36.86	141.5	61.1	FIs
13	IBP	14.76	103.75	59.62	FIs
14	GAIL	845.32	100	96.63	
15	BRPL	13.75	13.75	74.76	FIs & MFs

Note: * Price as on 18 February 1997 on the Bombay Stock Exchange.
Source: *Disinvestment Commission Report*, 1997: 68.

way of management contracts; some enterprises can be sold lock, stock and barrel; while a few others can be sold in phases. In some cases equity can be sold, in some others assets can be sold. In fact, each enterprise slated for privatization or part privatization needs a different modality depending upon its financial position, social obligations and market conditions.

The 1991–92 Budget suggested disinvestment of 20 per cent of equity in select PSEs; capital restructuring and rehabilitation schemes for chronically-sick PSEs; and a safety net for workers affected in the process. In this context, various questions were raised: would offloading up to 20 per cent of public sector shares increase efficiency? Could this be called privatization in the true sense? How would mutual funds and financial institutions figure in the whole scheme? Wouldn't there be conflicts of interest between the mutual funds and financial institutions as minority shareholders, and government as the majority shareholder? How could transferring a mere 20 per cent of shares to mutual funds result in greater autonomy for managers? And how could this system be made more accountable? How could the disinvestment in select PSUs (Rs18 288 crore in past nine years) yield adequate resources to cover the rise in expenditure on social sector to the tune Rs8175 crore during 1991–92 to Rs29 370 crore in 1998–99 and an estimated Rs32 380 crore in 1999–2000 (*The Financial Express*, 18 December 1999).

When the scheme was mooted in July 1991, no one could have believed that the government and the mutual funds could have behaved so competitively. By the end of December 1991 all the mutual funds and financial institutions had actually remitted Rs2500 crore on an account basis. Only 31 companies were taken up. Air India and Indian Airlines were dropped at the last moment for not having corporate status, while Steel Authority and Indian Petrochemicals were taken as last minute entrants. Everything was decided in haste. This change in the government's speed and substance remained an intriguing part of the sell-off drama (Killawala, 1992: 77–80).

Table 8.12 Bids by mutual funds and financial institutions

Institution	*Number of packages bid for*	*Estimated value (in crore rupees)*
State Bank of India	22	100
Canara Bank	25	131
Indian Bank	3	8.5
Punjab National Bank	1	3
Bank of India	Nil	Nil
General Insurance Corporation	95	300
Life Insurance Corporation	172	600
Unit Trust of India	489	1498
Total	807	2640.5

Source: *Business India*, 6–19 January 1992: 80.

Shares in the 31 companies were clubbed into packages of seven or eight companies; each package contained a mix of five or six profitable companies and one or two marginally profitable ones. A total of 47 different packages were prepared containing different amount of shares of each company. These were further sub-divided into a total of 825 packages, each requiring an investment of Rs3–4 crore. The job was carried out in a highly scientific and professional manner, with the scrip of all these companies likely to be soon listed on major stock exchanges (Table 8.13).

The objectives behind the disinvestment of 20 per cent equity in these select public sector enterprises were: broad-basing equity; improving management; and enhancing availability of resources. But privatization without effective competition and economic efficiency is likely to defeat the very purpose behind the changes in the economic policies. The government is now considering possibilities of breaking up some of the large public sector units so that they can compete with one another. For instance, the Narasimha Committee on Financial Reforms had favoured competition in the banking sector by allowing more foreign and private banks into India.

The banking sector in India has undergone rapid transformation in the past 20 years. The aftermath of nationalization showed a tremendous increase in the number of bank branches, particularly in rural areas, but also in deposits, advances and staff members. On the other hand, qualitative achievements deteriorated: efficiency was put at stake; house-keeping became problematic; quality of loan assets became poor; recovery efforts slackened; the number of bad debts increased; and the sense of belonging came to its lowest ebb. This state of affairs made it imperative for the World Bank and the IMF to exert pressure in favour of privatization. But, due to political reasons, the government has so far ruled out privatization in the sense of denationaliza-

Table 8.13 The Banking sector in India: watch them go!

Name of the Bank	*Issue price (In Rs.)*	*Date of Issue*	*Public issue size (Rs crore)*	*Over subscribed in times*	*Current Price (In Rs)*
Bank of Baroda	85	05.12.96	850	1.1	79.8
Bank of India	45	21.02.97	675	1.86	33.9
Corporation Bank	80	03.10.97	304	10.4	102.0
Dena Bank	30	28.10.97	180	1.13	21.5
State Bank of Travancore	600	08.12.97	69.24	2.5	1950
State Bank of India	100	15.12.93	750	1.9	209.4
State Bank of Bikaner	540	20.11.97	65.95	4.0	360.5

Source: Compiled by: Manish Mankad. *Business India*, 13–26 July 1998: 52.

tion. Rather, government is considering amending the acts governing Reserve Bank of India (RBI) and Industrial and Finance Corporation of India (IFCI) to allow partial privatization of these institutions. For instance, the State Bank of India (SBI) proposed to offer 30 per cent of its equity to the public in 1991. It was easier to denationalize SBI because its shares were held by the Reserve Bank of India (RBI) and not by the government; moreover, over 3 per cent of its shares were held privately.

In between nationalization and denationalization, the government can very well consider the consortium concept of privatization based on a tripartite mix of the government, the public and employees (Rao, 1991: 7). Bank employees can also be involved in the process of privatization; by offering them shares, they may become more involved, participative and efficient. In some sections, a novel scheme has been proposed to involve the private sector at the initial stages only. It is known as 'Build, Own, Operate and Transfer', or the BOOT scheme. Under this scheme a private sector agency can finance a project, operate it long enough to recover its investment along with a minimum return, and then transfer it back to the government. As a consequence an asset is created for public use, pays for itself and eventually reverts to the state itself. The BOOT scheme can also be considered for augmenting the country's foreign exchange requirements. So far the principle has been accepted for the oil exploration sector only (Pherwani, 1991: 6).

The last resort could be withdrawal from certain economic activities. For instance, the government might stop providing huge subsidies to the agricultural sector or simply close down sick PSUs. Chronically sick units such as National Bicycle Corporation, Cycle Corporation, Bharat Ophthalmic Glass Limited, Bharat Leather Corporation, Scooter India Ltd., Tannery and Footwear Corporation of India Ltd., Weighbird India Ltd., and Bharat Process and Mechanical Engineers Ltd. are being seriously considered by the government. All of them have been incurring heavy losses over recent years.

Out of 49 PSUs under the Industry Ministry, 21 are profit-making, while 28 are loss-making. The government is seriously thinking of winding up 14 sick units of National Textile Corporation (NTC) and amalgamating approximately 49 mills to a slim 21 to make them economically viable. If it is not possible to rehabilitate a unit on a viable basis, the government may think over partial or complete disinvestment of ownership through fresh issue of capital and control over management. When a unit starts making profits, the government can divest its equity in part to private promoters (Jhaveri, 1991: 14).

At one stage, the government also thought in terms of allowing civil servants extraordinary leave to work in private sector enterprises whether domestic or foreign, for a maximum period of five years. The move was designed to reduce the number of the officers on the government's payroll on one hand, and to provide the officers a chance to learn ways of improving efficiency and productivity on the other. On their return, these officers were supposed to transplant the privatization style to their parent organizations. At present government servants are only allowed to go on deputation to other government departments or foreign assignments.

A step forward

In 1998 budget, the Finance Minister, Mr Yashwant Sinha announced that his government was prepared to dilute its share in non-strategic PSUs down to 26 per cent, shut unviable units and sell their assets to meet the pending liabilities. He also proposed to set up a Special Purpose Vehicle (SPV) to bring the government holding in select PSUs to 49 per cent. The idea was to reduce the government stake in select blue chip PSEs such as the Industrial Development Bank of India to 40 per cent by transferring the surplus shares to the SPV. The SPV, in turn, was supposed to sell these shares to the financial institutions, banks and the general public. The idea was to disperse shareholding too widely to allow any effective say in the management of these blue chips by the shareholders. The former chief of the Disinvestment Commission expressed his reservations about the 'financial viability' and 'transparency' in SPV dealings (*The Times of India*, 8 September 1998: 15).

An evaluation

Politicians are the most practical people. They want to reap immediate benefits out of economic policies, and they know full well that they cannot survive if the economy fails. When a man is on the verge of falling, he does not think about long-term consequences. Similarly, when India found itself in a precarious situation with its credit rate plummeting, its foreign exchange reserves almost vanishing and political uncertainties looming large on the horizon, the first priority was to claw back to safety (Pherwani, 1991: 6).

Privatization assumed significance in this regard. The immediate concern was to obtain IMF loans to overcome the fiscal crisis, and liberalization, deregulation and privatization constituted the strings attached. Besides pressures from aid donors and multilateral agencies, the micro and macro-level reforms of the Indian economy also warranted it.

The questions arise: what are the long-term effects of privatization? Can the new package of economic reforms succeed? Will they be allowed to succeed? What are the political costs? What are the social costs? And what are the costs in terms of environmental degradation and deterioration of moral values? No doubt the recourse to free market mechanisms can liberate the energies of our entrepreneurs, can make them expand and diversify, stimulate savings and so on, but only by paying the penalties of initial dislocation (Waseem, 1991: 11).

The stabilization process advocated by multinational institutions and initiated by the Narasimha government involved a drastic adjustment of the budget. But stabilization cannot lead to sustainable growth automatically. On the other hand, it may very well lead to stagnation and hardships for the time being. When an economy finds itself in an acute crisis and seeks correction without allowing inflationary pressures to rise, there is no alternative but to contract economic activities. This is bound to affect some sections of society adversely (Sanghvi, 1991: 11).

Are we really prepared to bear hardships today for a better future tomorrow? IMF loans can only help in softening the adverse transitional impacts of stabilization and economic restructuring. It neither provides a magic wand nor a substitute for the transitional costs of macroeconomic restructuring which have to be borne by citizens themselves.

During the past 50 years, the profitability of unproductive rent-seeking activities has tended to overtake those of productive ones. Beneficiaries have consisted of industrialists, skilled professionals, government employees, industrial workers and rich farmers; organized sectors reaped the benefits at the cost of the unorganized segments of the economy. These very groups who have been recipients of rental benefits are likely to oppose economic restructuring to restore the rightful place of productive performance based on market forces. Instead of curtailing the benefits enjoyed by the upper strata of the society, the government is forced to protect their interests by sacrificing those of the poor and lower middle class. According to new estimates based on a consumption index, approximately 39 per cent of the population still stands below the poverty line (*The Times of India*, 30 December 1996: 10).

The very process of liberating the Indian economy from its physical bureaucratic and fiscal straightjacket is therefore fraught with dangerous consequences in a liberal political democracy built over the past five decades. Those who cite the examples of Korea and Taiwan in support of rapid liberalization in our own country, forget the hard truth that those nations have had a single culture with an authoritarian work culture, while India remains multicultural, multiethnic and a pluralistic society with well-established democratic norms and practices. It is not easy to carry out reforms imposed from above.

Every major economic reform is bound to have political consequences; it is bound to have gainers or losers, and the losers are bound to provide resistance too. And every political compromise involves economic costs in terms of sacrificing long-term goals, slowing down the pace of reforms and thereby increasing the duration of the transition period. If the government indulges in reaping immediate political gains, bows down to political pressures by various interest groups and lobbyists, economic reconstructing can never take place. For instance, the slashing of fertilizer subsidies is bound to foster political upheaval in rural areas, which any ruling party, lacking credibility, courage or political will, would like to avoid at all costs. According to some economists, the withdrawal of subsidies on food and fertilizers alone could bring down the deficit to the limits prescribed by the IMF. But it would definitely affect the poor farmers more than the better-off sections of the society since the withdrawal of subsidies is bound to lead to inflation. For instance, a rise of 30 per cent in fertilizer prices could result in a reduction in fertilizer use of 14 per cent and food grain output by 3.4 per cent, having an adverse effect on the entire economy (*The Financial Express*, 30 August 1991: 6).

Liberalization of the economy in general, and privatization in particular, is likely to further increase the economic disparities. It involves reduction in employment, capital expenditure and social infrastructure by the government, and implies a sharp shift in the distribution of income from working people to the entrepreneurial class. Even among the entrepreneurs, foreign investors are bound to have an edge over the domestic ones. Further, it would encourage traders at the cost of entrepreneurs. Instead of developing indigenous techniques, the private sector may indulge in importing cheap technology from abroad; most large companies in India already have imports much higher than their exports (Kothari, 1991: 26).

Furthermore, too much emphasis on market forces may tend to underline the predominance of non-priority items, amounting to sacrificing long-term development prospects for short-term interests. The new economic policies are elitist in orientation; they are meant to serve the interests of the industrial sector at the cost of the agricultural sector, and the rich sections of society at the cost of millions of those living below the poverty line. An attempt is being made to achieve economic efficiency at the cost of equity.

The questions arise: does the notion of a trade-off between equity and efficiency actually make sense? Does the notion of efficiency have the same status as that of equity? In the context of an equity-efficiency debate, it is quite possible to have an allocation of resources that is highly efficient but grossly inequitable, or one that is extremely equitable but highly inefficient. The logic behind it is that the two different objectives need not be reduced to a single one. Nor can one be a substitute for the other. A trade off can occur only between two primary objectives; in the developed world efficiency may be regarded as the prime objective, but in the context of emerging economies like India the notion of efficiency can acquire meaning only with reference to equity and not as a replacement for equity (Gupta, 1994).

However, if the country is not able to curtail the huge expenditures and waste of resources by the government itself, if the public sector does not turn efficient and self-sufficient, if the private sector is not able to compete at the international level by achieving ISO-9000 standards, if exports do not rise up to expectations, if we fail to attract investment by foreign nationals and NRIs, and if the government is not able to demonstrate a strong political will, the country might plunge into deeper crisis. Even if by removing all quantitative and fiscal constraints both in industrial and foreign trade policy the country is able to attract multinationals, they cannot be expected to fulfil social obligations towards the masses in India. They would certainly be less than concerned about the sociopolitical implications of the distortions in economic development through their forays, their sole purpose being to exploit cheap raw materials and labour.

Moreover, economic growth based on industrialization can lead to environmental degradation. Economists relate growth with economy, trade and stock prices, they do not give due importance to ecology. At best they may internalize ecological costs into their models. But sustainable economic growth cannot flourish in a sick, degraded, polluted and unsustainable environment (Khushoo, 1992: 4). Such growth calls for strict measures on the part of government to ensure population stabilization, agricultural growth, conservation of animal husbandry and fisheries, pollution-free energy systems, recycling of used materials and environment-friendly technologies. The costs of building a bio-industrial society could be too heavy for a country like India.

Moreover, with privatization the entire value system is likely to change, with self-interest bound to prevail over altruism. The privatization strategy is not adopted mainly with the motive of removing deficiencies in the public sector, it generally has the sole purpose of generating additional resources. It can have adverse effects on social welfare; either it can lead to poor quality of public services or reductions in expenditure on public services by the state. Therefore, it cannot be ruled out that the privatization strategy may backfire as and when its true social costs become apparent.

Lessons from India

Given the background of the public sector in India, it is doubtful that privatization will be accepted as an end in itself. So far there is no consensus in favour of market solutions and property rights; rather, the stress is on more efficient government. In a country where millions of people are forced to live in absolute poverty, the state cannot absolve of its social obligations. State intervention becomes imperative for the fulfilment of goals other than economic growth. Nor can development be seen merely in terms of economic growth. In fact, the ecological crisis requires a shift away from rising consumerism and growth if we want to sustain the world as a whole.

Just as socialism has failed to establish a veritable 'heaven on earth' (Gupta, 1987: 232), privatization cannot solve our economic problems *ipso facto*. Rather, it may become the source of a new set of problems. The report cards of the privatization experiences in advanced industrialized countries are not very encouraging; in developing countries it may lead to a rise in consumerism, inflation, unemployment or economic and regional disparities. Moreover, with the demise of communism it is difficult to say 'who will keep the capitalists honest now'. While the concept of a welfare state provided a new lease of life to the capitalist system, curtailment of public expenditure in the name of privatization may result in revolts from within – as and when the capitalist system becomes complacent.

At the most, privatization can be seen as a package of economic reforms and certainly not the only one. Therefore, an attempt should be made to revamp public enterprises by adopting certain short-term and long-term measures. Some short term measures might include reducing the size of the public sector by undertaking as few projects as are manageable; developing greater autonomy and accountability to public units' managers; restructuring the remaining potentially viable units through selective physical and financial rehabilitation, improving management and retrenching extra staff after providing adequate safety-nets and so forth.

Long-term measures might include providing competition to public sector enterprises by allowing private participation wherever feasible. Under the new industries and trade policies, the government has already invited private sector participation in core areas such as power, energy, communications, road and bridges. Apart from 18 industries of strategic importance, the government has decided to withdraw from other areas with the hope that the private sector will take up the slack in due course. It has also decided to liquidate chronically sick industries. The biggest gain could be by not launching new projects which are unlikely to be completed in time, owing to resource limitations. The emphasis has to be on profitability through efficiency.

There should not be any ambiguity or conflict about the basic goals of the public sector enterprises, where the PSEs owe high social obligations, profitability can be neither desirable nor feasible. In such cases the objectives should be specifically mentioned to enhance their utility and credibility.

In this context, memoranda of understanding with select public enterprises can play an important role in revitalizing the entire economy, acting as performance contracts between government and public enterprise. The government can provide clear guidelines for the mobilization of capital resources, expansion and diversification, without encroaching upon the autonomy of a given enterprise. A recent survey by SCOPE (Standing Conference of Public Enterprise) showed that there is perceptible interference from political quarters and bureaucracy via multiple reporting or otherwise. The chief executives of 83 state-owned enterprises held that unless and until autonomy is ensured, accountability could not be maintained. They were in favour of doing away with divestment beyond 49 per cent and handing over the management of the SOEs to professional groups (*The Times of India*, 7 December 1996: 17).

Whereas privatization encompasses a rolling back of government, memoranda of understanding allow the government to control economic activities in a more effective way. Whereas privatization involves a shift in the prevailing ideology, memoranda of understanding are rooted in a more technocratic and pragmatic approach to the same problems. Whereas privatization finds fault with the ownership pattern itself, memoranda of understanding find fault with the quality of the control mechanisms adopted by the government to manage public enterprises (Trivedi, 1990: i).

Usually these two are viewed as substitutes by policy-makers and not as complimentary. The proponents of privatization argue that it is the only way to take the country out of its deep financial crisis, and that it can help in generating extra-revenues for the state exchequer, increase efficiency and allow the government to concentrate on governing instead of running businesses. It can also help in globalizing the economy. The opponents of privatization, on the other hand, have argued that privatization would only mean taxing the future to meet present needs; colloquially, it means selling the family silver to pay the grocery bills. They are equally dubious that privatization would attract adequate investment from NRIs and foreign companies.

Despite very attractive terms and concessions, the NRIs have not responded in a big way. Nor is it possible to get much direct foreign investment for projects in India due to fiscal constraints worldwide following the Gulf War, the collapse of communism in Eastern Europe, German unification and the disintegration of the USSR. The integration of European markets in 1992 also posed further pressures on countries like India. Indian enterprises, public or private, have to achieve a certain level in terms of quality before they can hope to compete at the global level, and this quality cannot be improved overnight. Instead of focusing on superior cost strategies, it would be better to concentrate on superior service. India has an abundance of skilled human resources which can prove very cost-effective in terms of global competition (Das, 1996: 10). In certain sectors privatization of a function or service could be an important option (Vishwanathan and Chowdhury, 1994: 48).

Privatization is neither a quick-fix nor a magic wand. It cannot yield quick results in terms of economic efficiency, enhanced competition, de-bureaucratization and less government. Nor can disinvestment of equity in select public enterprises really solve our problem of resource limitations for ever. Nor can it lead to efficiency in the true sense of the term.

Even privatization, in the true sense of the term, cannot lead to economic growth and human development *ipso facto*. Nor can it be seen as a development strategy; rather, it has to be fitted within the framework of an overall development strategy. It does not call for a reduction in the role of the state in the Indian context; rather, it stands for an effective state in order to create conditions for growth with social justice. We can draw certain important and practical lessons from the Indian experiences in privatization:

1. Privatization has only limited scope in a country like India where vast diversity prevails. India has an open mind and no ideological inhibitions or reservations regarding privatization; yet it should not be carried away by the rhetoric of privatization in the same way that it was not carried away by the slogans of socialism in the past. India has always adopted a middle path and a cautious approach.
2. In the case of India, each SOE may warrant a different prescription, and it is better to adopt a case by case approach rather than prescribe the same

medicine to every patient. Protection may be needed in one case and competition in another. Each enterprise may have its own historical legacy or regional compulsions. In practice, it may suffice to reform, restructure or regulate a particular enterprise instead of privatizing it; and in many cases, privatization of style may suffice.

3. Where it is not feasible to resort to divestiture, major equities may be transferred from public to private hands. In the case of non-corporate forms of organization, a process of corporatization would be required before attempting privatization. In the case of India, the definition of the public sector also covers government-controlled enterprises which may not be in the form of limited liability companies or corporate entities (Ghosh, 1997).
4. It is not sufficient to rely on divestment alone as a privatization device. Nor should the proceeds from divestment be utilized for filling the gap in fiscal deficit. The motivation behind disinvestment in India seems to mobilize resources rather than reduce the role of government in the economy. No mutual fund or financial institution would like to subscribe to a public sector enterprise unless there is some guarantee of viable returns. The policy on divestment can prove to be dynamic in one set of economies and quite a disaster in another. A Disinvestment Corporation can restore public confidence in the wake of a number of scams in India, but a non-statutory disinvestment panel can have only a limited role.
5. It is desirable to have an independent and autonomous agency to look after the 'tedious' job of privatization in a developing economy. On 17 December 1999, the National Democratic Alliance (NDA) led coalition government created a new Disinvestment portfolio headed by Mr Arun Jaitley to provide momentum to the disinvestment process. Earlier, a Disinvestment Commission was formed in 1991 under the chairmanship of Mr G.V. Ramakrishna to draw up a comprehensive long term disinvestment programme, set up priorities and sequence to be followed besides supervising the entire process. During 1991–98, the government raised Rs1030 crore from disinvestment, whereas the target was to raise Rs2500 crore (Ganesh, 1998: 330). The new government has set a target of Rs10 000 crore through disinvestment itself during the financial year of April 1999 to March 2000. However, the disinvestment process cannot succeed unless and until adequate resources and autonomy are granted to the concerned authority.
6. In India, many SLPEs may have better scope of privatization than the central-level PSUs. The new privatization agency can also look into the problems of regional disparities in the wake of opening up the Indian economy. Privatization in India is bound to lead to a realignment of political and economic forces both at the global and the local level. India has already lost approximately 10 per cent of its trade with the former

USSR. The United States is now the biggest trading partner, whether we approve of its hegemony or not.

7. Conscious efforts are needed to make the public aware of the rationale, objectives, priorities and strategies of privatization. This is possible only when the government is clear in its direction. Most of the problems in India have arisen due to narrow and short-sighted approaches of government on disinvestment, and ill-defined, ambiguous and mismanaged policies towards privatization in general. The government has not been able to dramatize the euphoric of privatization, nor educate politicians and the masses alike about the need or inevitability of India's integration into the global economy. Nor has the media played a balanced role in highlighting the domestic constraints and international pressures, or the pros and cons of privatization in the sociocultural context.

   Most of the problems have arisen owing to prevailing myths among the elite and widespread ignorance among the masses. India's march to prosperity may not look very exciting right now, but it may prove very solid and consistent once its entrepreneurial potential is fully unleashed. The government must educate itself first before giving a clear direction to the emerging economy and democratic polity.

8. India's confidence can be built in a schematic way. First of all, the country needs to gain credibility by adopting monetary and fiscal policies consistent with the global economy and domestic environment. An open trading and monetary system can encourage competition in due course. Once this credibility is established, we can hope for more credits from external sources to follow. We might also expect sufficient foreign direct investment to flow into both the infrastructure and consumer goods. India provides a very good market to the developed world, but we cannot be selective in controlling the in or outflows. It will depend upon the market which cannot be fully planned. It will be necessary to take the calculated risks involved in the privatization process if we do not wish to be left out in the new global order. At the most, India can strengthen its public distribution system and social security network by involving the state, market and household. The debate cannot be on state versus market; it has to be focused on state *and* market.
9. India should learn from the experiences of other countries, without attempting a direct transplantation. We cannot achieve economic miracles by trying to emulate the experiences of either China or East and Southeast Asia. We should not forget that economic success came to East Asia in waves as an outcome of seismic transformations in the geopolitical ecology of the world. The rise of the market-oriented economies along the Asian and North American coasts of the Pacific coincided with the deindustrialization of the midwestern and northeastern provinces of the USA. US entrepreneurs invested in Japan to escape high taxes and ecological costs in their home country, and Japan has

played a strategic role in the rapid development of South Korea, Taiwan, Hong Kong and Singapore. Nor should we forget the negative effects of economic reforms in China. Despite double-digit economic growth, prices have risen alarmingly, the trade deficit has deepened, there are increasing trends of corruption and bribery, and untold misery for common men and women in China. The backlash of economic reforms includes growing regional disparities, a rise in popular discontent, a decline in moral values, and drastic cuts in social welfare. In order to avoid political confrontations associated with economic liberalization, China has preferred to use the term 'opening up' of the economy. China is still far away from liberal democracy, whilst the Indian economy has to cope with democracy. We cannot allow either the polity or the economy to disintegrate. The Russian experience of liberalization and privatization has been far from satisfactory. At the beginning of 1995 it sold approximately 500 SOEs worth US$200 billion in real prices for mere US$7.2 billion. These included 77 steel plants, 85 machine-building plants, 66 oil and gas enterprises and 65 chemical plants. Leohia Abalkin, the Director of the Institute of Economics under the Russian Academy of Sciences, has considered that if the trend continues Russia will convert itself into a raw material appendage to the highly developed countries and will have to face unsurmountable social tensions in the long run.

Russia would be bound to lose its economic sovereignty and national prestige in this process. If the magnitude and tempo of its economic destruction is not quickly halted, the process is likely to become irreversible. If it is allowed to continue it is bound to lead to further degeneration and disintegration. As such, it is in the interest of a country like India to look around and move cautiously, and we may have to bear with different levels of efficiency for the time being. The entire economy cannot be converted to become efficient, competitive and vibrant overnight; that would be an impossible task. Nor can a uniform policy be relied upon; a case-by-case approach is preferable.

10. India can certainly provide a new vision to the contemporary world. The taming and civilizing of market forces presupposes the development of social and political forces and institutions across the world, and these in return presuppose a global culture as distinct from a culture of globalization. This calls for the articulation of a new culture based on those values which take the real world of five billion people as the object of concern; the whole earth as the physical environment, with everyone concerned worldwide – consumers and producers alike – taking a common interest in collective action to solve global problems.

Privatization as the cause and consequence of globalization can provide only partial solutions to resolve fiscal problems. It cannot provide a lasting solution to our economic ills. Nor can we separate economic problems from the sociocultural and political context. To Joseph Schumpeter we can either begin or end our explanations with economic factors, but cannot do both. As such we will have to look beyond privatization if we want to highlight the very presence of human beings on this earth, not as predators, polluters and consumers, but as protectors, producers and caretakers (Gupta, 1996).

9
Beyond Privatization

The debate around the neoliberal themes of privatization, denationalization, deregulation and destatization is based on the 'new political economy' – economic politics applied to political markets (White, 1996: 31). It signifies political action in economic markets which aims at maximizing the profit and utility which underlines neoclassical economics. The waves of economic liberalization which swept the so-called first world, second world and third world alike during the 1980s and 1990s cannot be explained in straightforward political or ideological terms. Privatization experiences are not limited to the United States under Ronald Reagan or the United Kingdom under Margaret Thatcher, but include other parts of the world. Some forms of privatization have been adopted by the labour governments in New Zealand and Australia, socialist governments in France and Spain, and mixed regimes in Japan and Mexico.

The most striking shift towards privatization has taken place in the former USSR, Eastern Europe and China. The process of liberalizing their economies was launched by some communist governments even before the revolution actually began in 1989. Among the East European countries, Hungary was most receptive to private ownership as early as the 1960s and 1970s. The People's Republic of China launched a decollectivization movement in the early 1980s in agriculture, and introduced new incentives for profit-making in industrial sectors. Mikhail Gorbachev introduced *perestroika* and *glasnost* in the late 1980s which opened up new opportunities for private business cooperatives and independent decision-making by industrial enterprises. In 1990, Poland and the former Czechoslovakia introduced radical programmes of economic liberalization, rejecting the idea of a third way in the most tactical manner. After the collapse of communism in Eastern Europe and the disintegration of the former USSR, privatization became the hallmark of economic reforms in post-communist societies.

In fact, the move towards privatization in the developed and developing world has been so diverse in form and varied in settings that the causes and consequences are unlikely to be the same everywhere. If public ownership had diverse origins and designs, privatization is likely to have diverse origins and designs too. If there were reasons to support expanded government by politicians, bureaucrats and voters during the 1960s and 1970s, we must find the logic and rationale behind privatization gaining top priority on the political agenda during the 1980s and 1990s. While faster growth, higher efficiency and greater freedom have been cited as the primary objectives of privatization in the developed world, external debts and budgetary constraints were the main factors responsible for putting the privatization debate on the national agenda. In post-communist societies, privatization aimed at legitimization of the informal sector and mobilization of private investments from abroad in the form of joint ventures.

Privatization programmes and policies may also differ in their short-term and long-term objectives worldwide. In post-communist societies, the long-term objective could be the creation of markets and civil society; in capitalist countries the objective could be redrawing the public–private boundaries by either shifting some public responsibilities to the private sector or involving the private sector in carrying out public policies. For instance, in the United States the government is now trying to network the public and private sectors to promote trade at the global level. Attempts are being made to reinvent government, because the US government has now realized that competing on the global stage without adequate backup is 'like playing tennis at Wimbledon with an old wooden racket' (Tolchin, 1996: 7). For instance, the US government formed SEMATECH, a consortium of semiconductor manufacturing companies involving the private sector and the Defence Advanced Research Project Agency, now known as ARPA instead of DARPA; the Clinton administration decided to drop the word Defense to reap political benefits.

However, it would be foolish to locate the causes of privatization within the state itself (Starr, 1990: 46). Nor should privatization be seen as a simple matter of transferring public assets and services to the private sector mainly because politicians can hardly afford to be market-dependent (Laux, 1993: 398). Governments in the process of privatization purposefully participate in determining who will enter or exit the marketplace and under what conditions. Even the World Bank has now realized that the divestiture process adopted during the 1990s involved a political act. In most of the developing countries, the governments became engaged in tacit collusion with the newly-privatized enterprises to offer special benefits or, conversely, to oblige new owners to accept restrictions as the conditions of sale. As such, privatization became potentially useful as a broader effort to increase market forces (Shirley, 1988: 35); it allowed governments to build or rebuild coalitions to serve their own political goals. In the wake of marvelous innovations in science and technology, both the public and private sectors can even seek offshore connections to serve their vested interests.

The connection between privatization, globalization and offshore financial centres (OFCs) is not yet fully understood. An offshore centre can be defined as a centre that hosts financial activities that are separated from major regulatory units (states) by geography and or legislation. This may amount to a physical separation, in an island territory for example, or a legal separation within a city such as London or New York international-banking facilities (Hampton, 1994: 257). OFCs are often located in small or little known areas, and over the last few years global business offshore has risen tremendously. It aims at reaping the benefits of tax differentials, labour endowments and raw materials at a lesser cost than those prevailing in the home country. In fact, regional differences in the working of capitalism are now becoming more obvious and important.

Surprisingly, the globalization process has led to the formation of economic blocs at the regional level such as the European Union, NAFTA or ASEAN, each of these enjoys a number of satellite OFCs around it. While elites become integrated across the world, the masses feel insecure in the wake of globalization. Economic integration at the global level has certainly weakened the credibility and legitimacy of public agencies and social institutions. To Will Hutton (1995: 26):

> in most of the developing countries, the governments burgeoning international marketplace – destabilizing current flaws using offshore havens to avoid tax – is hostile to expressions of common and public interest. Private interests have too easily slipped the national leash and have used the ungoverned world beyond national frontiers to undermine what they regard as tiresome, inefficient and bureaucratic efforts to assert the moral and social dimension in human affairs.

In order to avoid heavy taxes and responsibilities towards environmental protection and social welfare, the business conglomerates have been demanding privatization and globalization since the 1970s. The synergy between the offshore interface, globalization and privatization has outpaced all attempts towards regulation either by business or government, and has become the chief source of onshore corruption by elities in certain countries (Hampton, 1996: 86). There are many reports of widespread corruption in China, Taipei, Hungary, India and many other countries in the wake of economic liberalization, deregulation and privatization.

Blurring of public and private boundaries

Neither nationalization nor privatization could have occurred without the consent of the elite forming the economic, political or social groups. And in both situations, public sector enterprises have been used as policy instruments. There can never be a full cycle of either nationalization or privatization at any given period of time or place. It is also a myth that the state symbolizes the private. Nor can we really say that 'public' relates to the general interests of the community, while the 'private' relates to selfishness and irresponsibility. In fact, it is self-interest and not selfishness which motivates both the public and the private, and self-interest may involve both selfish and unselfish goals and acts (Sales, 1991: 296).

Nor can we define the boundary or ideal relationship between public and private. The common interests of the public may be different from those of particular groups or individuals, yet the public can be seen as merely an extension of individual behaviour, or the realization of the private (Kaminski, 1991: 265). Both the public and private form important components of society as a whole. One sphere can gain only at the expense of the other. For instance, it is now being realized that the national interests of the United States suffered by relying more on markets and the private sector than government agencies and the public sector. The US had to pay a heavy price in terms of loss of jobs, national income, market share, decline in living standards, and an increase in the trade deficit and national debt for ignoring the reports of government agencies and relying excessively on the findings of private groups representing various vested interests (Tolchin, 1996: 2).

Once the world's leader in the manufacturing of machine tools and industrial machinery, the United States lost ground to Japan in nine out of 12 key technologies except semiconductors, aerospace and robotics according to a report of the US Department of Commerce in 1990. Soon other industries and technologies followed suit despite timely warnings from government agencies. But their findings were buttressed by private interests, and the United States has now realized that in the current global environment where money moves across the world in seconds, where companies are bought and sold without government interference, and where multinational corporations wield more power than most national governments, a strong state is needed once again to protect national interests. In the absence of adequate directions from government, various agencies – public as well as private – are likely to be set against one another. For instance, the Department of Commerce may stress economic promotion, while the Department of Defense might indulge in alliances with private business to promote arms sales.

As such there may be mutual infiltration between the public and private sectors in all societies depending upon their historical circumstances, socio-economic development and cultural traits. The private may call into question the public and reshape it, or the public may transform the private by helping it grow or by simply absorbing it. With the growth of civil society, the distinction between public and private is likely to be blurred (Lefort, 1991: 311).

In postindustrial and postmodern societies every organization is politicized, including private ones. No manager can ever succeed in running an enterprise, public or private, transnational or multinational, without understanding thoroughly the sociocultural and political environment in which he or she has to operate. The personnel working in a public, private, joint venture or multinational organization have to face similar sociocultural constraints. Nor can these organizations remain immune to public opinion and sensitivities. If any one of them neglects public safety or pollutes the environment, its public image may quickly become tarnished through media criticism, affecting its very growth and profitability.

With more and more globalization of economies, the whole debate about public versus private is becoming anachronistic. The focus is now on national versus multinational. New technologies have allowed financial markets to become integrated worldwide; and in high-tech societies, information and knowledge play a far more important role than raw-materials and capital endowments. There are some reports which suggest that there is virtually no difference between the performance of a public enterprise and a private company subject to an optimally designed regulatory and tax scheme. But even if there is some difference between the two it is not as sharp as sometimes suggested in the privatization debate. Through appropriate price policies and incentive mechanisms, even public enterprise can be made viable. If an enterprise's capital requirement poses a strain on the public sector borrowing requirement (PSBR), a mere shifting of these loans to the private sector cannot make an enterprise efficient (Mastrangelo and McPhail, 1993).

In fact, the basic difference in the programme of a public and a private enterprise lies in the collection of information about the costs and benefits of the enterprise concerned by the public and the private. While the private information remains private, public information can either be observed or verified by people concerned or third parties. Private and the public information may also vary around the external social benefits of an enterprise, the divergences between public interests and the interests of public officials, and the profitability of an enterprise. Just as the social benefits generated by public enterprises cannot be measured in terms of annual profits, similarly the private gains of the top bureaucrats and politicians in power cannot be calculated in fiscal terms. Since the latter have to function under constant political pressures, they cannot be expected to bear the immediate hardships and political costs for uncertain future gains. As such, it is difficult to say that private enterprises work only for profits, while public enterprises work only in the public interest. Only a public-spirited organization can work in the public interest, whether or not it is public, private or hybrid. Moreover, privatization may involve only the re-mixing of the mixed-economy (Laux, 1993: 400).

While in the UK it may imply shifting the balance from public to private, in the USA it may imply blurring the boundaries by associating private firms in the management of prisons, highways, the operation of bridges, sewage and water systems and social welfare. In a country like the United States, with a very small nationalized sector, privatization virtually amounts to the involvement of the private sector in carrying out the public responsibilities of the state.

In the era of bureaucratization of politics in lieu of politicization of bureaucracy, privatization has turned private enterprises and dominant groups into policy-makers. In other cases, privatization has not really helped in taking the load off governments in a bid to better government (Savas, 1987). What has been relinquished is the 'doing' part of the job only. Prior to privatization, the conceiving, planning, goal-setting, standard-setting, performance-monitoring and evaluating parts still remain with the government. If these are done badly, public interests still suffer; as such, privatization cannot be a cure for government incompetence (Gupta, 1996a). Even after privatization the government's workload is not really reduced; only the nature of the job changes. Instead of running an enterprise, it is not required to regulate it.

There are therefore two ways in which the boundaries between the public and private become blurred:

1. The government may set the policy, even if the private sector provides the services. But as partners in implementation, the private providers also usurp the policy-making power to some extent.
2. Once the private firms or the NGOs become the recipients of public funds, they become subject to governmental controls and scrutiny. As such, they may become less and less private in the process.

Both these processes of privatization have actually led to the weakening and blurring of the distinction between public and the private (Starr, 1990: 40).

Competition or cooperation?

It is doubtful whether competition will remain the guiding force even in the twenty-first century. Nor can we say with certainty that competition always leads to economic or technical efficiency. A public monopoly can be converted into a private one through privatization, as the United Kingdom did in the case of British Telecom, or a government may liberalize without resorting to privatization *per se* as the United States did in the case of deregulation of telecommunications. Some governments may resort to privatization and liberalization simultaneously by selling SOEs and deregulating entry into markets. Both privatization and liberalization aim at achieving economic efficiency through competitive markets.

But markets are not perfect in themselves; nor do they always lead to competition. The deviation from perfect competition and the extent to which production and consumption processes generate external economies and diseconomies are to be well-understood. Where technologies give rise to economies of scale, only large monopolistic or oligopolistic enterprises are viable, and markets do not conform to the competitive ideal. Nor can it be claimed that competition would always lead to economic efficiency. For instance, the manufacturing of ordinary shoes may be a low-profit operation because of the high degree of competition at both domestic and international levels, whereas hand-crafted or designer shoes may be more profitable, being less-competitive. In today's world, the shift has already taken place from mass production to quality production.

In fact, markets are to be seen not only as economic institutions but also as political and sociocultural. Real market prices are determined by political processes and the real political strategies are determined by the network of market processes. Both of them create culture and are created by culture (Wallerstein, 1991: 374); there is no such thing as an economically natural or market price. For instance, in 1990 when Iraq invaded Kuwait, oil prices immediately rose worldwide. Of course it can be explained in terms of demand and supply, but the invasion of Kuwait was in itself a political act with serious economic consequences. The price of oil depended on geo-political *rapport de forces* at the global level, since nature has not fixed any price for oil as such.

It is obvious that markets do not fix the price of a commodity or a service on their own; political forces are also involved. It is the government which regulates prices to suit the socioeconomic conditions prevailing in a given polity. During the 1950s and 1960s, bureaucracy-controlled extensive production systems provided high growth rates and led to the expansion of the world economy. During the 1970s, artificial attempts had to be made to sustain the expanding world economy in industrialized countries, but in vain. During the 1980s this arrangement began to break down. The growing debt burden became unsustainable in the sagging world economy and a call was made to revert to market forces. But the market is too blunt a weapon to discipline financial institutions which are thinly capitalized and closely linked through myriads of transactions with other institutions (Kaufman, 1990).

In fact, markets can foster as well as thwart human development. They not only allocate resources and distribute income, they also shape our culture. As such, economic growth and development should be seen as the consequence and not the precondition for satisfying human needs – the needs of food, clothing and accommodation along with other non-material needs of human dignity, cultural identity and social participation. The stress has to be on being rather than becoming, as the very essence of human being. As such, an individual cannot be treated simply as a producer or a consumer; he or she has to be seen as a member of the 'social whole' (Braun, 1990: 55–6). The market remains an important economic and social institution, but not the only one. Similarly, privatization can be seen as an important tool of the market-edifice, but certainly not the only one. Even if it leads to efficiency and competition, it may backfire when its true social and political costs are revealed.

Some recent research has shown that markets may be a useful mechanism for coordinating economic activities and competition necessary for promoting economic efficiency and growth, but neither market incentives nor competition are enough. Markets may benefit individual actors but not society as a whole. It is now being held that better results can be achieved through cooperation in lieu of competition. For instance, Lane Kenworthy (1996) has suggested nine types of cooperation to reap economic benefits. To him, cooperation at the macro level among various firms, trade unions, government and interest groups can reduce rent-seeking, restrain wages, and lead to coherent and productive government policies. Cooperation at the meso level among various investors, suppliers, purchasers and competing firms can lead to hightened communication, greater willingness on the part of investors to invest, and productivity. It can also lead to savings on research and development by pooling resources, diffusion of technology, training employees and standard-setting. Cooperation at the micro level among management, employees and other functional departments within firms can lead to better work culture and mutual understanding (Kenworthy, 1996: 56).

In his recent book, *Trust*, Francis Fukuyama (Free Press N.Y.) has also highlighted the role of cooperation in explaining the differences in economic performance at the global level in general, and in the Asia Pacific region in particular. He believes that a high degree of coordination between government and business has paid rich dividends in terms of economic growth in Japan, France and South Korea. On the other hand, Austria, Germany, Norway, Sweden, Finland, Denmark, Belgium and Netherlands have also shown an extensive amount of cooperation among labour and business associations; but owing to a lesser degree of intergroup centralization and coordination, these countries have been comparatively more successful in achieving macro level cooperation than those countries based on highly individualistic and atomistic economies (Kenworthy, 1996: 55). The United States, the UK and Canada fall in the latter category.

According to a survey, the nations with the best performance record in terms of productivity growth are those which have been able to balance competition with cooperation, such as Japan, Austria, Germany and Italy; while those faring the worst in terms of a misery index based on unemployment and inflation happen to be those who have predominantly relied on competition, such as the United States, Canada, the UK, Australia and New Zealand (Kenworthy, 1996: 55).

In the present era of interdependence and interconnectedness, the key to economic success lies in economic cooperation and systematic tolerance of vast differences prevailing across the world (Gupta, 1996b: 15). We have examples of widespread complementary cooperation in many East Asian countries where inter-firm and intra-firm networking is quite common. Interorganizational cooperation in East Asia is so widespread that it can provide a model for others. For instance, in the 1970s almost all of the Japanese joint ventures in Singapore and Malaysia were with the local Chinese, and approximately 90 per cent of the Japanese joint ventures in Indonesia and Thailand were made possible through Chinese middlemen. Both the Japanese and Chinese companies sought government links to serve and promote their own vested interests.

Impact on sovereignty

Over the past few years the world has changed dramatically. While the integration of economic forces at the global level has made privatization acceptable at that level, it has affected the political freedom of the nation state in internal and external affairs. It has led to two types of turbulence on policy-making processes: external turbulence is generated by transnational actors who are particularly visible in monetary issues and financial volatility; and domestic turbulence is fed by domestic counter-reactions and maladaptations to the globalization of economic forces in general, and privatization in particular. Liberalization, deregulation and privatization have not only freed domestic economies from state regulation, but they have also exposed them to greater internal and external vulnerability (Massey, 1992). This has led to domestication of international policies and internationalization of domestic economies (Gupta, 1994).

Aida Soedimoto, of the United Nations University of Tokyo, aptly observed in his opening statement at the symposium on *Science and Praxis of Complexity* (1985):

> In the process of inter-dependence, we have all become vulnerable. Our societies are permeable to decisions taken elsewhere in the world. The dynamics of inter-dependence might better be understood if we think of the globe not in terms of a map of nations but as a meteorological map, where weather systems swirl independently of any national boundaries and low and high fronts create new climatic conditions far ahead of them.

Consequently, political actors at the national level can adopt altogether different strategic policies. They can either resort to cooperation and coordination, or conflictual negotiations and isolationist threats. Both these strategies have been used by political actors at various discussions on GATT, the Maastricht Treaty and the WTO. While some governments may succeed in managing domestic constraints to reap benefits from international-led turbulence, others may use international constraints to seek support from influential groups at the domestic level to support their fiscal and political policies.

For instance, Greece and Italy are now resorting to external constraints to introduce certain economic policies at the domestic level (Campanella, 1992: 196). As such, globalization and privatization have definitely led to a shift in the role of the state, government officials and political actors. But it is a misconception to say that the nation-state has declined or has become irrelevant or obsolete. It is important to realize that the state is not anathema to the market; nor is there any dichotomy between them. Both are complementary to each other. States are very much needed to regulate markets (Beteille, 1995: 10), and only the state can provide a context for the interaction of private agents (Gintis, 1992: 47).

In an era of breathtaking speed and scope, the notion of the nation-state defined as 'the power whose acts are not subject to control by another' needs rethinking. The interplay of economic forces and the speed of technological change have terminally eroded traditional concepts such as sovereignty, security, geopolitics and economic progress. So far, the notion of sovereignty has generally been taken as a statist as well as a static concept. In fact, it is not the notion of sovereignty but its conceptualization in abstract and divisive terms which has become vulnerable to postmodern deconstruction. We also find an inherent contradiction between the liberal concept of state and sovereignty: to be sovereign is to be free, and in the liberal tradition to be free implies equality. While liberalism is the first theory to embrace the universal notion of freedom and equality, the liberal state is the first form to deny that force (Gupta, 1995).

In international law and affairs, all states enjoy the same status in terms of sovereignty, but in practice we find hierarchical relations dominating both national and international politics – the strong suppressing the weak. To transcend the abstract notion of sovereignty we will have to build up its universal and egalitarian features. For this we will have to sever the concept of sovereignty from that of the state by reconceptualizing the concept of sovereignty in terms of governability rather than in statist terms. Under the new framework it may not be necessary for all the constituent units to have the same level of authority. We may have different shades of sovereignty or different levels of autonomy. In today's world of interdependence, even national interests can be best served through consolidation of common interests across borders. Through mutual cooperation and coordination, policy-makers can balance their national and international interests and adapt governmental organizations befitting their new roles.

In future, we may find power shifting from political parties and trade unions to new state agencies. The traditional monopoly of the Ministry of External Affairs may be challenged by these new state agencies or NGOs. In some countries, regional and subregional units may assume more powers than those entrusted to them initially. Even privatization can be instrumental in integrating the domestic economy at the global level, making it difficult for the government at the central level to regulate the economy effectively. In future, we may require supranational institutions to regulate the market economy in the global interest.

The various structures in a civil society can play an important role in promoting the culture of globalism in order to sustain the globalization of economy (Gupta, 1995). We cannot move into the direction of globalization in the sense of true globalism, if our attitudes and thinking remain pre-global. Privatization can exert psychological, institutional, operational, social, political and cultural impacts on civil society but in a limited way. Civil society can also control the adverse effects of privatization. Elements of opposition to the socially disruptive consequences of privatization are already visible in the form of emerging women's, environmental and peace movements.

Welfare effects of privatization

The integration of affluent political elites and economic powers at the global level in the wake of destatization and privatization has caused a lot of anxiety, distress and insecurity among the non-affluent majority. The major driving force in the globalization process has been the 37 000 to 40 000 MNCs who virtually control one-third of the world's private-sector assets and sales amounting to approximately US$5500–6000 billion (Ghosh, 1996). The powers of the MNCs and TNCs have become consolidated due to their close alliance with multinational banks and international institutions such as the World Bank and the IMF. The availability of cheap labour, natural resources and lack of liabilities or concern for environmental pollution was responsible for the shift of finance capital and a large number of economic activities from the developed world to the developing one. But the effects of globalization, destatization and privatization have been neither symmetrical nor homogeneous. They have led to an increase in economic and regional disparities on the one hand, and cut-backs on social security, health and education on the other.

The socially disruptive consequences of economic integration of markets at the global level during the 1980s are becoming more obvious and visible during the 1990s. The electronic conquest of distance enhanced by fast data processing, not only transforms local markets into worldwide networks, but also magnify local problems into world security problems, transmute local poverty into world development problems, and convert the ecological behaviour of individuals into global environmental threats (Cleveland, 1993). The growth of violence, individual and collective, has also assumed a global dimension in recent years.

The crisis in human security is now found to be more serious than generally perceived. In today's world, the threat to human life can come from militarism, environmental pollution, ethnic chauvinism, religious extremism or drug-related crimes. Today we are forced to live in a world that is injured by the everyday tragedies of Bosnias and Somalias on the one hand, and abject poverty, hunger and disease on the other. Today we also live in a world where wide economic disparity prevails. In the 1960s, the total income of people in the richest 20 per cent bracket worldwide was 30 times higher than the lowest 20 per cent. In the 1990s it has become 60 times higher (Streetan, 1995).

We find globalization of prosperity on the one hand, and globalization of poverty on the other. Despite tremendous progress made in various fields during the last 50 years, we still live in a world where a fifth of the developing world's population goes hungry every night, a quarter lacks access to safe drinking water, and a third lives in a perpetual state of abject poverty. This is even more shocking when we find multiple expressions of moral indifference and comfortable self-righteousness towards the plight of others.

The affluent are no longer bothered about the problems of hunger, disease, ignorance, illiteracy and homelessness of the hundreds of millions of people, the 'wretched on the earth', constituting almost two-thirds of the global population and occupying almost half of the land. They believe that poverty is the fault of the poor, exclusion the responsibility of the excluded and equality of outcome – an impossible task (Gupta, 1994). Not only the poor but the rich are also afflicted by growing human distress owing to the weakening social fabric – a rising crime rate, ethnic and civil strife, political terrorism, environmental pollution, the spread of narcotic drugs, restlessness among the youth, private corruption by public officials, mafia operations, alienation and loneliness. These phenomena cannot be explained merely in terms of overload or fiscal crisis. They have to be explained in terms of crass behavioural changes reflected in the distrust of social policies as public goods. In fact, methodological individualism is proving to be antistructural, antifunctional, antinormative and antisociological. Once again we are at a crossroad. Humanity has been through many transitions during its long history on this planet, but this time we are involved in a very difficult and crucial transition. It is difficult because of the time factor involved. While innovations in science and technology have made rapid change possible, it is difficult to change values at the same speed.

If we wish to improve the quality of life, we have to change the very perceptions and attitudes towards our own lives and those of our fellow beings. Economic man, so modern in his freedom, is only quasi-modern in his obligation towards society. He is responsible for his own fate, to the degree of the economic model of economic choice followed by him, with very little or no concern for others. (Wolfe, 1989: 50). To create a society as modern as the individuals who compose it, we must look beyond the notion of self-in-isolation to the notion of self-in-group (Gupta, 1994: 15).

This requires a paradigm shift in the perception based on cooperation in lieu of competition, convergence in lieu of conflict, and holism in lieu of hedonism (Singh, 1994: 67). The need of the hour is to strike a balance between rising materialism and sagging spiritualism if mankind is to come out of the morass of moral crisis and emotional emptiness. We must chisel the contours of our minds before it is too late.

The question arises: will privatization lead to a further decline in moral values? In fact, one needs an ultra-modern mind to understand the sociocultural implications of economic and political policies undertaken under domestic constraints or international influence. But one thing is certain – changes in economic and political policies do affect the sociocultural behaviour of an individual. Privatization is bound to bring an industrial culture which extols the role of the entrepreneur as a hero, of profits and success and conspicuous consumption and social status as the most cherished goals of life. What is lacking is the moral dimension which produces genuine heroes and a sense of community purpose (Woodward, 1991). It is now being held that the more one is privatized, the less likely he or she is to take part in collective action (Reddy, Selvarary and Kumar, 1991: 2–7).

Privatization has the most adverse effects on the welfare activities of the state. Owing to resource limitations and the shift in attitudes of people towards social welfare, the consensus on the responsibility of the state towards human well-being seems to be over. Even in advanced economies it is no longer possible to keep the commitments made during the period of economic boom towards social security and well-being. Reaganomics and Thatcherism, reflected in the market-friendly ideology of privatization, have led to the drastic decline of egalitarianism in the realm of economic thought (Vyasulu, 1991: 13).

Practically, we find a sharp decline on social expenditure in major OECD countries during the 1980s and 1990s. But a passive, non-interventionist and less-powerful state cannot cope with the unfolding crisis in terms of widening economic and regional disparities and the decline in moral values. Nor can it provide the much needed guidance for the human development essential for future economic growth. The right wing economic policies can benefit only the few at the top, but at a price so heavy that the victories cannot be celebrated even by the winners (Bowles, Gordon and Weisskopf, 1991: 6).

Economic growth, environmental conservation and human development

If communism failed for lagging behind in terms of economic growth, neoconservatism may fail too for breeding excessive consumerism, to the neglect of humane aspects of development. Neither socialism, which tends to favour the public relation, nor liberalism which tends to place private relations foremost, can lead to all-round human development. What is required is an ideal balance between public and private, leading to economic growth with social justice (Piachaud, 1991: 204–25).

In the absence of social justice, we may only have economic growth without any development, depending on how we interpret the term development. It is the usual practice to define underdevelopment not in terms of what people are or what they would like to be, but in terms of what they do not have and what others think they should become. Once the problem has been defined as low income, the only solution lies in economic and not holistic development.

But the traditional one-dimensional approach of measuring development in terms of GDP or GNP has already been replaced with a more complex but multidimensional measure of human development, based on variables such as literacy, life expectancy and personal freedom. The Human Development Index is a derivative of earlier indices such as the International Human Suffering Index, Physical Quality of Life, and so on. But it does not mean that human development and economic growth have no connection whatsoever; in fact, economic growth needs to be seen both as the cause and a consequence of human development, and vice versa. If human development is seen as the ultimate objective, economic growth can be seen as the surest way of achieving it. But the myths of unfettered economic growth have to be shed by all means possible (Srinivasan, 1992: 8).

Infinite growth in a world of finite resources is neither possible nor desirable. In lieu of Rambo economics, what we need is sustainable growth – growth which satisfies present needs without risking the needs of future generations (World Commission on Environment and Development, 1987: 46). Only sustainable growth can ensure the survival of humanity in the long term, because only a humane approach to development can avert environmental catastrophe and ameliorate poverty. In this regard, the World Bank's prognosis is indeed a cause for alarm (Gurtov, 1994: 198):

> Under present productivity trends, and given projected population increases, developing country output would rise by 4–5 per cent a year between 1990 and 2030 and by the end of the period would be about five times what it is today. Industrial country output would rise more slowly but would still treble over the period. World output by 2030 would be 3.5 times what it is today . . . If environmental pollution and degradation were to rise in step with such a rise in input, the result would be appalling environmental pollution and damage. Tens of millions more people would become sick or die each year from environmental causes.

Environmentalists and Greens all over the world are now pressing for punitive action for environmental pollution and degradation, making pro-marketeers environmentally accountable. They are demanding that polluters be made to pay for damages inflicted upon innocent people, and for a comprehensive charter of amenity rights for citizens and nomination of an environmental ombudsman to enforce rules and regulations related to environment conservation (Mishan, 1993: 237). The idea is to tax private polluters in order to encourage the use of anti-pollution technology and devices on the one hand, and to raise additional resources for social development on the other.

But the costs of disrupting already existing industrial units or reducing their size and changing their structure in the wake of anti-pollution legislation can be too high. Sometimes it may not be feasible to detect the hazardous spillovers arising from rapid innovations in science and technology and marketization of new products at an early stage. Moreover, in a highly competitive world governments may not act swiftly or they may deliberately avoid penalizing their polluting enterprises in order to avoid cost advantages in international trade.

Sometimes social regulations may not reflect the public values of the people, or they may conflict with their private values as consumers (Farber, 1989;

1039). Nor can the agglomeration of private interests lead to a grey future of green hopes. In the absence of rigid control, private or privatized enterprises cannot be expected to follow the logical choice of a sustainable environment in the public interest (Heilbroner and Milberg, 1995). As such, excessive materialism and conspicuous consumption have to be checked if they really want to avoid the environmental disaster threatening the survival of 'spaceship earth' (Simonis, 1990: 118). In pursuit of economic growth to the neglect of humane development, modern technology has failed to take care of the inner limits of human society and the outer limits of spaceship earth. As such, it has disturbed the ecological equilibrium, jeopardized the ecosystem's stability and the quality of life with regard to both physiobiotic and sociocultural aspects (Mohan, 1993: 39–41). Privatization is likely to further affect this equilibrium in an adverse manner.

Growth is important, but contentment is still more important. Instead of pursuing a path of abundance, we must learn to delimit our needs and desires. On the threshold of the twenty-first century when we are moving into a highly uncertain and ambivalent future, we need to rely on a new perspective that goes beyond the state and the market. The pursuit of inner growth and humane development is far more important than the mere pursuit of external goods and comforts. In fact, the well-being of an individual depends upon his or her happiness, and the happiest person on earth remains the one who is the most content – the luckiest are those who know they have enough.

Happiness does not always lie in attaining power, position or materialistic goods. It is a personal experience, varying from individual to individual, depending upon his or her temperament, biological inheritance, aspirations, abilities, upbringing and circumstances around. In fact, it is an inner experience that comes in the form of mental serenity and emotional equilibrium. It is the mind alone that is the abode of human health, happiness and harmony. Encouragement of self-interest in the tradition of economic liberalization and privatization cannot lead to human development and human welfare. The linear approach towards a market economy worldwide, marked by increasing cultural, psychological, social and ideological homogenity and politico-economic centralization, can pose a serious threat to the very notion of individualism.

Paradoxically, economic progress may impede inner growth and holistic development of individuals, and the market economy may lead to the corporatization of society and the diminution of self (Whiston, 1991: 163–78). Market-based efficiency may bring surplus wealth and wider choice, but at the cost of freedom of mind. The market economy makes us think in a single predetermined direction, sacrificing many creative talents on the way. Therefore, corporatism should be questioned in all its facets – economic, political, sociocultural or ecological. The feminist theory also aims at deconstructing the very public-private dichotomy to expose the psychic opposition between male and female. In fact, true emanicipation lies in attaining power over the self.

A creative society need not be sacrificed at the altar of mass society, nor should individuals be treated as conforming ants rather than potential gods. Nor should any nation be subsidized at the economic expense of others. At the individual level, too, the pursuit of economic growth can be a worthwhile exercise only if it leads to a positive contribution to human development. In this context, privatization can only be considered as an important device of economic management, political strategy or as an administrative tool, but certainly not an end in itself. Privatization forces simply cannot be unleashed without concern for their management according to prevailing sociocultural values, economic development, political norms and administrative capabilities.

A uniform policy of privatization at the global level is neither feasible nor desirable. Nor can one policy last forever. Nothing is constant and permanent except change itself. Change is the law of life; Tennyson writing that '*the old order changeth, yielding place to new*' and Carlyle that *Change indeed is painful, yet needful*.

Men can make their own history but under circumstances directly found, given and transmitted from the past. The economic motive may play a predominant part in history but it does not mean that there are no other causes at work. Non-economic motives can also influence the individual psyche in important ways. That is why the Marxist idea of economic determinism was discredited by scholars like Schumpeter. History has proved that it was a mistake to believe that the dictatorship of the proletariat would lead to communism *ipso facto*. Nor did Marxist predictions of a withering away of the state, or the inevitability of the fall of capitalism and revolution in the industrial societies of the UK and the USA come true. On the other hand, many unforeseen developments have taken place at the global level since the fall of the Berlin Wall in 1989. Who could have expected that its fall would set the stage for the fall of communism in Eastern Europe and the disintegration of the former USSR? Who could have foreseen the market reforms in the People's Republic of China under the leadership of the Communist party, or the formation of regional blocs like the EU, NAFTA or SAFTA in the wake of globalization? Who could have thought in terms of the decline in sovereignty, governability and democracy?

Prior to the globalization thrust, the role of the state was conceived as a buffer protecting national economies from disruptive external forces. But the priority has now shifted to adapting national economies to the perceived exigencies of the world economy (Cox, 1991: 337). No single, national economy, not even the largest, can control the world market or determine its orientation. The hyper-liberal model asserting the separation of the state from the market has led to a conflict in the dual role of government: (1) promoting efficient and competitive markets at the domestic and global level, and (2) balancing the welfare of social group – youth, women, immigrants, minority groups or the marginalized. The long-term viability of the model which separates the state from the market has become an open question.

The dangers of political mobilization by marginal groups, women and environmentalists are foreshadowed in the writings of the neoliberal ideologues. These groups are no longer powerless or fragmented, they are becoming organized and mobilized pitting democratic legitimacy against economic efficiency. Either the corporatist processes will need to be insulated against democratic pressures, or an alternative model of development will have to be formulated. To curb the polarization effects of globalization and privatization, an emphasis will have to be laid on collective action for collective goods. Instead of globalization embedded in a market economy, we shall need globalization based on social well-being.

Under these circumstances, indiscriminate privatization can fuel reactionary trends and backfire. While the lure of certain benefits may bring forward domestic and foreign investors, distorting concessions may create new sources of economic and regional disparity paving the way for re-regulation. As such, privatization can be seen as both the cure and cause of economic ills.

This is not an argument against privatization *per se*, but a warning to look beyond the figures which define growth as a surrogate measure of economic and social welfare. To make an enterprise more market-responsive and open to technological change, privatization is not always warranted. In fact, each country's situation is uniquely different and requires different solutions. It remains to be seen whether a country needs to move away from the state and what adjustments may be made within existing frameworks.

In fact, with rapid integration of the economy at the global level, the whole debate about 'public' and 'private' sector is becoming anachronistic. In the era of joint ventures, transnationals and multi-nationals, it is no longer the question of 'public' versus 'private' or 'state' versus 'market'. It is a myth to say that the state symbolizes the 'public' and the 'market' symbolizes the 'private'. Nor can we really say that the 'public' always relates to the general interests of the community or 'private' relates to selfishness and irresponsible behaviour. The truth is that it is 'self-interest' which guides both the 'public' and the 'private' sector. Nor can we really equate 'self-interest' with 'selfish-interest'.

In post-industrial and post-modern societies, every organization is highly politicized, including the NGOs and private ones. No manager can ever succeed in running an enterprise 'public', 'private' or 'non-governmental organization' it may be, without understanding the socio-cultural and political environment in which he or she has to operate. The basic difference lies in the collection of information. Whereas the private information remains 'private', the public information can be observed and verified both by the private and third parties. It makes a lot of difference as far as the economic efficiency of an enterprise is concerned.

Moreover, the information collected by 'public' and 'private' sources may also differ in terms of social benefits and profitability of an enterprise. Just as the social benefits generated by public enterprises cannot be measured in terms of annual profits, similarly the 'private gains' of the top bureaucrats and politicians in power cannot be calculated in fiscal terms. In fact, neither 'privatization' nor 'nationalization' could have occurred without the consent of the respective elite in a given society comprising the economic, political, administrative or social nexus. While the 'waves of nationalization' signified expansion in the role of the state, privatization signifies contraction (Siegmund, 1996: 5).

As such, privatization should be seen as an 'ideology of transformation' rather than the 'transformation of a theory'. Privatization cannot be considered merely as an outcome of groups in power but it also helps in forming and shaping these groups. It amounts to 'recapitalization of capitalism' or 're-mixing of the mixed economy'. With privatization the very ownership patterns get changed. Whereas under public sector, the public acts as the 'principal', the politicians, bureaucrats and businessmen acts as the 'agents'.

After privatization, the very 'principal agent' relationship is altered. Now the managers are required to act as 'principals' and shareholders become the 'agents' in lieu of the citizens *per se*. But the problems of citizens pertaining to rising consumerism, economic and regional disparities, mafia and violence, restlessness among the youth and loneliness among the aged in the wake of hi-tech and post-modern societies cannot be solved by mere economic efficiency, competition or wider choice.

On the onset of the 21st century, the thrust has to be on 'cooperation' in lieu of 'competition', 'convergence' in lieu of 'conflicts' and 'holism' in lieu of 'hedonism'. What we need is the 'culture of globalism' in lieu of the 'thrust of globalization'. The stress has to be on the 'being model' of development in lieu of 'having model'. In the new millennium, the growth and development of an individual is likely to be judged in terms of the 'humanitarian values' and 'inner growth' acquired by him or her, rather than in terms of acquisition of power, position and materialistic goods. As such, privatization can be considered at the most an economic device, political strategy or administrative tool for economic growth and development, but certainly not an 'end in itself'.

Bibliography

Abelson, P. (ed.) (1987) *Privatization: An Australian Perspective*, Sydney: Australian Professional Publications.

Abromeit, H. (1986) 'Privatization in Great Britain', *Annals of Public and Cooperative Economy*, vol. 57 (April–June).

Accountancy, September (1989) Journal of the Institute of Chartered Accountants of England and Wales.

African Association for Public Administration and Management (1987) *Public Enterprises: Performance and the Privatization Debate*, New Delhi: Vikas Publishing House.

Aggarwal, R. and M. Mejstrik (1992) 'Privatization and Capital Market Development in Eastern Europe: Lessons from the Czechoslovak Experience'. *C.E.R.G.E. Working Paper*: (14), Prague: Charles University, Centre for Economic Research.

Ahmad, M. (1982) 'Political Economy of Public Enterprises', in L. Jones (ed.), *Public Enterprises in Less Developed Countries*, Cambridge: Cambridge University Press.

Ahmed, R.Z. (1996) 'Thatcherites Bloom in Labour Colour', *The Times of India*, New Delhi (24 October).

Aiyar, S.S.A. (1991) 'Managing Exit Policy: Mass Transfer, Not Mass Retrenchment', *The Times of India*, New Delhi (7 November).

Alam, A.M.Q. (1989) 'Privatization Policy and Problems of Industrial Developments in Bangladesh', *South Asia*, vol. xii (2).

Anand, V. (1994) 'Implementation Issues and Privatization Plans', *Public Enterprise*, vol. 4 (1–2).

Anon (1985) 'People's Capitalism does not Impress the IMF', *Islamic World Review*, no. 5 (October).

— (1985) 'Privatization: Everybody is Doing it Differently', *The Economist*, 12 December.

— (1985) 'What is ahead of Privatization', *Institutional Investor* (April).

Arnold, N.S. (1990) 'Economists and Philosophers as Critics of the Free Market Enterprises System', *Monist*, vol. 73.

Aschein, K. and R. Garelick (1990) 'General Economics and Post-Modern Capitalism', *Yale CR Studies*, vol. 78.

Ascher, K. (1987) *The Politics of Privatization: Contracting out Public Services*, London: Macmillan.

Asian Pacific Trade Union Co-ordination Committee (1988) 'Privatization in Asia-Pacific Region – A Capitalist Offensive', Calcutta (14 November).

Athreya, M.B. (1991) 'Alternative Models for Privatization–Peoplization', Centre for Economic and Industrial Research, New Delhi (March).

Austin, J.E., L.H. Wortzell and J.F. Coburn (1986) 'Privatizing State-Owned Enterprises: Hopes and Realities', *The Columbia Journal of World Business*, vol. 21 (3).

Aylen, J. (1987) 'Privatization in Developing Countries', *Lloyds Bank Review*, vol. 16 (3) (January).

Ayub, M. and S.O. Hedstad (1987) 'Management of Public Industrial Enterprises', *World Bank Research Observer*, vol. 2 (January).

Azhar, L. (1990) 'Las Transiciones des de el Autoritarismo en Venezuela. El Proyecto de Accion Democratica y Sus Efectos Sobre el Sistema Sociopolitico', *Desarjollo Economico*, vol. 117, Buenos Aires.

Bagchi, A. (1991) 'The Fiscal Challenge: Reducing Budget Deficits', *Monthly Commentary*, vol. 32 (12) (July–August).

Baig, M.A. (1991) 'Liberalization: Rural Sector Key to Success', *The Economic Times*, 16 November. See also Y.K. Alag (1991) 'Is Agriculture getting a Raw Deal?'. Same issue.

Balz, Manfred: Rechtseinheit als Grundlage für die soziale und wirtschaftliche Einheit–recht–liche Hindernisse bei der Bewältigung der Treuhandaufgaben. In: Bitburger Gespräche, Jahrbuch 1991/92.

Bardhan, P. (1991) 'Avoidable Tragedy of the Left in India', *Economic and Political Weekly*, 19 October.

Baxi, U. (1991) 'On Privatization', *Mainstream*, New Delhi (6 July).

Becker, G. (1990) *Business Week*, 24 November.

Beesley, M.E. (1993) *Privatization, Regulation and Deregulation*, London: Routledge.

Beesley, M.E. and S. Littlechild (eds) (1987) *Public Enterprise Policy in India and UK in 1980s*, Bombay: Himalaya Publications.

— (1989) 'Privatization: Principles, Problems and Priorities', in V.V. Ramandham (ed.), *Privatization in Developing Countries*, London: Routledge.

Bennet, A.H.N. (1988) 'Theoretical and Practical Problems in Determining Criteria for the Performance Evaluation of Public Enterprise', *Public Enterprise*, vol. 8 (1).

Berg, E. (1989) 'Privatization: Developing a Pragmatic Approach', *Economic Impact*, no. 57.

Berg, E. and M. Shirley (1987) 'Divestiture in Developing Countries', *World Bank Discussion Paper no. 11*, Washington DC: The World Bank.

Berger, P.L. (1992) 'The Uncertain Triumph of Democratic Capitalism', *Journal of Democracy*, vol. 3 (3).

Bery, S.K. (1990) 'Economic Policy Reforms in Developing Countries: The Role and Management of Political Factors', *World Development*, vol. 18 (8), Washington DC.

— (1990) 'Economic Policy in Developing Countries: The Role of Management of Political Factors', *World Development*, vol. 18 (8).

Beteille, A. (1995) 'Between State and Market', *The Times of India*, New Delhi (18 January).

Bharat Ram, V. (1991) 'Privatization: The Great Debate', *The Times of India*, New Delhi (25 April).

Bhatt, M. (1991) 'Gujrat Ports: Courting the Private Sector', *The Financial Express*, New Delhi (13 December).

Bidwai, P. (1996) 'Privatization Perils: Bringing the State Back In', *The Times of India*, New Delhi (19 December).

Bienen, H. and J. Moore (1987) 'The Sudan Military Economic Corporation', *Armed Forces and Society*, vol. 13 (4) (Summer).

Bienen, H. and J. Waterbury (1989) 'The Political Economy of Privatization in the Developing Countries', *World Development*, vol. 17 (5) (May).

Bishop, M. and J.A. Kay (1989) 'Privatization in the United Kingdom: Lessons from Experience', *World Development*, vol. 17 (5) (May).

Bishop, M., J. Kay and C.P. Mayer (1995) *The Regulatory Challenge*, Oxford: Oxford University Press.

Blanden, M. (1988) 'Murder on the Privatization Express', *The Banker* (April).

Blum, U. (1992) 'Recent Experiences with Privatizing State Enterprises in the former GDR: The Case of the Treuhandanstalt', a paper presented to the SOG Conference on 'Regime Transition, Elites and Bureaucracy', Hamburg, 23–25 April.

Bohm, A. and G. Kreacic Vladimir (eds) (1991) *Privatization in Eastern Europe*, Yugoslavia: International Centre for Public Enterprise in Developing Countries.

Bös, D. (1988) 'Arguments in Privatization', Cologne: unpublished mimeo (June).

— (1991) 'Privatization and the Transition from Planned to Market Economy: Some Thoughts About Germany', *Annals of Public and Cooperative Economics*, vol. 62.
— (1991) 'Privatization in East Germany: A Survey of Current Issues', *Fiscal Affairs Department*, IMF Working Papers, November.
Bowden, A. (1994) 'Investing in Europe: Anyone for Seconds?', *The Investors Chronicle*, 22 April.
Bowles, S., D.M. Gordon and T.E. Weisskopf (1991) 'Right Wing Economics Backfired', *Challenge*, vol. 34 (1) (July–August).
Braun, G. (1990) 'The Poverty of Conventional Development Concepts', *Economics*, Germany: Institute of Scientific Cooperation.
Bremer, J. (1986) *Options for Privatizing Agricultural Parastatals in Developing Countries*, Washington DC: Heritage Foundation.
Breuel, B. (1994) *Die Rolle der Treuhandanstalt*, Germany: Kiel Institute of World Economics.
Brittan, S. (1984) 'Politics and Economics of Privatization', *Political Quarterly*, (April–June).
— (1985) 'Two Cheers for Self-Interest: Some Moral Prerequisites of a Market Economy', London: Institute of Economic Affairs.
— (1986) 'Privatization Comment', *The Economic Journal: 96.*
Bruce, A. (1986) *State of Private Sector Disinvestment: The Case of Sealink*, Oxford: Phillip Allan.
Bryson, L. (1992) *Welfare and the State: Who benefits?*, London: Macmillan.
Buchanan, J.M. (1987) 'Liberty, Market and State', *Economic Impact*, vol. 58 (2).
Buckhaus, J. (1990) 'Privatization and Nationalization: A Suggested Approach', *Decision*, vol. 17 (3–4) (July–December).
Buckland, R. (1987) 'The Cost and Returns of the Privatization of the Nationalized Industries', *Public Administration*, no. 55.
Bureau of Public Enterprise (1990–96) *Annual Reports*, New Delhi: Government of India.
Burton, J. (1991) 'Selling off from Strength', *International Management*, vol. 46 (December).
Business Week, 1994 December 12, 'America's New Watchword: If it Moves, Privatize it'.
Butler, E. (ed.) (1988) *Mechanics of Privatization*, London: Adam Smith Institute.
Butler, S.M. (ed.) (1985) *The Privatization Option: The Strategy to Shrink the Size of Government*, Washington DC: Heritage Foundation.
Cairncross, F. (1990) 'Sternness Without Efficiency', *Social Studies*, TLS, 9–15 March.
Calder, K.E. (1988) 'Public Corporations and Privatization in Modern Japan'. A paper presented at the workshop on 'Privatization' at Princeton, New Jersey.
Calvert, P. (1991) 'The Ethics of Privatization'. A paper presented at the XV World Congress of International Political Science Association held at Buenos Aires, Argentina, 21–25 July.
Campanella, M.L. (1992) 'The Effects of Globalization and Turbulence on Policy-making Processes', *Government and Opposition*, vol. 24 (4) (Autumn).
Cardos, E.A. (1991) 'Privatization Fever in Latin America', *Challenge*, vol. 34–5 (September–October).
Carlin, W. (1994) 'Privatization and Deindustrialization in East Germany', in Saul Estrin (ed.), *Privatization in Central and Eastern Europe*, London: Longman.
Carlin, W. and C. Mayer (1994) 'The THA Privatization by State and Market', in O.J. Blauchard, K.A. Foot and J. Sachs (eds), *The Transition in Eastern Europe*, Chicago: University of Chicago Press.
— (1995) 'Structure and Ownership of East German Enterprises', *Journal of the Japanese and International Economics*, vol. 9 (1).
Carnoy, M. (1984) *The State and Political Theory*, Princeton: Princeton University Press.

Carsberg, B. (1986) 'Regulating Private Monopolies and Promoting Competition', *Long Range Planning*, no. 19.

Carsberg, B. and S. Lumby (eds) (1985) 'Privatizing British Airport Authority: Policies, Prospects and Procedures', *Public Money*, vol. 5.

Catherine, P. (1986) 'Privatizing British Gas: Is the Regulating Framework Adequate?', *Public Money*, vol. 6 (1).

Chakravorty, N. (1991) 'World Bank for Privatizing Coal Sector', *The Hindustan Times*, New Delhi (20 November).

Chapman, C. (1990) *Privatization*, London: Business Books.

Charap, J., K. Dyba and M. Kupka (1992) 'The Reform Process in Czechoslovakia: an assessment of recent developments and prospects for the future', *Communist Economies and Economic Transformation*, vol. 4 (1): 3–22.

Charbonnier, V. (1995) former Director of Bayer AG, Treuhandanstalt, quoted by E. von der Heyden, 'Privatization in East Germany: The Delivery of an Economy', *The Columbia Journal of World Business*, vol. xxx (3) (Fall).

Chary, S.N. (1991) 'When Will We Go Global?', *The Financial Express*, New Delhi (29 November).

Chattopadhaya, P. (1991) 'Privatization – Missing the Trees for the Wood', *Fortune India*, vol. ix (6) (16 January).

— (1991) 'Pangs of Privatization', *Facts for You*, 9–16 December.

Chelliah, R. (1991) 'Need to Divest Government of Vast Economic Powers', *The Times of India*, New Delhi (29 March).

Chenoey, K.A.M. (1991) 'Privatizing India', *Mainstream*, New Delhi (2 August).

Chidambram, R.M. (1989) 'Justification for Privatization', *Third Concept*, New Delhi (December).

Christiansen, R.E. (1989) 'Editor's Introduction on Privatization', *World Development*, vol. 17 (5) (May).

Claudon, M.P. (ed.) (1991) *Comrades Go Private: Strategy for Eastern Europe Privatizations*, New York: New York University Press.

Cleveland, H. (1993) *Birth of a New World: An Open Moment for International Leadership*, USA: Jossey Bass.

Commander, S. and T. Killick (1988) 'Privatizations in Developing Countries: A Survey of Issues', *Privatization in Less Developed Countries*, Hemel Hempstead: Harvester Wheatsheaf.

Convery, F. and Moore McDowell (eds) (1989) *Privatization: Issues of Principle and Implementation in Ireland*, UK: Gill and Macmillan.

Cook, M. and J. Piggotto (1989) 'The Sharing Society', *Contemporary Reviews*, 25–30 January.

Cook, P. and C. Kirkpatrick (1988) *Privatization in Less Developed Countries*, New York: Harvester Wheatsheaf.

Cornuelle, R. (1991) 'New Work of Invisible Hands', *Times Literary Supplement*, 5 April.

Corrias, A. (1991) 'The IRI Formula of Privatization', *Public Enterprise*, vol. iv (1–4).

Cowan, G. (1988) *Privatization: A Technical Assessment*, USA: Agency for International Development.

— (1990) *Privatization in the Developing World*, UK: Greenwood Press.

Cox, R.W. (1991) 'The Global Political Economy and Social Choice', in D. Drache and M.S. Gertler (eds) *The New Era of Global Competition, State Policy and Market Power*, McGill: Queens University Press.

Crozier, M., S.P. Huntington and J. Watanuki (1975) *The Crisis of Democracy: Report on the Governability of Democracies to the Trilateral Commission*, New York: New York University Press.

Curwen, P.J. (1986) *Public Enterprises: A Modern Approach*, UK: Wheatsheaf.
Dandekar, V.M. (1988) 'Indian Economy since Independence', *Economic and Political Weekly*, 2–9 January.
Dandavate, M. (1992) 'Budget: Some Crucial Issues', *Janata*, 23 February.
Das, A.N. (1992) 'Brave New Words: Fallout of Structural Adjustments', *The Times of India*, New Delhi (8 January).
Das, G. (1996) 'Nation and Corporatism: Indian Companies in the Global Market', *The Times of India*, New Delhi (11 December).
Datta, R. (1991) 'External Debt Trap and Policy Options', *The Financial Express*, New Delhi (8 August).
Davidson, P. (1993) 'A Billion-dollar Off', *The Banker*, vol. 10 (1), October.
Davies, S. (1987) 'Towards the Remoralization of Society', in M. Loney (ed.) *The State or the Market?*, London: Sage.
Demone, H. (1989) *Services for Sale – Purchasing Health and Human Services*, UK: New Brunswick.
Dempsey, J. (1993) 'A High Price to Pay for High Wages in the East', *The Financial Times*, 22 February.
Department of Energy (1987) *Sale of Government Shareholding in British Gas*, London: HMSO, HC paper no. 22.
Department of Environment (1986) *Privatization of the Water Authorities in England and Wales*, London: HMSO, Cmnd 9734.
Dey, P.K. (1988) 'Public Sector and Indian Economy', *Business Standard*, 10 December.
Dhameja, N. (1991) 'Privatization in India: Various Problem Areas', *MDI Management Journal*, vol. 4 (1), January.
Dherse, L-J. (1986) 'Moving Towards Privatization in Developing Countries', *The Bank's World*, April.
Dikshit, S. (1989) 'Don't Privatize, Streamline', *The Financial Express*, New Delhi (24 April).
Djondo, K. (1988) 'Anatomy of a Privatization Scheme: The Togo Example', *African Business*, 16–18 February.
Dodason, J.S. (ed.) (1988) *Bus Regulation and Privatization: An International Perspective*, UK: Avebury.
Donahue, J.D. (1989) *The Privatization Decision: Public Ends, Private Means*, Basic Books Inc. Publishers.
Donnison, D.V. (1984) 'The Progressive Potential of Privatization', in Julian Le Grand and R. Robinson (eds) *Privatization and the Welfare State*, UK: Routledge.
Drum, B. (1993) 'Privatization in Africa', *The Columbia Journal of World Business*, Spring.
Dunlewy, P.R. (1986) 'Explaining the Privatization Boom: Public Choice Versus Radical Approaches', *Public Administration*: 54, Spring.
Dutt, R.C. (1988) 'Public Sector: Soft Option of Privatization', *Mainstream*, 27 February. New Delhi.
Dutt, Rudra (1991) 'Public Sector Performance: Turning from Black to Grey' *Mainstream*, 21 July.
El-naggar, Said ed. (1989) *Privatization and Structural Adjustment in the Arab Countries*, Washington DC: International Monetary Fund.
Ensor, P. (1986) 'South Korea's Unwieldly Public Enterprises', *Far Eastern Economic Review*: 129(29).
Erasaari, R. (1990) 'The Problem of Welfare: Is There a Welfare Civilization?', *World Futures*: 28(1–4).
Erginsoy, O. (1990) Quoted by Richard Molz. 'Privatization in Developing Countries', *The Columbia Journal of World Business*, Spring/Summer.

Estrin, S. (1994) *Privatization in Central and Eastern Europe: Key Issues in the Realignment of Central and Eastern Europe*, London and New York: Longman.
Evans, G. (1992) 'Treuhand's Tricks of the Trade', *Euromoney*, September.
Ezekier, H. (1992) 'Shut Sick Industries to Raise Employment', *The Times Of India*, New Delhi (28 January).
Farber, Daniel A. (1989) 'Environmentalism, Economics and the Public Interest'. *Stanford Law Review*. April.
Featherstone, Mike ed. (1988) *Post Modernism: A Theory, Culture and Society*. London: Sage Publication.
— (1990) *Consumer, Culture and Post Modernism*. London: Sage Publication.
— ed. (1990) *Global Culture: Nationalism, Globalization and Modernity*. London: Sage Publication.
Feigenbaum, H.B. and J.R. Henig (1992) 'Reciprocal Relations Between State and Society: Privatization and Democracy'. A paper presented at the annual meeting of APSA. September 2–6.
— (1994) 'The Political Underpinnings of Privatization: A Typology'. A paper presented at the XVI IPSA World Congress held at Berlin from August 21–25.
Feldman, D.R. (1986) 'Privatization and the State Statutory Framework: A Key to Success'. *The Privatization Review*: 2(1). Winter.
Finley, Lawrence K. ed. (1989) *Public Sector Privatization*. UK: Quorum Books.
Fischer, Wolfram, Herbert Flax and Hans Karl Schneider eds. (1996) *Treuhandanstalt: The Impossible Challenge*. Berlin: Akademie Verlag.
Fischer, W. and H. Schröter (1996) 'The Origins of the Treuhandanstalt', in W. Fischer, H. Flax and H.K. Schneider (eds), *Treuhandanstalt: The Impossible Challenge*, Berlin: Akademie Verlag.
Fitch, L.C. (1988) 'Rocky Road to Privatization'. *American Journal of Economics and Sociology*: 47(1).
Fitzgerald, Ronald (1988) 'The Real Global Revolution: Privatization', *Reader's Digest*. July.
— (1988) *When Government Goes Private: Successful Alternatives to Public Service*. New York: Pacific Research Institute of Public Policy.
Flynu, Norman (1989) 'The New Right and Social Policy'. *Policy and Politics*: 17(2).
Forrest, Ray and Alan Nurie, (1987) *Moving the Housing Market: Council Estates, Social Changes and Privatization*. UK: Avebury.
— (1988) *Selling the Welfare State: The Privatization of Council Housing*. London: Routledge.
Forsyth, M. (1982) *Barriers to Privatization*. London: Aims of Industry.
Foster, C. (1984) 'Privatizing British Airports: What's to be Gained?' *Public Money*: 3(4).
Francis, D.R. (1985) 'US stepping up Push for Free Enterprise via Third World Aid', *Christian Science Monitor*, 30 May.
Fraser, Robert ed. (1988) *Privatization: The UK Experience and International Trends*. Longman. Kelsing's International Studies.
French, M. (1987) 'Crash Lesson for Privatizers'. *Euromoney*. December.
Friedmann, Robert, Neil Gilbert and Mosche Snerer eds, (1987) *Modern Welfare States: A Comparative View of Trends and Prospects*, Brighton: Wheatsheaf.
Frinerman, James V. (1991) 'Economic and Legal Reform in China'. *Problems of Communism*: XL. September-October.
Fruin, Mark W. and Toshihiro Nishiguchi (1993) 'Supplying the Toyota Production System' in Bruce Kogut ed. *Country Competitiveness*. New York: Oxford University Press.
Fruin, M.W. (1995) 'Prospects for Economic Cooperation in Asia-Pacific Region', *Asian Survey*, vol. xxxv (9).

Frydman, R. and A. Rapaczynsky (1991) 'Markets and Institutions in Large Scale Privatization: An Approach to Economic and Social Transformation in Eastern Europe' in V. Corbo ed. *Reforming Central and Eastern European Economies*. Washignton DC.

Fukuyana, Francis. (1995) *Trust*. New York: Free Press.

Gabel, H.L. (1987) 'Privatization: Its Motives and Likely Consequences'. European Institute of Business Administration Working paper No. 37.

Gabel, R. (1986) *Privatization of Public Services*. Agency for International Development. February 17–19.

Gallo, Luis S. (1993) 'The Value Added of Investment Bankers in Privatizations'. *The Columbia Journal of World Business*. Spring.

Gandhi, Jagdish P. (1991) 'Passenger Road Transport: Privatization – A Panacea?' *The Financial Express*. September 20. New Delhi.

Ganesh, G. (1998) *Privatisation Experience Around the World*. New Delhi: Mittal Publications.

Ganesan, K.P. (1991) 'Dynamics of Human Resources', *Financial Express* (20 July): 7.

Garner, M.R. (1988) 'Has Public Enterprise Failed' in V.V. Ramandham ed. *Privatization in the UK*. UK: Routledge.

Gay, Andrew and William Jenkins (1991) 'Public Administration and Government'. *Parliamentary Affairs*: 44(1).

Gayle, J. Dennis and Goodrich, N. Jonathan eds. (1990) *Privatization and Deregulation in Global Perspective*. UK: Pinter.

Ghose, Arun (1992) 'Management of Economy and IMF Conditions'. *Economic and Political Weekly*. January 4–11.

Ghosh, D.N. (1996) 'Swadeshi vs. Videshi', *The Times of India*, New Delhi (16 April)

Ghosh, Partha S. (1997) 'Vision and Strategy Should Guide Reforms'. *The Times of India*. January 4, New Delhi.

Gillespie (1989) 'Naked Face of Capitalism'. *The Times of India*. April 17. New Delhi.

Gintis, Herbert (1992) 'New Economic Rules of the Game'. *Challenge*. September–October.

Glade, W. (1983) 'The Privatization and Denationalization of Public Enterprises' in G. Ram Reddy ed. *Government and Public Enterprise*. Bombay: N.M. Tripathi.

— ed. (1985) *State Shrinkage: Comparative Inquiry into Privatization*. Austin: University of Texas Press.

— (1989) 'Privatization in Rent Seeking Societies'. *World Development*: 17(5). May.

Goldstein, Carl. (1991) 'More Haste Less Speed'. *Far Eastern Economic Review*. August 29.

Goodrich, J.N. (1988) 'Privatization in America'. *Business Horizon*: 31(1).

Gopal, Ajit S. (1989) *Social Responsibility of Public Sector*. New Delhi: Centre for Public Sector Studies.

Gopalkrishnan C.V. (1991) 'IMF World Bank: Shattering of Keynes Dream'. *Mainstream*. July 20. New Delhi.

Gorbachev, Mikhail (1987) *New Thinking for Our Country and the World*. London: Collins.

Gormely, William T. ed. (1991) *Privatization and its Alternatives*. UK: University of Wisconsin Press.

Gouri, G. (1989) 'Economic Liberalization in India and Efficiency in Public Enterprises: Some Issues', in T.L. Sankar *et al.* (eds), *Privatization: Diversification of Ownership of Public Enterprise*, Hyderabad: Institute of Public Enterprise.

— ed. (1991) *Privatization and Public Enterprise: The Asia Pacific Experience*. Hyderabad: Institute of Public Enterprise.

Government of India (1956) *Industrial Policy Resolution: Guidelines for Industries*. New Delhi.

— (1986) *Report (Draft) of the Economic Advisory Council on Public Enterprise in India*. New Delhi.

Government of Malaysia (1985) *Guidelines on Privatization*. Economic Planning Unit. Kuala Lumpur.
Grabher, Gernot (1994) 'The Elegance of Incoherence, Institutional Legacies, Privatization and Regional Development in East Germany and Hungary'. Social Science Research Centre. June. Berlin.
Grand, Julian Le and Ray Robinson (eds) (1985) *Privatization and the Welfare State*. London: George Allen & unwin.
Gray, S. (1985) 'Easing Strain on Economy: Privatization'. *The Financial Times*. May 20. New Delhi.
Great Britain (1987) *Privatization in the United Kingdom*, London: HMSO.
— (1988). *Privatizing Electricity*, London: HMSO.
Green, D. (1982) *The Welfare State for Rich or for Poor?* London: Institute of Economic Affairs.
Green, Richard and Catherine W. Price (1995) 'liberalization and Divestiture in the UK Energy Sector'. *Fiscal Studies*: 16(1).
Gretton, J., A. Harrison and D. Beeton (1987) 'How Far have the Frontiers of the State been Rolled Back between 1979–887?' *Public Money*, vol. 17(3).
Goyal, S.K. (1987) 'Privatization of Public Enterprises: Some Issues for Debate', in M. Beesley and S. Littlechild (eds), *Public Enterprise Policy in India and UK in the 1980s*, Bombay: Himalaya Publications.
Griffiths, B. and H. Murray (1985) *Whose Business?* Institute of Economic Affairs. London.
Grimstone, Gerry (1989) 'Privatization: Macroeconomics and Modalities' in V.V. Ramandham ed. *Privatization in Developing Countries*. London: Routledge.
Grosfeld, I. and G. Ronald (1995) 'Defensive and Strategic Restructuring in Central European Enterprises'. CEPR Discussion Paper 1135.
Grout, P.A. (1988) 'Employee Share Ownership and Privatization: Some Theoretical Issues'. *Economic Journal*: 98 September.
Guha, Seema (1991) 'Summer of Discontent Ahead'. *The Times of India*. July 4. New Delhi.
Gupta, Asha (1987) *Socialism in Theory and Practice: Narendra Deva's Contribution*. New Delhi: Geetanjali.
— (1988) 'Ideology in the Third World'. *Janata*. December 11. Bombay.
— (1989) 'Welfare State and Privatization'. *Economic and Social Change Quarterly*. June. New Delhi.
— (1990) 'Why Privatization?' *Janata*. April. Bombay.
— (1990) 'Will Privatization Lead to Efficiency?' *Monthly Commentary*. February. New Delhi: Indian Institute of Public Opinion.
— (1990) 'Welfare State and Privatization in Canada'. *Indian Journal of Public Administration*. October-December. New Delhi.
— (1991) 'Will Disinvestment Lead to Privatization?' *Financial Express*. March 18. New Delhi.
— (1992) 'Socio-Cultural Dimension of Privatization'. *Financial Express*. April 22. New Delhi.
— (1993) 'Pitfalls on the Road to Privatization'. *Financial Express*. January 7. New Delhi.
— (1993) 'Will Privatization Lead to Debureaucratization?' *Janata*. June. Bombay.
— (1994) 'Structural Adjustment, Privatization and the Public Bureaucracy' in R.B. Jain and Heinz Bongartz eds. *Structural Adjustment, Public Policy And Bureaucracy in Developing Societies*. Friedrich Ebert Stiftung. New Delhi: Har Anand Publications.
— (1994) 'Privatization in Canada: Lessons for India' in M.P. Singh and Chandramohan eds. *Regionalism and National Identity: Interdisciplinary Perspectives*. New Delhi: Pragati Publications.

— (1994) *Changing Perspectives of the Welfare State: The Issue of Privatization*. New Delhi: Pragati Publications.
— (1994) 'Role of Advanced Economies in Promoting Welfare at the Global level'. A paper presented at the International Conference of ICSW held at Tampere, Finland (July).
— (1995) 'Need for Evolving a Consensus on Global Welfare'. *Janata*. February-March. Bombay.
— (1995) 'Who's Job Is It Anyway?' *Financial Express*. June 1. New Delhi.
— (1995) 'Privatization of Electricity in India'. *SAR Economist*. February-March. New Delhi.
— (1995) 'Should Higher education be Privatized?' *The Indian Dominion*. June. New Delhi.
— (1995) 'Beyond Sovereignty', *Third Concept*, no. 100, New Delhi (June).
— (1996) 'Global Welfare and Global Development: An Indian Perspective'. *Yojana*. Government of India Publication. March. New Delhi.
— (1996) 'Privatization: An Economic Device or a Political Strategy?' *The Journal of Institute of Public Enterprise*: 19(1–2). Hyderabad.
— (1996) 'Structural Adjustment, Privatization and Public Bureaucracy', *Journal of Institute of Public Enterprise*, Hyderabad (February).
— (1996) 'Asia's Future and the Future of Asianization', a paper presented at JAIR-ISA International Conference held at Makuhari, Japan, 20–22 September.
— (1996) 'From Public Administration to Public Management: A Shift in Paradigm', a paper submitted to the Third International Conference of the International Institute of Administration Schools, held at Beijing, 8–11 October.
Gupta, Uttam (1989) 'Towards Low Cost Economy: Challenges and Constraints'. *The Economic Times*. April 17. New Delhi.
Gurtov, Mel (1994) *Global Politics In Human Interest*. London: Lynne Reinner Publishers
Guru, Sutanu (1991) 'Why Not Privatize the Private Sector First?' *The Times of India*. March 22. New Delhi.
Haggard, Stephen (1988) 'Privatization in the Philippines' in Raymond Vernon ed. *The Promise of Privatization: A Challenge for US Foreign Policy*. New York: Council on Foreign Relations.
Haggard, S. (1988a) 'The Philippines: Picking up after Marcos', in R. Vernon (ed.), *The Promise of Privatization*, New York: Council on Foreign Relations.
Haggard, Stephen and R. Kaufman (1988) *The Politics of Stabilization and Structural Adjustment*. Prepared for the NBER Project on Developing Country Debt. Cambridge: NBER.
Haggani, S. (1985) 'Undoing Nationalization: The Task in Pakistan'. *Far Eastern Economic Review*: 129 (29).
Hall, John A. (1988) *Liberalism: Politics, Ideology and the Market*. London: Paladin.
Hampton, Mark P. (1994) 'Treasure Islands or Fool's Gold: Can and Should Small Island Economies Copy Jersey?' *World Development: 22(2).*
— (1996) 'Where Currents Meet: The Offshore Interface Between Corruption, Offshore Finance Centres and Economic Development'. *IDS Bulletin*: 27(2).
Hanke, Steve H. (1996) 'The Privatization Option: An Analysis'. *Economic Impact*: 3.
— (1986) 'Strategies Employed in Successful Privatization Efforts'. US Agency for International Development. February 17–19. Washington DC.
Hans, Jaswant. (1991) 'Rediscovering Competition'. *The Financial Express*. December 12. New Delhi.
Haque, I. (1988) 'Privatization of the Economy: The Factors that Have Kept the Pace Slow'. *Dawn*. January 16–22. Karachi.

Hariharan, R. (1991) 'Part Privatization of PSUs: Practical Problems'. *The Financial Express*. December 12. New Delhi.
Harris, J. (1987) *The State in Retreat*. Institute of Development Studies. Sussex.
Harris, R. (1980) *The End of Government?* Institute of Fiscal Studies. London.
Harrison, B. (1987) 'Privatization: A European Perspective'. *British Economy Survey*: 18(2).
Haveman, R. and J. Margolis eds. (1977). *Public Expenditure and Policy*. Chicago: Rand McNally.
Hawarth, Nigel (1992) 'National Sovereignty, Deregulation and the Multinational: New Zealand in the 1980s' in John Deeks and Nick Perry eds. *Controlling Interests*. Auckland: Auckland University Press.
Heald, David (1982) 'Privatizing Public Enterprises: An Analysis of the Government's Case'. *Political Quarterly*: 53.
— (1983) *Public Expenditure: Its Defence and Reforms*. Oxford: Basil Blackwell.
— (1984) 'Privatization: Analysing Its Appeal and Limitations'. *Fiscal Studies*: 5(1).
— (1987) 'Performance Measurement of Public Enterprises: Resolving Conceptual Issues'. International Institute of Public Finance: 25. Paris.
— (1987) 'United Kingdom: The End of Nationalization and Afterwards?' A paper presented at a seminar held at Auffield College. November 13–14. Oxford.
— (1990) 'The Relevance of Privatization to Developing Countries'. *Public Administration and Development*: 10.
Heath, John ed. (1990) *Public Enterprises at Crossroads*. London: Routledge.
Heilbroner, Robert and Williams, Milberg. (1995) *The Crisis of Vision in Modern Economic Thought*. New York: Cambridge University Press.
Heller, Peter and Christian Schiller (1989) 'The Fiscal Impact of Privatization: Some Examples from the Arab Countries'. *World Development*: 17(5). May.
Heller, Haus and Mansoor Ali (1986) 'Review of the Fiscal Impulse Measure'. *International Monetary Fund Occasional Paper No. 44*. Washington DC.
Helm, D. (1987) 'RPI minus X and the Newly Privatized Industries'. Public Money: 7(1).
—1987. 'Nuclear Powers and the Privatization of Electricity Generation'. *Fiscal Studies*: 8(4).
Hemming, R. and A. Mansoor. (1988). 'Privatization and Public Enterprise'. *International Monetary Fund Occasional Paper: 56*. Washington DC.
Henderson, P.D. (1977) 'Two British Errors: Their Probable Size and Some Possible Lessons'. *Oxford Economic Papers*. July.
Henig, Jeffrey R. (1990). 'Privatization in the United States: Theory and Practice'. *Political Science Quarterly*: 104 (4).
Henney, A. (1987) *Privatized Powers: Restructuring the Electricity Supply Industry*, London: Centre for Policy Studies.
Hensley, M.L. and E.P. White (1993) 'Privatization Experience in Malaysia: Integrating Build–Operate–Own and Build–Operate–Transfer Techniques within the National Privatization Strategy', *The Columbia Journal of World Business* (Spring).
Hewitt, Martin. (1992) *Welfare, Ideology and Need: Developing Perspectives on the Welfare State*. UK: Harvester Wheatsheaf.
Heyden, E. von der (1995) 'Privatization in East Germany: The Delivery of an Economy', *The Columbia Journal of World Business*, vol. xxx (3) (Fall).
Hinton, W. (1991) *Privatization of China: The Great Reversal*. London: Earthscan.
Hirschoff, P. (1986) 'The Privatization Drive'. *Africa Report*. July–August.
Holzmann, R., C. Thimann and A. Petz (1993) 'Pressure to Adjust: Consequences for the OECD Countries from Reforms in Eastern Europe', a paper presented at the Empirical

Economic Policy Forum on 'Consequences of Eastern European Reform: Are the OECD Countries Ready for their Economic Adjustments?' held at Vienna, 18 October, mimeo.
Hopper, David W. (1995) 'India's Economic Reforms and Long-term Development: Observations by an Outsider'. *Liberalization*. New Delhi: Allied.
Howell, D. (1986) *Blind Victory: A Study in Income, Wealth and Power*. London: Hamish Hamilton.
Humphrey, Clare E. (1991) *Privatization in Bangladesh: Economic Transition in a Poor Country*. Oxford: Westview.
Hutton, W. (1995) *The State We're In*. London: Jonathan Cape.
Ikenberry, C.J. (1990) 'The International Spread of Privatization', in E.N. Suleiman and J. Waterbury (eds), *The Political Economy of Public Sector Reform and Privatization*, Westview.
Inotai, Andras (1992) 'Experience with Privatization in East Central Europe', in Horst Siebert ed. *Privatization*.
Isenstien, Howard (1986) 'Privatization is Not for Foreigners'. *Euromoney*. November.
Iyer, Ramaswamy R. (1988) 'Sectoral Corporation: Some Organizational Experiments in Public Sector in India'. *Economic and Political Weekly*. February.
Jain, A.K. (1988) 'Public Sector: Profile and Steps to Improve Performance'. *Mainstream*. New Delhi.
Jain, R.B. and Heinz Bongartz eds. (1994) *Structural Adjustment, Public Policy and Bureaucracy in Developing Societies*. New Delhi: Friedrich Ebert Stiftung and Har Anand Publishers.
Jalan, Bimal (1991) *Indian Economic Crisis: The Way Ahead*. New Delhi: Oxford University Press.
Jatar, S.C.N. (1990) 'Privatization of the PSEs'. *The Financial Express*. March 28. New Delhi.
Jenkinson, T. and C. Mayer (1988) 'The Privatization in France and UK'. *European Economic Review*: 32.
Jha, P.S. (1988) 'Need for Privatization'. *The Hindustan Times*. March 11. New Delhi.
Jhaveri, N.J. (1991) 'Privatization: The Nuts and Bolts Issues', *Monthly Commentary* (October).
Johnson, Christopher (1987) 'Power to the People'. *Lloyds Bank Economic Bulletin*: (107).
— ed. (1988) *Privatization and Ownership*. UK: Printer Press.
— (1990) 'Pricing the Family Silver'. *The Financial Times*. March 29. London.
Johnson, G. and J.G. Hailman (1987) 'Meta Policy Transition and Policy Implementation: New Federalism and Privatization'. *Public Administration Review*. November–December.
Johnson, Norman (1991) *Reconstructing the Welfare State: A Decade of Change*: 1980–1990. UK: Harvester Wheatsheaf.
Jonas, M. (1985) 'Socialism Changes Course With Re-Privatization'. *African Business*: (85).
Jones, Lervy P. (1985) *Performance Evaluation for Public Enterprises*. Boston University.
Jonquieres, G. de (1986) 'Best-seller with a Choice of Ending'. *The Financial Times*. December 10.
Joshi, Sharad (1991) 'The IMF Loan: Time to Axe the Drumstick Tree'. *The Times of India*. July 19. New Delhi.
Joshi, Navin Chandra (1990) 'Privatization: The Need of the Hour'. *Surya India*. July. New Delhi.

Kalra, Rajesh (1992) 'A Glossary of Liberalese'. *The Sunday Times of India*. February 9.
Kamerman, Sheila B. and Alfred J. Kahn (1989). *Privatization and the Welfare State*. New Jersey: Princeton University Press.
Kaminski, Antoni Z. (1991) 'The Public and the Private: Introduction'. *International Political Science Review*: 12 (4).
Kanesalingam, V. (1991) *Privatization: Trends and Experiences in South Asia*, New Delhi: Macmillan.
Kang, S. Il (1988) *Korea's Privatization Plans and Past Experience*, Seoul: Korea Development Institute.
Kapp, K.W. (1978) *The Social Cost of Business Enterprise*. Nottingham: Spokesman.
Kaufman, Henry. (1990) 'After Drexel, Wall Street is Headed for Darker Days'. *International Herald Tribune*. February 24. New York.
Kaul, B.N. (1991) 'Crux of India's Economic Crisis: A New East India Company Set in Motion'. *Women's Era*: 18 (43). November, Second.
Kaushik, Surendra (1991) 'India's Democratic Transformation', *Challenge*, September–October.
Kay, J.A. and D.J. Thompson (1986) 'Privatization: A Policy in Search of a Rationale'. *The Economic Journal*: 96.
Kay, J.A., Mayer Colins and David Thompson (1986) *Privatization and Regulation: The UK Experience*. December. UK: Oxford University Press.
Kent, Calvin ed. (1987) *Entrepreneurship and the Privatizing of Government*. New York: Quorum Books.
Kenworthy, Lane (1996) 'Balancing Competition and Cooperation'. *Challenge*. July–August.
Keohane, Robert O. (1984) 'The World Political Economy and the Crisis of Embedded Liberalism' in John N. Goldthorpe ed. *Order and Conflict in Contemporary Capitalism*. Oxford: Clarendon Press.
Keynes J.M. (1926) *The End of Laissez Faire*. London: Hogarth Press.
Khare, Harish. (1991) 'Politicians versus Economists: Sabotage from Within Inevitable'. *The Times of India*. July 17. New Delhi.
Khathate, Deena (1991) 'Privatization Linked to Human Development'. *The Times of India*. December 12. New Delhi.
Khushoo, T.N. (1992) 'Ecology must Blend with Economy'. *The Times of India*. January 4. New Delhi.
Killawala, Alpana (1992) 'All is Well that Ends Well'. *Business India*. January 6–19.
Killick, Tony and Simon Commander (1989). 'State Divestiture as a Policy Instrument in Developing Countries'. *World Development*: 17(5).
Kikeri, Sunita, John Nellis and Mary Shirley (1992) *Privatization: The Lessons of Experience*. Washington DC: World Bank.
King, L. (1987) 'Lessons of Privatization'. *Long Range Planning*: 20(6).
Kirpekar, Subash. (1991) 'Few Coal Mines May Go to Private Sector'. *The Times of India*. November 20. New Delhi.
Klein, R. (1984) 'Privatization and the Welfare State'. *Lloyds Bank Review*. January 12–29.
Klinz, W. (1992) 'Venture Capital Companies, MBO/MBI Funds. Introduction', in Treuhandanstalt *et al.* (eds), *Privatization – Together into the Social Market Economy*, Cologne.
Kloepfer, M. and J. Friedrich (1996) 'The Treuhandanstalt Under Public Law', in W. Fischer *et al.* (eds), *Treuhandanstalt: The Impossible Challenge*, Berlin: Akademie Verlag.

Koch, Alexander Kochi (1992) 'Employees in the Privatization Process'. Proceedings of workshop on 'Main Aspects and Objectives of Privatization'. Cologne: Deutscher Institute Verlag.

Kojima, Makoto (1991) 'Steel Industry in India: A Case Study'. *Privatization: Options and Challenges*. Center for Economic and Industrial Research. New Delhi.

Kokalz, L. and P. Hufner. (1994) 'Management Buy Out/Management Buy In'. Working paper no. 54. Stuttgart: Des Institutes für Mittelstandsforschung, Schaeffer-Poeschel.

Konig, Klaus. (1988) *Developments in Privatization in FRC*. Speyerer, Forscungsberischte.

Kopp, Karel (1991) 'Privatization in Czechoslovakia'. *Czechoslovak Economic Digest*. February.

Kothari, K.K. (1991) 'Privatization: Some Issues'. *The Financial Express*. December 2. New Delhi.

Kothari, Rajni (1991) 'Our Emerging Future: Economic and Political'. *Mainstream*. August 31.

Kristof, C.D. (1986) 'Privatization and Environment: Taxing the Future'. *The Privatization Review*: 2 (3).

Kristof, Nicholas D. (1991) 'Capitalism with a Red Face in China'. *The Times of India*. December 24. New Delhi.

Kulkarni, U.G. (1985) 'Singapore Steps Away from State Capitalism'. *Far Eastern Economic Review*: 129 (29).

Kumar, Ravindra (1992) 'The Political Economy of Liberalisation'. *The Times of India*. February 26. New Delhi.

Kuznetsov, V.I. (1993) 'The Market and Privatization', *Mirovaia ekonomika i mezhdunarodnye otnosheniia*, vol. 7, Russian text, I.M.E.M.O.

Labour Research Development (1987). *Privatization: Paying the Price*. London: LRD Publication.

Lakhotia, R.N. (1987) 'Public Sector in 2001 A.D.' *The Economic Times*. June 29. New Delhi.

Lal, Deepak (1983) *The Poverty of Development Economies*. London: Institute of Economic Affairs.

— (1985) 'Nationalism, Socialism and Planning'. *World Development*. June.

— (1987) 'Political Economy of Economic Liberatization'. *World Bank Economic Review*: 1 (2). January.

— (1992) 'Social Policy After Socialism' in H. Siebert ed. *The Transformation of Socialist Economies*. Germany: Tübingen.

Laux, Jeanne Kirk (1993) 'How Private Is Privatization?' *Canadian Public Politiques*: 19 (4).

Laux, J. and M. Molot (1988). *State Capitalism*. New York: Cornell University Press.

Lawless, John (1991) 'The State of the Century'. *International Management*: 46. December.

Lawson, N. (1987) *The Observer*. October 25.

Laxman, Srinivas (1991). 'Privatization Sparks Off Debate'. *The Times of India*. October 15. New Delhi.

Lee, B. and Nellis, J. (1990) 'Enterprise Reform and Privatization in Socialist Economies'. Discussion paper 104. Washington DC: World Bank.

Leeds, Roger S. (1988) 'Turkey: Rhetoric and Reality' in Raymond Vernon ed. *The Promise of Privatization*. New York: Council on Foreign Relations.

— (1988) *Malaysia: The Shifting Balance Between the Public and Private Sector*. John Kennedy School of Government. Harvard University.

— (1989) 'Malaysia: Genesis of Privatization Transaction'. *World Development*: 17 (5). May.

— (1989) *Privatization of National Commercial Banks of Jamaica: A Case Study*. Centre for Business and Government. Harvard University.
Lefort, Claude (1991). Quoted by Arnaud Sales. *International Political Science Review*: 12 (4).
Lehmbruch, Gerhard (1994) 'The Process of Regime Change In East Germany: An Institutionalist Scenario for German Unification'. *Journal of European Policy*: 1 (1). June.
Letwin, Oliver (1988). *Privatizing the World: A Study of International Privatization in Theory and Practice*. London: Cassell.
Lieberman, Mayrol (1989) *Privatization and Educational Choice*. London: Macmillan.
Lightman, E. *et al.* (1989) 'A Transatlantic View: Privatization Canadian Style', in J.D. Donahue (ed.), *The Privatization Decision: Public Ends, Private Means*, New York: Basic Books.
Lipton, D. and J. Sachs (1990) 'Privatization in Eastern Europe: The Case of Poland'. *Brookings Papers on Economic Activity*: 2.
Loney, Martin (ed.) (1991) *The State or the Remoralization of the Society*. London: Sage.
Luders, Rolf J. (1991) 'Massive Divestiture and Privatization: Lessons from Chile'. *Contemporary Policy Issues*, vol. ix.
MacPherson, C.V. (1964) *The Political Theory of Possessive Individualism*. Oxford: Oxford University Press.
Madarassy, Andrea (1990) 'Private Investment Rebounds in Developing Countries'. *Finance and Development*. June. Washington DC.
Madsen, P. (1985) *Dismantling the State: The Theory and Practice of Privatization*. National Centre for Public Analysis. Texas.
Manser, W.A.P. (1982) 'Nationalization or Privatization: The Case For Each'. *Banker*. December.
Mansoor, A. (1988) 'The Fiscal Impact of Privatization', in P. Cook and C. Kirkpatrick (eds), *Privatization in Less Developed Countries*, Hemel Hempstead: Harvester Wheatsheaf.
Marathe, S.S. (1986) *Regulation and Development: India's Policy Experience of Control Over Industry*. New Delhi: Sage.
Marsh, D. and P. Betts (1986) 'Privatization in France: Socialists Try to Stop the Bandwagon'. *The Financial Times*. January 13. New Delhi.
Mascarenhas, R.C. (1993) 'Building an Enterprise Culture in Public Sector: Reform of the Public Sector in Australia, Britain and New Zealand'. *Public Administration Review*: 53 (4). July–August.
Mason, Joanne (1991) 'European Privatization Party'. *International Management*: 46. December.
Masser, I. (1983) 'Privatization is the Only Alternative to State Provision'. *PTRC Education and Research Services*. London.
Massey, Andrew (1992) 'Managing Change: Politicians and Experts in the Age of Privatization'. *Government and Opposition*: 24 (4). Autumn.
Mastrangelo, Teressa B. and Robert J.F. McPhail. 1993. 'Serving Those Going Private: The Role of Accountancy in Privatization'. *The Columbia Journal of World Business*. Spring.
Mattelart, Armand (1991) *Advertising International: The Privatization of Public Space*. London: Routledge.
May, T. Jr. (1985) 'Selling Financial Assets: Techniques and Financial Implications'. *Fiscal Studies*: (6).
Mayee, C. and S. Meadoweraft (1985) 'Selling Public Assets: Techniques and Financial Implications'. *Fiscal Studies*: 6(42).
Mayo, Chandrika (1989) 'To Privatize or Not: The Transport Problem'. *The Times of India*. April 16. New Delhi.

Mayo, P. (1983) 'The Privatization of Road Freight Transport'. *PTRC Education and Research Services*. London.

McCartny, Daniel and Sheila M. Puffer (1995) 'Diamonds and Rust on Russia's Road to Privatization'. *The Columbia Journal of World Business*. Fall.

McCracken, Paul W. (1991) 'Thoughts on Marketing State-managed Economies'. *The Financial Express*. New Delhi.

Mclachlan, Sandy (1989) 'The National Freight Buy-out'. Quoted by V.V. Ramandham ed. *Privatization in Developing Countries*. London: Routledge.

Mehta, Fredie A. (1991) 'Will the Reforms Package Succeed?' *The Economic Times*. November 23. New Delhi.

Menon, K.T.R. (1991) 'Indian Airlines Plunges Deeper into the Red'. *The Times of India*. April 15. New Delhi.

Milanovic, B. (1989) *Liberalization and Entrepreneurship*. New York: ME Sharpe

Milanovic, B. (1990) *Privatization in Post-communist Societies*. Washington DC: World Bank.

Miller, Alan N. (1995) 'British Privatization: Evaluating the Results'. *The Columbia Journal of World Business*. Winter. vol. xxx, No. 4.

Miller, A.H., W.M. Reisinger and V.L. Hesli (eds) (1993) *Public Opinion and Regime Change: The New Politics of Post Soviet Societies*. Boulder CO: Westview Press.

Millward, Roben and D. Parker 1983. 'Public and Private Enterprise: Comparative Behaviour and Relative Efficiency' in Millward *et al. Public Sector Economies*. London: Longman.

Milne, R.S. (1992) 'Privatization in ASEAN States: Who Gets What, Why and With What Effects?' *Pacific Affairs*. Spring.

Min, Shinn C. (1988) *Privatization of Public Enterprises in Korea*. Korea: Chung Ang University.

Mishan, E.J. (1993) 'Economics versus the Greens: An Exposition and A Critique'. *The Political Quarterly*. Oxford: Blackwell.

Mishra, R.K. and R. Nandgopal (1991) 'Public Sector: A State of Confusion'. *The Economic Times*. December 9. New Delhi.

Misra, S.N. (1997) 'Polity and Economy: The Indian Experience from Innocence to Confusion' in Bijoyini Mohanty and S.C. Hazare eds. *Political Economy of India: Retrospects and Prospects*. New Delhi: A.P.H. Publishing.

Mitchell, Bernard (1994) 'Post Fordism, Transnational Production and the Changing Global Political Economy' in Richard Stubbs and Geoffrey R.D. Underhill (eds), *Political Economy and the Changing World Order*. Toronto: McClelland & Stewart.

Mitra, Ashok (1991) Quoted in 'Need to Divest Government of Vast Economic Powers'. *The Times of India*. March 29. New Delhi.

Mla'dek, J. (1994) 'Czech Privatization Process: Time for Corporate Governments', revised version of a paper prepared for the IIASA Conference held at Laxenburg, Austria, 18–20 November 1993, mimeo.

Moe, Ronald C. (1987) 'Exploring the Limits of Privatization'. *Public Administration Review*. November.

Mohan, Madan (1993) 'Ecology and Development'. *Third Concept*. January.

Mohanty, D.K. (1997) 'Problematics in Defining New Trends in India's Political Economy' in Mohanty and Hazare eds. *Political Economy of India: Retrospects and Prospects*. New Delhi: A.P.H. Publishing.

Mohnot, S.R. (ed.) (1991) *Privatization: Options and Challenges*. New Delhi: Centre for Industrial and Economic Research.

— (1991) 'Peoplization via Privatization'. *The Financial Express*. May 5. New Delhi.

— (1993) in V. Ramananadham (ed.), *Constraints and Impacts of Privatization*, London and New York: Routledge.
Molz, Richard (1990) 'Privatization in Developing Countries'. *The Columbia Journal of World Business*. Spring/Summer.
Moore, Barrington (1966) *The Social Origins of Dictatorship and Democracy*. Boston: Beacon Press.
Moore, John (1983) *Why Privatize?* London: H.M. Treasury.
— (1986) *Privatization in the United Kingdom*. London: Aims of Industry.
Morris, Robert (1988) *Testing the Limits of Social Welfare*. London: Branches University Press.
Morris, Sebastian (1991) 'Holding Companies, Performance Contracts and Task Orientation in Public Sector'. *Economic and Political weekly*, vol. xxvi (8).
Mosley, Paul (1987) 'On Persuading a Leopard to Change his Spots: A Study of World Bank Structural Adjustment Lending: 1980–85'. *Princeton Essays in International Finance*. New York: Princeton.
— (1988) 'Privatization, Policy-based Lending and World Bank Behaviour' in Paul Cook and Colin Kirkpatrick eds. *Privatization in Less Developed Countries*. New York: Harvester Wheatsheaf.
Mujumdar, N.A. (1996) 'Public Policy and the Financial System: A Dilemma of Two Cultures'. *Economic and Political Weekly*. December 14.
Muller, Jurgen (1996) 'Structural Effects of Privatization by the THA' in Wolfram Fischer, Herbert Flax and Hans Karl Schneider eds. *Treuhandanstalt: The Impossible Challenge*. Berlin: Akademie Verlag.
Mukhopadhyay, J.K. (1988) *The Privatization Phenomenon and Its Relevance to Developing Countries*. Bombay: Forum of Free Enterprise.
Murthy, K.R.S. (1990) 'MOU: More Memorandum Than Understanding'. *Economic and Political Weekly*. May 26. Bombay.
Nankani, Helen B. (1990) 'The Rhetoric and Reality of Privatization: Recent experience and Emerging Perspectives'. *Decision*: 17 (34).
— (1990) 'Lessons of Privatization in Developing Countries', *Finance and Development*. March. IMF: World Bank Publication.
National Audit Office (1987) *Report on the Sale of Government Shareholding in British Airways*, London: HMSO, paper no. 37.
Naqvi, Nawab Haider and A.R. Kemal (1991) 'The Privatization of Public Industrial Enterprises in Pakistan'. *The Pakistan Development Review*: (2).
Nellis, John R. (1994) 'Successful Privatization in Estonia: Unusual features'. *Transition: 5 (5)*.
Nellis, John R. (1986) *Public Enterprises in Sub-saharan African*. Washington DC: World Development Discussion Paper.
Nellis, John R. and Sunita Kikeri (1989) 'Public Enterprise Reform: Privatization and the World Bank'. *World Development*: 17 (5). May.
Neuberger, J. (ed.) (1987) *Privatization: Fair Shares for All or Selling the Family Silver?* London: Macmillan.
Newman, R. (1986) *The Selling of British Telecom*, London: Holt Rinehart & Winston.
Nielsen, Richard (1988) 'Cooperative Strategy'. *Strategic Management Journal*: 9.
Nigam, R.K. (1986) 'Indian Public Sector at the Crossroads'. *Tender Times*. March 27.
— (1992) 'Public Sector to Vacate Commanding Heights in Economy' in Jagdish Prakash ed. *Privatization of Public Enterprise in India*. Bombay: Himalaya Publishing.
Oakeshott, Robert (1983) 'Privatization and Workers Buy-outs'. *Public Money*. December.
— (1998) 'The Beginnings of an Employee-owned Sector' in Christopher Johnson ed. *Lloyds Bank Annual Review: Privatization and Ownership*: 1. London: Pinter Publishers.

Ohasi, T.M. and T.P. Roth (1988) *Privatization – Theory and Practice*. Vancouver: Fraser Institute.
O' Higgins, Michael (1984) 'Privatization and Social Security'. *Political Quarterly*. April–June.
Okun, B.R. (1986) 'Deregulation is Good Business'. *Span*: 27. December.
Olaf, H.S. and J. Newport (1987) *Management Contracts: Main Features and Design Issues*. Washington DC: World Bank.
Oliver, E. (1987) 'Privatization and C.I.P.F.A.', *Public Finance and Accountacy*, 12 June.
Ollard, W. (1988) 'Buy-Outs Take hold in Europe'. *The Italian Monthly of International Finance*. March.
Olson, M. (1982) 'The Rise and Decline of Nations'. *New Haven*.
— (1984) 'The Development Dilemma'. *New Republic*. July.
Pack, J.R. (1987) 'Privatization of Public Sector Services in Theory and Practice'. *Journal of Policy Analysis and Management*: 6.
Palat, Ravi Arvind (1996) 'Pacific Century: Myth or Reality?' *Theory and Society*: 25 (3).
Palkhiwala, Nani (1991) Quoted in 'Palkhiwala on the Good, Bad and Ugly'. *The Times of India*. October 1. New Delhi.
— (1992) 'The Union Budget: Committee Needed to Examine Changes'. *The Times of India*. March 6. New Delhi.
Palmer, J. (1993) 'Europe in the Block'. *Barron's*: 14. June.
Panda, G. (1990) 'Privatization in Less developed Countries: Rationale, Policy Options and their Compulsions', in V.K. Vaid Raizada and M.R. Rana (eds), *Public Enterprises in India*, New Delhi: Anmol Publications.
Papps, I. (1988) *Deregulation and Privatization*. Oxford: Philip Allen.
Paranjape, H.K. (1988) 'Privatization or Perestroika: Towards Socialist Objectives'. *The Economic Times*. July 3. New Delhi.
Parekh, Bhikhu (1990) 'When Will the State Whither Away?' *Alternative*, vol. xv.
Parker, David (1993) 'Privatization and the International Business Environment', Working papers in Commerce: 93 (15). October.
— (1993) 'Unravelling the Planned Economy: Privatization in Czechoslovakia'. *Communist Economies and Economic Transformation*: 5 (3).
Parker, Richard (1993) 'Delusions of Shock Therapy'. *Dissent*. Winter.
Parry, Richard (ed.) (1990) *Privatization: The UK Experience and International Trends*. UK: Jessica Kingsley.
Patel, I.G. (1987) 'On Taking India Into Twenty-First Century'. *Modern Asian Studies*: 21 (2).
— (1992) 'New Economic Policies: A Historical Perspective'. *Economic and Political Weekly*. January 4–11.
— (1994) 'Limits of the Current Consensus on Development'. Proceedings of the World Bank Annual Conference on Development Economics, Washington DC: World Bank.
Patnaik, Prabhat (1990) *Economics and Egalitarianism*. New Delhi: Oxford University Press.
Patted, Mohan N. (1991) 'Privatization Holds the Key'. *The Financial Express*. October 3 New Delhi.
Paul, S. (1988) 'Privatization: A Review of International Experience'. *Economic and Political Weekly*. February 2.
Peacock, Allen (1984) 'Privatization in Perspective'. *The Banks Review*: 144. December.
Pendse, D.R. (1985) 'Privatization: An Economic Growth'. *The Financial Express*. June 10–11.
— (1985) 'Some Reflections on the Role of Donor Agencies in the Privatization Process'. *National Westminster Bank Quarterly Review*. November.

— (1988) 'Privatization: Myths and Realities'. *The Financial Express*. August 15–17.
Pennathun, Krish (1991) 'Privatization Will Be Sabotaged'. *The Times of India*. May 1. New Delhi.
Pereira, Lulz Carlos Bresser, J.M. Maravall and A. Przeworski (1993) *Economic Reforms in New Democracies: A Social Democratic Approach*. New York: Cambridge University Press.
Pfeffermann, Guy P. and Andrea Madarassy (1989) *Trends in Private Investment in Thirty Developing Countries*. Washington DC: International Finance Corporation.
Pherwani, M.J. (1991) 'Privatization: Road to Economic Repair'. *The Illustrated Weekly of India*. February 23.
Piachaud, David (1991) 'Revitalizing Social Policy'. *The Political Quarterly*: 62 (20). April–June.
Pierson, Christopher (1991) *Beyond the Welfare State*: Cambridge: Polity Press.
Pirie, Madsen (1988) *Privatization: Theory, Practice and Choice*, Avebury: ASI Publications.
Plant, Raymond C.F. (1989) 'Ruled by the Regulator'. *The Times*. November 27.
Platzer, R. (1986) 'The Privatization Debate in Austria'. *Annals of Public and Cooperative Economy*: 57. April–June.
Poole, R.W. (ed.) (1988) *Federal Privatization: Towards Resolving the Deficit Crisis*. Santa Monica: Reason Foundation.
Prabhu, A.N. (1991) 'Privatization: How to Make it Work Here'. *The Hindustan Times*. September 4. New Delhi.
Prakash, Jagdish (ed.) (1992) *Privatization of Public Enterprises in India*. Bombay: Himalaya Publishing.
Price Waterhouse (1987) *Privatization: The Facts*. London: Price Waterhouse.
Privatization Newsletter of Czechkoslovakia (1991–92) Prague: Charles University, Center for Economic Research and Graduate Education.
Prosser, T. (1986) *Nationalized Industries and Public Control*, Oxford: Blackwell.
Pryor, Fredric L. (1985) 'Growth and Fluctuations of Production in OECD and East European Countries'. *World Politics*: 37.
Prybyla, Jan S. (1991) 'The Road From Socialism: Why, Where, What and How?' *Problems of Communism*. January–April.
Przeworski, A. and M. Wallerstein (1982) 'Democratic Capitalism at the Crossroad'. *Democracy*: 2.
Raizada, V.K. Vaid and M.R. Rana compiled (1990) *Public Enterprises in India*. New Delhi: Anmol Publications.
Ramachandran, K.S. (1991) 'Global Support For Domestic Reform?' *The Financial Express*. November 30. New Delhi.
— (1992) 'Markets Should be Poor and Not Just Market-Friendly.' *The Financial Express*. January 11. New Delhi.
Ramana, G.V. (1991) 'Privatization: The Wrong Route', *The Economic Times* (23 September): 7.
— (1991) 'Privatization: Need for Safety Mechanism'. *The Economic Times*. December 7. New Delhi.
Ramanadham, V.V. compiled (1988) *UNDP Report on the Inter-Regional Workshop on Privatization*. May. Oxford: Templeton College.
— (ed.) (1988) *Privatization in the U.K.*, London: Routledge.
— (ed.) (1989) *Privatization in Developing Countries*. London: Routledge.
— (1991) *The Economies of Public Enterprises*. London: Routledge.
— (1991) 'The Comparative Advantage of Public and Private Enterprise: A Conceptual Analysis' in S.R. Mohnot ed. *Privatization: Options and Challenges*. New Delhi: Centre for Economic and Industrial Research.

— (1995) *Privatization and Equity*. London and New York: Routledge.
Ramanath, Narayanaswamy (1986) 'Socialism and the Market'. *Economic and Political Weekly*: 21 (4).
Rangnekar, Sham S. (1992) 'Changing Styles'. *Business World*. January 1–14.
Rao, B. Ramachandra (1991) 'Consortium Concepts of Privatization'. *The Financial Express*. September 4. New Delhi.
Rao, G.V. (1991) 'How to Prepare for Privatization?' *The Times of India*. May 27. New Delhi.
— (1991) 'Privatization: Is India Ready For It?' *The Financial Express*. June 9. New Delhi.
Rao, V.L. (1989) 'Economic Management: Ideology versus Pragmatism'. *Mainstream*. February 25.
Rawcliffe, Michael (1990) *The Welfare State: Weighing Up the Evidence*. UK: Dryad Press.
Raza, Asmi (1989) 'Privatization Cannot be Our Economic Panacea'. *The Times of India*. May 10. New Delhi.
Reddy, T. Chandramohan, V.M. Selvarary and S.V. Kumar (1991) 'The Privatized Workers in the Millieu of Collective Action'. *Indian Journal of Industrial Relations*: 27 (1).
Reddy, Y.V. (1988) 'Privatization of Public Enterprises: Scope and Units' in T.L. Sankar and Y.V. Reddy ed. *Privatization: Diversification of Ownership of Public Enterprises*. Hyderabad: Institute of Public Enterprise.
— (1989) 'State, Market and Privatization' in Sankar and Reddy eds. *Privatization: Diversification of Ownership of Public Enterprises*. Hyderabad: Booklinks Corporation.
Redwood, John (1987) *Privatization: The Case of Britain*. San Francisco: Institute for Contemporary Studies.
Rees, J. (1986) 'Is There an Economic Case for Privatization?' *Public Money*: 5 (1). March.
Rees, J. and M. Synnott (1986) 'Are the Water Authorities an Attractive Proposition?'. *Public Money*: 6 (1).
Revzin, P. (1988) 'North Africa's Cities Full of Jobless Youths Cast Shadow on Europe'. *Wall Street Journal*. November 8.
Richardson, J.J. (ed.) (1989) *Privatization and Deregulation in Canada*. US: Dartmouth.
Ringlien, Wayne (1990) *Privatization of Farming Activities in Hungary*. Washington DC: Finance and Development.
Roberts, Paul Craig (1991) 'Privileged Privatization'. *Reason*: 26.
Robson, J. (1985) 'Putting Italy on the Market.' *Euromoney*. December. London.
Rocco, J. (1986) 'The Privatization Challenge'. *Institutional Investor*. July.
Roe, Mark. J. 'Political and Legal Restraints on Ownership and Control of Public Companies'. *Journal of Financial Economics*: 27.
Rohwedder, Detlev (1990) His speech before the Volkskammer on September 13.
Rosa, Jean Jacques (1992) Comments on Jan Winiecki's 'The Political Economy of Privatization' in Horst Siebert (ed.), *Privatization*. Germany: Kiel Institute of World Economics.
Rose, R. (1988) 'Privatization: A Question of Quantities and Qualities', a paper presented at the Conference on 'A Supply-side Agenda for Germany', 29–30 June, Cologne.
Rose, R. and C. Haerpfer (1994) 'Mass Response to Transformation in Post-Communist Societies', *Europe-Asia Studies*, vol. 46 (1).
Rose, Richard and W.T.E. Mishler (1994) 'Mass Reaction to Regime Change in Eastern Europe: Polarization or Leaders and Laggards?' *British Journal of Political Science*.
Ross, Randy (1990) *Government and the Private Sector: Who Should Do What?* New York: Crane Russak.

Roth, G. (1987) *The Private Provision of Public Services in Developing Countries*. Oxford: Oxford University Press.

Rueschmeyer, D., Hubert E. Stephens and J.D. Stephens (1992) *Capitalist Development and Democracy*. Chicago: University Press of Chicago.

Ryan, Mick and Tony Ward (1989) *Privatization and the Penal System: The American Experience and the Debate in Britain*. Buckingham: Open University Press.

Sachs, Jeffrey D. (1991) 'Accelerating Privatization in Eastern Europe'. World Bank Annual Conference on Development Economics. April 25–26. Washington DC.

— (1991) Quoted by Etzoini Amitai in 'Eastern Europe: The Wealth of Lessons'. *Challenge*. July–August.

— (1991) 'Crossing the Valley of Tears in East European Reforms'. *Challenge*. September–October.

Sales, Arnaud (1991) 'The Private, the Public and Civil Society: Social Realms and Power Structures'. *International Political Science Review*: 12 (4).

Salim, Abdul Rauf (1989) *Issues and Problems in Privatization*. Hyderabad: Asian and Pacific Development Centre and Institute of Public Enterprise.

Samson, Colin (1994) 'Three Faces of Privatization'. *Sociology*: 28 (1).

Sandberg, Dani (1994) 'The Pirate Privateers'. *New Internationalist*. September.

Sanghvi, Vijay (1991) 'Political Cost of Liberalization'. *The Hindustan Times*. July 19. New Delhi.

Sankar, T.L. et al. (1985) 'State Level Public Enterprises in India: An Overview'. *Economic and Political Weekly*. February 25.

Sankar, T.L. and Y.V. Reddy (eds) (1989) *Privatization: Diversification of Ownership of Public Enterprises*. Hyderabad: Institute of Public Enterprise and Booklinks Corporation.

Sankar, T.L., R.K. Mishra and R. Nandgopal (1990) 'Can State Level Enterprises in India Earn a Rate of Return?' *Economic and Political Weekly*. November 24.

— (1991) 'Do State Level Public Enterprises Need Memorandum of Understanding?' *Economic and Political Weekly*. August 31.

Sankar. T.L. and Y.V. Reddy (1991) 'Privatization of Activities and Enterprises in the Public Sector in India', in Geeta Gouri ed. *Privatization and Public Enterprise: The Asia Pacific Experience*. Hyderabad: Institute of Public Enterprise.

Sarmad, Khwaya (1991) 'Is the Private Sector More Productive Than the Public Sector?' *The Pakistan Development Review*. 30 (4).

Sathe, Vasant (1989) *Restructuring the Public Sector in India*. New Delhi: Vikas Publishing.

— (1991) Quoted in 'Need to Divest Government of Vast Economic Powers'. *The Times of India*. March 29. New Delhi.

Savas, E.S. (1987) *Privatization: The Key to Better Government*. New Jersey: Chatham House.

— (1990) 'A Taxonomy of Privatization Strategies'. *Policy Studies Journal*: 18 (2).

— (1992) 'Privatization in Post-Socialist Countries'. *Public Administration Review*: 52 (6).

Scarpaci, Joseph (ed.) (1991) *Health Services: Privatization in Industrial Societies*. London: Jessica Kingsley.

Scheunry, S.M. (1986) *Will China Go Capitalist*? London: Institute of Economic Affairs.

Schelling, Corrina S. (ed.) (1984) *Public Private Partnership: New Opportunities For Meeting Social Needs*. Cambridge: Ballinger.

Schmidt, Klaus-Dieter (1996) In a personal interview with the author on June 22, at the Kiel Institute of World Economics.

Schmidt, Klaus-Dieter and Uwe Siegmund (1996) 'Privatization Strategies', in Wolfram Fischer et al. eds. *Treuhandanstalt: The Impossible Challenge*. Berlin: Akademie Verlag.

Schmieding, Holyer (1992) 'Alternative Approaches to Privatization: Some Notes on the Debate', in Horst Siebert ed. *Privatization.*

Schultz, George (1986) Quoted by Tony Killick. 'Twenty Five Years in Development: The Rise and Impending Decline of Market Solutions'. *Development Policy Review:* 1 (2). June.

Sclar, Elliot D. (1994) 'Public Service Privatization: Ideology or Economics?' *Dissent.* Summer.

Sen, Anikendra Nath (1991) 'Deregulating Indian Skies'. *The Times of India.* July 19. New Delhi.

Sethi, J.D. (1991) *Indian Economy under Siege.* New Delhi: Vikas Publishing.

Shackelton, J.R. (1986) 'Privatizing in the Third World'. *Banca Nationale del Lavaro.* December.

Sharma, Tyagraj (1989) 'Scope for Public Sector Elimination in Select Area'. *The Economic Times.* November 19. New Delhi.

Sharp, M. and G. Shepherd (1987) *Managing Change in British Industry.* International Labour Office. No.5. Series on Employment, Adjustment and Industrialization.

Sharp, M. and William Walker (1991) 'Thatcherism and Technical Advance: Reform Without Progress?' *Political Quarterly: 62 (3).* July–September.

Shekhar, Chandra, former Prime Minister of India (1992) 'Indian Political Economy in ill form'. *SAR Economist.* New Delhi. September.

Shirley, Mary M. (1983) 'Managing State Owned Enterprises'. World Bank Staff Papers No. 577. Washington DC: World Bank.

— (1988) 'The Experience with Privatization'. *Finance and Development.* September.

Shiva, Ramu S. (1987) 'Privatization of Public Enterprises: The Ripple Effect' in T.L. Sanker et al eds. *Public Enterprises Policy in India and U.K. in 1980s.* Bombay: Himalaya.

Short, R.P. , R.H. Floyd and C.S. Gray (1984) *Public Enterprise in Mixed Economies: Some Macroeconomic Aspects.* Washington DC: International Monetary Fund.

— 1988. 'Public Enterprises: A Statistical Comparison' in Robert H. Floyd, Clive S. Gray and Robert P. Short eds. *Public Enterprise in Mixed Economies: Some Macroeconomic Aspects.* Washington DC: International Monetary Fund.

Sicherl, P. (1983) *The Role of Public Enterprises in National Development.* Ljubljana: International Centre for Public Enterprises in Developing Countries.

Siddiqui, Kalim (1991) 'Free Market-Capitalism versus Planning'. *Third Concept* August. New Delhi.

— (1992) 'Myths and Reality About the US Economic Decline'. *Third Concept.* January. New Delhi.

Siegmund, Uwe (1996) 'Are There Nationalization-Privatization Cycles? – A theoretical Survey and First Empirical Evidence'. Kiel Working Paper: (757).

Simonis, U.D.O.E. (1990) 'A Development Strategy for the 1990s', *Inter Economics, May–June.*

Sing, W.G. (1983) 'The Implications of Privatization for Ethnic Minorities'. London: PTRC Education and Research Service.

Singh, Karan (1994) 'Transition to the Global Society: Towards A *Dharma* for the New Milennium'. *Trends in Social Science Research:* 1 (2). December.

Singh, R.D. (1986) 'State Intervention, Foreign Economic Aid, Savings and Growth in LDCs: Some Recent Evidence' in Shackleton. 'Privatizing in the third World'. *Banca Nationale del Lavaro.* December.

Singhvi, G.C. (1991) 'Economic Democracy'. *The Financial Express.* September 12. New Delhi.

Sivaram Krishnan, K.C. (1991) 'Move From Private to Public Transport'. *The Times of India*. October 4. New Delhi.
Smith J.G. (1986) 'Social Ownership and Reforms of the Nationalized Industries: The Labour Party's Plan'. *Public Money*. December.
Soltys, Michael (1991) 'Privatization Going Out of Fashion?' *Buenos Aires Herald*. March 10.
Sood, A. and A. Rigo (1989) *Report on Techniques of Privatization of State Owned Enterprises*. Washington DC: World Bank.
Spechler, Martin C. (1995) 'Privatization is Not the Key to Successful Transition'. *Challenge*. January–February.
Srinivasa, Alam (1991) 'Will Vayudoot be Put Up for Sale?' *The Times of India*. March 13. New Delhi.
Srinivasa, Raghavan T.C.A. (1991) 'Privatization: Where Will the Money Come From?' *The Economic Times*. May 31. New Delhi.
Srinivasan, T.N. (1992) 'Human Development: UNDP's Flawed Index'. *The Economic Times*. January 1. New Delhi.
Stacey, R. 1993. *Strategic Management and Organizational Dynamics*. London: Pitman.
Stackhouse, M.L. (1994) 'The Global Future and the Future of Globalization', *Christian Century*, vol. iii (4), 2–9 February.
Starkie, D. and D. Thompson 1985. 'Privatizing London's Airports'. London: Institute of Fiscal Studies.
Starr, Paul (1987) 'The Limits and Privatization' in Steve H. Hanke ed. *Prospects for Privatization:* 36 (3). New York: Proceedings of Academy of Political Science.
— (1988) 'The Meaning of Privatization'. *Yale Law and Policy Review:* 6.
— (1990) 'The New Life of the Liberal State: Privatization and the Restructuring of State-Society Relation' in Suleiman and Waterbury eds. *The Political Economy of Public Sector Reform and Privatization*. USA: Westview Press.
Steel, D and D. Heald (eds) (1984) *Privatizing Public Enterprises: Options and Dilemmas*. London: Royal Institute of Public Administration.
Stephenson, A. (1988) 'Prospects for Privatization'. *Accountancy:* 102. February.
Stockton, Lord (1985) quoted in *The Sunday Times,* 10 November.
Streeten, Paul (1995) 'Human Development: The Debate About the Index'. *International Social Science Journal:* 143.
Suleiman, E.N. and Waterbury, J. (1968) 'Market and Industries'. *International Encyclopedia of Social Science:* 9.
Suleiman, Ezra N. and Waterbury (1990) *The Political Economy of Public Sector Reform and Privatization*. Boulder: Westview Press.
Sundquist, James L. (1984) 'Privatization: No Panacea For What Ails Government' in Schelling ed. *Public Private Ownership: New Opportunities For Meeting Social Needs*. Cambridge: Baillinger.
Swamy, Dilip (1991) 'Privatization: Only For Avoiding Losses'. *Mainstream*. June 29. New Delhi.
Swann, D. (1988) *The Retreat of the State: Deregulation and Privatization in the U.K. and U.S.A.*, Hemel Hempstead: Harvester Wheatsheaf.
Swierezek, Frederic William (1988) 'Privatization Policy and Market Issues: An Example From Thailand'. *Public Enterprise:* 8 (3). Yugoslavia.
Syker, A. and C. Robinson (1987) *Current Choices: Good Ways and Bad Ways to Privatize Electricity*. London: Centre for Policy Studies.
Tandon, B.C. (1987) 'Leasing Out Public Enterprises: An Alternative of Privatization'. *The Financial Express*. December 17–18. New Delhi.

Taniuchi, M. and Y. Taguchi (1990) 'Privatization and Deregulation in Asia-Pacific Region', a paper presented at Pacific Economic Cooperation Conference held at Osaka, Japan, 28–30 March.

Teece, David (1993) 'The Dynamics of Industrial Capitalism: Perspectives on Alfred Chandler's Scale and Scope'. *Journal of Economic Literature:* 31 (1). March.

Tendulkar, Suresh D. (1991) 'Economic Reform: Hostages of Interest Groups'. *Monthly Commentary:* 36 (12). September.

Thakore, Dilip (1991) 'Public Sector Disinvestment is a Must'. *The Pioneer.* December 26. New Delhi.

Thanner, Benedikt (1993) 'The "Simple" Micro Approach in East German Privatization: The Inevitability of Macro Contradiction'. *Economic Problems of National Unification.* Seoul, Korea.

Thanulingam, M. (1990) 'Techniques of Privatization', in V.K. Raizada and M.R. Rana (eds), *Public Enterprises in India,* New Delhi: Anmol Publications.

Thapar, L.M. (1991) 'Privatization: A Pragmatic Approach' in S.R. Mohnot ed. *Privatization: Options and Challenges.* New Delhi: Centre for Economic and Industrial Research.

Tolchin, Susan J. (1996) 'The Globalist From Nowhere: Making Governance Competitive in the International Environment'. *Public Administration Review:* 56 (1). January–February.

Treuhandanstalt (1995a) *Daten Zum Management Buy Out I,* Auszuge aus der VA-Datenbank der Treuhandanstalt, Stand, Berlin: Unveroftenlichtes, internes manu-skript.

— (1995b) *Daten Zum Management Buy Out II.*

— (1995c) *Daten Zum Management Buy Out III.*

Trivedi, P. 1989. 'Public Enterprise Performance Improvement and Holding Companies'. *Indian Journal of Public Enterprise:* 4 (17). December. Allahabad.

— (1990) *Decision,* vol. 17 (34).

Tyler, William G. (1988) 'Technical Efficiency in Production in a Developing Country: An Empirical of the Brazilian Plastics and Steel Industries'. *Oxford Economic Papers:* 31 (197).

UNDP Report on the Inter-regional Workshop on Privatization. 1988. May 23–27. Oxford: Templeton College.

Uddley, Stephen (1991) *Technology and the Welfare State: The Development of Health Care in Britain and America,* London: HarperCollins.

United Nations (various years) *World Development Report,* New York: UN.

United Nations (1991) World Economic Survey, New York: UN.

Veljanovski, Cento. 1987. *Selling the State: Privatization in Britain.* London: Weidenfeld and Nicolson.

Venkataraman, R. (1991) *Public Sector Management: An Approach to Review and Redesign of Management Control Systems* in Vernon Raymond ed. 1988. *The Promise of Privatization.* New York: Council on Foreign Relations.

— (1988) 'Twilight of State-Owned Enterprises'. World Bank EDI Working Papers. June.

Vickers, John and George Yarrow (1985) *Privatization and National Monopolies.* London: Public Policy Centre.

— (1988) 'Regulation of Privatized Firms in Britain'. *European Economic Review:* 32.

— (1988) *Privatization: An Economic Analysis.* London: MIT Press.

— (1989) In Paul MacAvoy *et al* eds. *Privatization and State Owned Enterprises: Lessons From United States, Britain and Canada.* Boston: Kluwer Academic.

Vickers, John and Vincent Wright (1989) 'The Politics of Industrial Privatization in Western Europe: An Overview'. *Politics of Privatization in Western Europe.* London: Frank Cass.

Vishwanathan, R. and S. Roy Chowdhury (1994) 'Restructuring the Public Sector: The Privatization Option'. *Public Enterprise:* 14 (1–2).

Volkhart, Vincentz (1994) 'Privatization in East Germany: Regulatory Reform and Public Enterprise Performance' in V.V. Ramandham ed. *Privatization: A Global Perspective.* London and New York: Routledge.

Vuylsteice, Charles (1988) 'Techniques of Privatization of State Owned Enterprises in Vol. I: Methods and Implementation'. World Bank Technical Paper no. 88. Washington DC: World Bank.

Vyasulu, Vinod (1991) 'The Decline of Egalitarianism'. *The Economic Times.* November 17. New Delhi.

Waish, Mary Williams (1995) 'Going Private: The Profit and the Pain'. *Los Angeles Times.* January 10. World Report.

Walker, Alan (1984) 'The Political Economy of Privatization'. *Privatization and the Welfare State.* George Allen and Unwin.

Walker, M. (ed.) (1988) *Privatization: Tactics and Techniques.* Vancouver: Fraser Institute.

Walker, W. and M. Sharp (1991) 'Thatcherism and Technical Advance: Reform without Progress?', *The Political Quarterly,* vol. 62 (3) (July–September).

Walle, Nicolos van de (1989) 'Privatization in Developing Countries: A Review of the Issues'. *World Development:* 17(5). May.

Wallerstein, Immanual (1991) 'Capitalist Markets: Theory and Reality'. *Social Science Information.* London: Sage.

Waseem, Saba (1991) 'Waiting for Growth'. *The Economic Times.* November 25. New Delhi.

Waterbury, J. (1988) 'The Political Context of Public Sector Reform and Privatization in Egypt, India, Mexico and Turkey', a paper presented at the Workshop on Privatization at Princeton, New Jersey.

Webb, G.R. and J.C. Mc Master (1987) *Privatization in Asia and South–East Asia.* National Australia Bank. June.

Welfeus, P. (1991) 'The Economic Challenge of Privatization and Foreign Investment in Europe', a paper presented at the Annual Conference of the Society of Government Economists on 'East European Economies in Transition' held on 23 May, Washington DC.

Whiston, T.G. (1991) 'Forecasting the World's Problems: The Corporatization of Society and Diminution of Self'. *Futures.* March. London: Butterworth-Heineman.

White, Barbara Harris (1996) 'Liberalization and Corruption' in B.W. White and Gordon White eds. *IDS Bulletin:* 27 (2).

Whitehead (1990) Quoted by Suman K. Bery. 'Economic Policy Reform in Developing Countries: The Role of Management of Political Factors'. *World Development:* 18 (8).

Whitfield, Dexter (1991) *The Welfare State: Alternative Strategies for the 1990s,* London: Pluto Publishing.

Williamson, O.E. (1985) *The Economic Institutions of Capitalism.* New York: Free Press.

Wilson, Ernest (1986) 'The Public Private Debate'. *Africa Report.* July–August.

— (1987) *Privatization in Cote D'Ivoire: Three Case Studies.* Cambridge: Centre for Business and Government, Kennedy School of Government.

— (1988) 'Privatization in Africa: Domestic Origins, Current Status and Future Scenarios'. *Issue: A Journal of Opinion:* 16 (2).

Winiecki, Jan (1988) *The Distorted World of Soviet Type Economics.* London: Routledge.

— (1992) 'The Political Economy of Privatization' in Horst Siebert ed. *Privatization: Symposium in Honour of Herbert Giersch.* Kiel Institute for World Economics.

Wolf, Charles Jr. (1993) *Markets or Government: Choosing Between Imperfect Alternatives: A Rand Research Study* Cambridge MA: MIT Press.

Wolf, Alan (1989) *Whose Keeper?* Berkeley: University of California Press.

Wolfe, Joel (1989) 'Reorganizing Interest Representation: A Political Analysis of Privatization in Britain' in J. Wolfe and R. Forglesong eds. *The Politics of Economic Adjustment.* New York: Greenwood.

Woodward, Nick (1990) 'Public Enterprise, Privatization and Cultural Adaptation' in John Heath ed. *Public Enterprise at the Crossroad.* London: Routledge.

— (1991) 'Management as a Cultural Artefact' *Gestion 2000:* vol. 65.

World Commission on Environment and Development (1987) *Our Common Future,* New York: Oxford University Press.

Wortzel, H.V. and Lawrence H. Wortzel (1989) 'Privatization: Not the Only Answer'. *World Development:* 17 (5). May.

Yotopoulos, Pan A. (1989) 'The (Rip) Tide of Privatization: Lessons from Chile', *World Development:* 17 (5). May.

Young, Peter. (1986) 'Privatization in Great Britain', *Government Union Review:* 7 (2). Spring.

Yoder, Richard A., Philip L. Borknolder and Brians Friesen (1991) 'Privatization and Development: The Empirical Evidence', *Journal of Developing Areas,* April.

Index